German Democracy

German Democracy

From Post-World War II to the Present Day

Gert-Joachim Glaessner

Oxford • New York

First published in 2005 by

Berg

Editorial offices:

1st Floor, Angel Court, 81 St Clements Street, Oxford OX4 1AW, UK

175 Fifth Avenue, New York, NY 10010, USA

Berg is the imprint of Oxford International Publishers Ltd.

Library of Congress Cataloging-in-Publication Data

Glaessner, Gert-Joachim, 1944-

German democracy : from post-World War II to the present day / Gert-Joachim Glaessner.

p. cm.

Includes bibliographical references and index.

ISBN 1-85973-876-1 (pbk.) – ISBN 1-85973-871-0 (cloth)

1. Germany–Politics and government–20th century. 2. Democracy–Germany.

I. Title.

JN3971.A58G58 2005

320.943--dc22

2005009760

British Library Cataloguing-in-Publication Data

A catalogue record for this book is available from the British Library.

ISBN-13 978 1 85973 871 9 (Cloth)

978 185973 876 4 (Paper)

ISBN-10 1 85973 871 0 (Cloth)

1 85973 876 1 (Paper)

Typeset by JS Typesetting Ltd, Porthcawl, Mid Glamorgan

Printed in the United Kingdom by Biddles Ltd, King's Lynn

www.bergpublishers.com

Contents

Appendices

Preface

Sixty years after the end of World War II, Germany has become a solid democratic state and a universally accepted member of the commonwealth of Western democracies. The second German democratic state – despite difficult conditions at the outset, the extraordinary circumstances of the Cold War and its divided nation status – did not take the same route as the first, unsuccessful German experiment with democracy, the Weimar Republic, which lasted only fifteen years.

The central question of this book is how West Germany managed to develop into a stable democracy despite the pressures it had to withstand as part of a divided nation. Unlike other modern democracies, such as those of Great Britain, the United States or France, West German democratic elites had to cope with a series of disadvantages and shortcomings which resulted from recent history. First and foremost, the unprecedented crimes of the Nazi dictatorship had not only made Germany a pariah among civilized states, but also cut all links to the positive elements of national history. Second, democracy had no roots in many sectors of German society; many, if not most, Germans had supported National Socialism without great reservations. Last but not least, a democratic system had to be established under difficult international conditions. The very idea of a German national state was discredited by the hubris of the Wilhelmine Empire and 'National' Socialism. Germany was divided into two political systems, which developed on the basis of widely differing fundamental principles. In the West a democratic political order emerged, while in East Germany a 'new type' of political system developed, which relied upon the ideology of the Marxist-Leninist Party. That is why this book not only deals with West Germany but also considers the developments in East Germany up to and after 1989.

The Federal Republic in the West and the German Democratic Republic in the East owe their forty-year existence from 1949 to 1989 to the confrontation and constant regime clash between East and West. Germany, which lay on the brink of the East–West conflict, was an exposed playing field for the enemies in the Cold War. Both German states were involved in this conflict in an exceptional way. As products of the Cold War, they were adversaries and, at the same time, dependent upon one another. Both were directly dependent on the political developments and atmosphere of the enemy camp. Both defined themselves through disassociation from the other. Their eventual and unexpected reunification was the result of an international political constellation in which the Soviet Union was no longer prepared or able to continue its hegemonic control over Eastern and Central Europe through military force while popular revolutions were breaking out on all sides.

A book on German Democracy from post-World War II to the present day has to take these extraordinary historical and political circumstances into account. To provide a deeper understanding of present-day Germany, one must not only tell the story of West-German democracy but also assess the legacies of authoritarianism and dictatorship and acknowledge the value of the only successful democratic political revolution in German history.

This book starts from the assumption that German unification, which came about in 1990 through the accession of East Germany to the Federal Republic, marked a third historical turning point after the end of World War II in 1945 and the creation of two German states in 1949 and should be interpreted as the second foundation of the Federal Republic. The solid foundations for a successful democratic order in Germany were laid in West Germany in 1949 with the help, and under the auspices, of the United States, Britain and France. The political order in united Germany is legitimated by forty-five years of democratic development and the establishment of a civil society in the West and by the credentials of the democratic revolution of 1989 in the East.

In writing this book I had a good deal of help from various people I would like to thank. Valuable and relevant comments were also made by anonymous readers. I have to give special thanks to Professor Ian Wallace for critical comments on earlier versions of this book. Kathleen May from Berg Publishers supported me with suggestions and critical remarks which helped me to come up with a concise text, and she made a tremendous effort to polish my English.

But first and foremost I would like to thank my European and overseas students of two master's programs, 'Euromasters' and 'Trans-Atlantic Masters,' and European exchange students at Humboldt University who encouraged me to write a comprehensive textbook on Germany.

Chronology

1945	May 8	Unconditional surrender of Nazi Germany.
	June 5	Berlin Declaration. The Allied powers assume supreme authority with respect to Germany.
	June 9	The Soviet Military Administration (SMAD) is established as highest authority in East Germany.
	July 11	The Inter-Allied Military Authority (Kommandantura), consisting of the four commanders-in-chief, takes full control over the Berlin Area.
	July17–August 2	Potsdam Conference. The three Allied powers, USA, UK and USSR, decide on the future of Germany during a transitional period.
	August 30	The Allied Control Council is established as governing body of the Allies.
1948	June 16	The Allied Control Council collapses after the Soviet Union withdraws.
	June 20–21	Monetary reform in West Germany, the deutsche mark (DM) is introduced as legal tender.
	June 23–May 12, 1949	Berlin Blockade. The Soviet Union interrupts all traffic from West Germany to Berlin. An Anglo-American 'air lift' (Luftbrücke) starts on June 26 and supplies West Berlin with food, heating material etc. until the very end of the blockade.
	September 1	The Parliamentary Council is established to draft a constitution for West Germany.
1949	May 23	Foundation of the Federal Republic of Germany. The Basic Law comes into being on May 24.
	August 14	First general election.
	August 15	Konrad Adenauer, aged 73, is elected first chancellor of the Federal Republic.
	September 12	Theodor Heuss is elected first president of the Federal Republic.
	October 7	Foundation of the German Democratic Republic (GDR).

	October 31	The Federal Republic joins the Organization for European Economic Cooperation (OEEC), which later became the OECD.
1950	June 25	The Korean War starts.
	September 28	The GDR becomes a member of COMECON, the Eastern European economic area under Soviet control.
1952	April 18	France, Italy, the Benelux countries and West Germany found the European Community for Coal and Steel.
	May 27	France, Italy, the Benelux countries and West Germany sign a treaty to create a European Defence Community (EDC). This plan, aiming at a supranational European army, finally collapsed in 1954, when the French parliament did not ratify the treaty.
1953	June 17	A public uprising in East Germany is crushed by Soviet tanks.
1955	May 9	West Germany becomes a member of NATO.
	May 14	The GDR becomes a member of the Warsaw Pact.
1957	March 25	Treaties of Rome. The European Economic Community (EEC) and the European Atomic Energy Community (EURATOM) are founded by France, Italy, the Benelux countries and West Germany. The United Kingdom is invited to join but refuses.
	September 15	Federal elections in West Germany, the CDU/CSU gains an absolute majority in parliament.
1958	July 10–16	The 5th Party Congress of the SED declares the final transition of the GDR into a fully fledged Soviet-style socialist society.
1960	September 12	After the death of the first president, Wilhelm Pieck, Walter Ulbricht is elected as chairman of the State Council of the GDR and becomes officially the most powerful figure in East Germany.
1961	August 13	The Wall is erected in Berlin and the borders to West Germany are finally sealed off.
	September 17	Federal elections in West Germany. Chancellor Adenauer loses his absolute majority in parliament. The charismatic leader of the SPD and mayor of Berlin, Willy Brandt, gains national status.

1962	October 26	Government action against the news magazine *Der Spiegel* triggers a political crisis and leads to public protests. Konrad Adenauer is forced to reshuffle his cabinet.
1963	January 15–21	6th Party Congress of the SED in East Berlin calls for the advancement of the socialist society and introduces a new system of central economic planning.
	January 22	Franco-German Treaty of Friendship signed by Konrad Adenauer and Charles de Gaulle.
	October 15	After fourteen years as chancellor, Konrad Adenauer steps down. The former minister for economics, Ludwig Erhard, is elected as chancellor.
1966	December 1	Due to an economic crisis and internal conflicts the Erhard government collapses. A so-called grand coalition of CDU/CSU and SPD is formed. Kurt Georg Kiesinger becomes chancellor and the leader of the Social Democrats, Willy Brandt, foreign minister.
1968	April 2–3	Over Easter thousands of students protest in many German cities. The year of 1968 is – as in other countries – marked by protest demonstrations and riots of young people, later called the generation of 1968.
	April 6	The East German parliament passes a new 'socialist constitution' for the GDR.
	August 21	Soviet and Warsaw-Pact troops crush the Prague Spring.
1969	September 28	Federal elections in West Germany. For the first time the SPD leads a coalition government, with the Liberals as junior partner.
	October 21	Willy Brandt is elected chancellor.
1971	May 3	Walter Ulbricht is forced to step down as leader of the SED. Erich Honecker is elected as his successor.
	June 15–19	8th Party Congress of the SED claims the GDR is a separate 'socialist nation.'
	August 12	The Federal Republic and the Soviet Union sign the Moscow Treaty.
	September 3	Four Power Agreement on Berlin.
	December 7	Signing of the Warsaw Treaty.

1972	April 27	The governing coalition loses its majority in the Bundestag. The Christian Democrats fail to win a vote of no confidence against Chancellor Willy Brandt.
	November 19	Early elections. Willy Brandt wins a landslide victory.
	December 21	Basic Treaty signed by the Federal Republic and the GDR.
1973	September 18	The Federal Republic and the GDR become members of the United Nations.
	December 11	Prague Treaty.
1974	May 6	After a political crisis, triggered by GDR espionage, Willy Brandt quits office. Helmut Schmidt is elected as his successor on May 16.
	October 7	GDR constitution revised.
1975	August 1	The two German states sign the final declaration of the Conference on Security and Cooperation in Europe at Helsinki.
1977		Terrorist attacks by the 'Red Army Faction' in cooperation with Palestinian terrorists lead to controversial anti-terror measures.
1982	September 17	The coalition of SPD and Liberals collapses after differences over finances and the budget.
	October 1	The leader of the CDU, Helmut Kohl, is elected as federal chancellor. He forms a coalition with the Liberals.
1983	March 6	Early federal elections. The CDU/CSU nearly gains an absolute majority in parliament.
1987	September 7–11	After years of negotiation, the leader of the GDR, Erich Honecker, pays an official visit to the Federal Republic.
1988		The SED leadership distances itself from reforms initiated by the CPSU under Mikhail Gorbachev. Political dissidents in East Berlin protest against state repression and are protected by the Protestant Church.
1989	May 2	Hungary announces the dismantling of the 'Iron Curtain' at its border with Austria.
	July–August	Tens of thousands of GDR citizens use summer vacations in Poland, Hungary and Czechoslovakia to seek refuge in West German embassies. After complicated diplomatic negotiations, most of them are transferred to West Germany.

August 19	Hundreds of East Germans use the occasion of a 'Pan-European picnic' at the Hungarian–Austrian border to cross the Iron Curtain. That particular event encourages thousands of East Germans to follow them. This mass exodus proved to be one of the decisive moments of the destabilization of the GDR.
September 4	For the first time since 1953 GDR citizens took to the streets in Leipzig to protest against the government. This was the beginning of the so-called 'Monday demonstrations,' which, in the weeks to follow, spread all over the GDR.
October 16	More than 100,000 citizens of Leipzig take to the streets chanting: 'We are the people.'
October 18	Erich Honecker is dismissed as General Secretary of the SED. Egon Krenz becomes his successor.
November 4	Biggest mass demonstration in the GDR since June 17, 1953. More than half a million people demand fundamental political change and democracy.
November 9	In an attempt to calm down public outrage, the SED opens the Wall. This proved to be the beginning of the end of communism in East Germany.
November 18	A new government is elected in East Germany, which later includes members of the opposition.
December 3	The Politburo of the SED resigns.
December 7	First meeting of the 'Round Table.'
1990 March 18	First democratic elections in the GDR. Lothar de Maizière, CDU, becomes prime minster on April 12.
June 17	The GDR parliament decides to join the Federal Republic.
July 1	Monetary, Economic and Social Union of the Federal Republic and the GDR comes into place.
September 12	Instead of a final peace treaty with Germany, the Two-Plus-Four Treaty is signed by the foreign ministers of the USA, USSR, United Kingdom, France, and the Federal Republic and the prime minister of the GDR.
September 20	Both German parliaments pass the Unification Treaty, which provides detailed regulations for German unification.

	October 3	Through the accession of the GDR to the Federal Republic, German unification is achieved.
	December 2	First all–German democratic elections since 1933. The Christian–Liberal coalition succeeds in holding onto power. Helmut Kohl is reelected as German chancellor.
1991		German–Polish treaty solves remaining differences between the two states. Treaties with Hungary and Czechoslovakia are to follow.
1992	February 7	Treaty of Maastricht. New provisions in the German constitution pave the way for further European integration.
1994	August 31	The last Russian troops leave German soil.
	November 15	As a consequence of German unification, changes in the Basic Law, proposed by a joint commission of the Bundestag and Bundesrat, are implemented.
1998		After sixteen years, Helmut Kohl is voted out of office by federal elections. Gerhard Schröder is elected as chancellor of a red–green government.
1999	July 1	The German capital moves from Bonn to Berlin.
	October 16	For the first time since World War II, German troops take part in military actions outside Germany, in Kosovo.
2002	September 22	In an unexpected victory, the red–green government succeeds in federal elections. Gerhard Schröder is reelected as chancellor.

1949 and 1989 – New Democratic Beginnings and Continuity

In 1989 two German states – the democratic Federal Republic of Germany (FRG) and the communist German Democratic Republic (GDR) – celebrated their fortieth birthdays. 'Seldom has a state emerged in such a manner,' remarked President Richard von Weizsäcker in his speech on May 24, 1989 at the fortieth anniversary celebration of the enactment of the Basic Law. Four years after the unconditional surrender of the German Reich on May 8, 1945 and the total defeat of the National Socialist regime, the Western Allies paved the way for a democratic order to be established in West Germany, while the Soviet Union created a communist 'satellite system' in East Germany.

Post-war Germany and the Foundation of Two German States

In 1945 the highest governmental power in Germany was taken over by the four Allies: the United States, the Soviet Union, Great Britain, and – after the Potsdam conference of July/August 1945 – France. A constitutional German political order became extinct, and it was unclear when it might resurface in the future, if at all.

Just four years later the Federal Republic of Germany and the German Democratic Republic were created. Both were unintended polities. Neither the Yalta Conference in early 1945, nor the Potsdam Conference which took place after the war in Europe had ended, led to binding decisions by the Allied powers about the future of Germany after the transitional period during which the four Allies governed over a divided country. The foundation of two alien German states in 1949 was the consequence of growing divisions and rising hostilities among the former Allies. The Federal Republic of Germany and the German Democratic Republic were children of the Cold War. When the Cold War ended in 1989/90 there was no historical legitimization to uphold the division of Germany any longer.

When the Federal Republic was created in 1949, it was not a state in the traditional sense, but a 'transitorium,' as the first president, Theodor Heuss, would put it. Or, in the words of Carlo Schmid, a leading Social Democrat, it was an 'emergency formation.' After twelve years of National Socialist tyranny and four years of military occupation, the western part of Germany, with the concurrence of the three Western

1

occupying powers, was allowed to adopt a liberal democratic constitution, which proved able to guarantee a stable political future for the German people in the West.

German politicians were naturally hesitant about this highly unusual state formation. They feared that the formation of a separate state would impede the reunification of Germany, which at that time was divided into four occupied zones administered by the Allies. But the occupying forces of the United States, the United Kingdom and France greatly desired a democratic West and used their position of power to bring their influence to bear upon the new Germany. At the time no one believed that this provisional structure would last nearly half a century.

In 1949 few political pundits dreamed that the newly created state – forced upon the Germans by their Western victors – would develop into a stable, democratic political order supported by its citizenry. A Western protectorate seemed to be the logical outcome of war, not a 'semi – sovereign state' that would, within less than a decade, become a respected member of the commonwealth of democratic nations.

The Federal Republic of Germany was founded as a separate state but with reference to all of Germany. The preamble of the West German constitution – the Basic Law – laid claim to all German people. It set out to 'give new political order for a period of transition ... on behalf of those Germans to whom participation was denied,' i.e. the people in East Germany and in those parts of the former German Reich now administered by Poland and France. The preamble called upon the 'entire German people ... to achieve in free self-determination the unity and freedom of Germany.' The formula 'in free self-determination' meant unification under democratic terms. Reunification was officially the prime goal of West German politics but not at any price: 'unity in liberty' was the shibboleth of the time that allowed for a firm integration of the Federal Republic into Western institutions, which, during the period of the Cold War, contradicted reunification.

This political order drew its normative and institutional ideas from modern democratic theory and practice. The framers of the constitution and most of the political actors relied heavily on British, American and French experiences and the advice given by the representatives of the Western Allies. Even more important for German democrats were the lessons drawn from the failure of the first German democracy – the Weimar Republic – which literally gave itself up and surrendered in 1933 to Nazism. In addition, some of the political actors or their advisors came back from exile with an in-depth knowledge of the functioning and the mechanisms of a liberal democracy.

By its fortieth birthday, the Federal Republic was well regarded for its stable political and economic system. It had evolved into a liberal democracy that provided the institutional framework which ultimately allowed for the previous divisions between the two Germanies to be overcome and the dream of reunification to be realized. When in 1989 German unification was unexpectedly on the national and international political agenda, the ideas of democratic order formulated in the Basic Law and its supplements provided the blueprint for a new political order. When the GDR officially reunited with the Federal Republic on October 3, 1990, this symbolized the death of the old Federal Republic. But it did not initiate the new political order. The latter's roots were firmly planted in the constitution of 1949 and strengthened by the political culture of Germany's second democracy.

How did the Federal Republic manage to develop into a stable democracy? This can largely be explained by the political conditions, which were quite different from those surrounding the first German democracy. The Weimar Republic did not even last fifteen years before it was overrun by National Socialism. In the midst of a global economic crisis that left millions of people unemployed and without hope for the future, the Weimar Republic collapsed at its weakest point. Populist political movements, first and foremost communism and National Socialism, used the dire political situation to gain support at the expense of the democratic parties. The democratic political elites failed to defend the Republic against concerted attacks from its adversaries and, in 1933, handed power to the Nazis.

In comparison to the conditions surrounding the birth of the Federal Republic, the origins of the Weimar Republic were fairly promising. World War I ended in German defeat in the fall of 1918, and the Versailles Treaty called for massive reparations that would burden Germany for several years. Revolution in November 1918 successfully destroyed the former authoritative regime and, after a period of civil unrest, led to the establishment of parliamentary democracy. The internal development of Germany, with the exception of restrictions on military expansion, was in the hands of German politicians. Nevertheless, the new democracy was overshadowed by the suspicion that it had been forced upon the Germans by politicians who had betrayed the people by complying with the harsh regulations of the Versailles Treaty and by renouncing German interests.

The situation during the early years after World War II, however, was quite different. The victory of the Western Allies and the Soviet Union and the unconditional surrender of Nazi Germany signified a fundamental break in the history of the German nation state. The country was occupied. The victorious powers held supreme authority over Germany: the Allied Control Council for Germany was established as supreme power. Germany was divided into four zones of occupation, ruled by Allied military governments. Even after the foundation of the Federal Republic (and the German Democratic Republic) in 1949, some 'reserve powers' of the four Allies concerning Berlin and the future of Germany remained. It was only with the unification of Germany in 1990 that these remnants of World War II were finally abolished. The Allies determined the process by which, and the degree of freedom with which, German politics could be formed. Growing conflicts between the Allies led to divisions within the German state and the emergence of two Germanies. The political order of the Federal Republic was a democracy, formed under the conditions and expectations of the Western Allies, while the GDR represented a Soviet-style political and social system and the German outpost of the new Soviet Empire.

The West German state came into existence in a period of post-war economic and social chaos that can only be described as catastrophic. The fear of social unrest and political instability was, understandably, widespread. Despite this ominous start, a combination of favorable circumstances helped ensure that its democratic development proceeded in marked contrast to that of the Weimar Republic. Unlike during the Weimar Republic, a retrogressive transfiguration of the former political regime was not possible. National Socialism was so thoroughly discredited in the post-war period that only extremist groups on the fringe openly acknowledged solidarity to it.

The Cold War led to an unexpected and rapid integration of West Germany into the international community of free nations, while the GDR fell into the 'socialist camp,' those states ruled or dominated by the Soviet Union. Both German states had no choice but to function as 'outposts' for the enemies on opposite sides of the political and military blocs. It was the Cold War that transformed the 'negative control' of the Federal Republic by the occupying powers into the positive control of a political and social order welcomed into the community of states in the West.

Like West Germany, the GDR was the product of the disintegration of the coalition against Nazi Germany, the Cold War and the changing geopolitical interests of the superpowers. In sharp contrast to the Federal Republic, East Germany was always an 'occupation regime,' a political system under the control of its Soviet occupiers. The East German regime was directly linked to the Soviet Union both politically and militarily. The Soviets were determined to support and defend the GDR in a crisis, and they did so with their tanks in 1953 when they crushed a popular uprising. But they did not do so in 1989.

West Germany's early inclusion in the existing Western European and trans-atlantic communities created the ideal conditions for rebuilding its economy, which would lead to the elimination of poverty and create the conditions required for the 'economic miracle' of the 1950s. The integration of the Federal Republic into the West facilitated the growth of Western values as well as the process of European integration. This integration was not only a meaningful stabilizing factor within the East–West conflict, but also provided a significant contribution to the new political and cultural self-awareness of the Federal Republic. Next to a solid constitutional backing, the Westernization of the Federal Republic signified the strongest security measure against attempts at authoritarianism.

A second factor, not to be underestimated, was the position of the new democracy in opposition to communism. For over forty years, both German states, and in particular Berlin, stood at the center of a battle – often coming close to a military confrontation – between the superpowers of the United States and the Soviet Union. This battle coincided with another – a debate between Marxist-Leninist ideology on the one hand and the ideals of liberal democracy on the other. Germany was on the front line of this political and ideological war, which passed through the heart of Berlin.

The Federal Republic and the GDR represented two contrary political and socio – economic orders as well as political cultures. Both were products of the victorious powers. But the Federal Republic was given the chance to establish a liberal democratic order based on the freely expressed will of its people, while the GDR was deprived of its democratic legitimacy by the Soviet Union. International political conditions and the unique origins of the two German states forced both states to disassociate from one another and challenge the other's right to exist.

The West was concerned that the Soviet Union would threaten the democratic order in Western states such as France and Italy, both with strong communist parties. Naturally, West Germany was deemed especially vulnerable to the spread of communism due to its status as a divided nation, even though the Communists never gained much support in democratic elections. Communism was generally perceived to be democracy's 'mortal enemy,' just as National Socialism and fascism had been previously. The destruction of the Weimar Republic and the specter of Nazism hung heavily over the new democracy. The National Socialist reign of terror in Germany, Stalinism in the Soviet Union in the 1930s, and the Hitler–Stalin Pact of 1939 together promoted the perception of National Socialism and Soviet-style communism as 'totalitarianism.' The Weimar experience, National Socialism and Stalinism essentially determined the antitotalitarian consensus within the young Federal Republic, with the natural exception of the KPD (the Communist Party of Germany).

After the war, the question of how to manage a defeated German Reich occupied the Allies. Conflicts of interest were apparent as early as the Potsdam Conference in the summer of 1945, and came to the fore after the war-coalition of the four powers disbanded in 1948. Debates about the Marshall Plan and currency reform and crises such as the Berlin Blockade and the Soviet Union's withdrawal from the Allied Control Council made the answer obvious: build a divided state under the supervision of the respective victorious powers.

The Western Allies pushed ahead with the establishment of a democracy in their zones of occupation. In the Cold War the differences between the three Western powers' concepts of the new order, which can be explained by the differing constitutional traditions of each country, quickly lost significance. In the beginning, the politicians of the Soviet Union and the GDR successfully gave the impression that their state was only an answer in response to Western imperialism's plans to divide Germany in the interest of the 'monopoly of the bourgeoisie.' Not without success did they reclaim the idea of an undivided nation. Only the failure of their socio-economic experiment – forcing them to seal off their borders and build the Berlin Wall in August 1961 – revealed the hollowness of their rhetoric.

The Federal Republic and the GDR as Political and Societal Antipodes

The two periods of state foundation in post-war German history, 1949 and 1989/90, were periods in which a new political order and a new political culture were built.

In 1949 neither West Germany nor the GDR could link itself to the handed-down political and cultural model, be it of the Bismarck regime, the Wilhelmine Empire, or the Weimar Republic. Both had to be established on a new basis: the ideas of liberal democracy in the West and Marxist-Leninist ideology in the East.

The newly founded West German democracy had to examine the political and cultural traditions which had contributed to the failure of the first German democracy. Democratic convictions and behavior had no solid foundation in Germany. The tradition of antidemocratic thinking and the intellectual after-effects of National Socialism, whose scope and consequences the democrats were very well aware of, were a burden for the young Federal Republic. The establishment of a democratic political order took place under the patronage of the Allies, who installed protections against an authoritarian or totalitarian backlash by means of the reserve powers they continued to hold. In the immediate post-war period and the first few years of the Federal Republic the emergence of a workable, democratic, basic consensus, without which a democracy cannot survive, was not secured. It took over two decades before the ideas of liberal democracy were universally accepted by the West Germans.

In East Germany the break with the past was at first glance much more radical and principled than in the Federal Republic. The GDR portrayed itself an 'antifascist democratic order' which had learned the lessons of history. Not only was the political system revolutionized, but the socio-economic order was as well. The Communists in East Germany promised not only a new form of democracy, but in addition a total and final break with the cultural hegemony of the bourgeoisie and the establishment of a new culture of the previously suppressed majority of the population, the workers and farmers. Without compromise, antifascism became the state doctrine.

The break with the past seemed to be complete in 1948. It is often overlooked that at this time there existed traditional ties to the political culture of an authoritarian state in Germany. These ties were not broken and, in fact, produced a particularly peculiar political, social and cultural environment for the seventeen million Germans in the East. A strange mix of traditional German authoritarianism and Marxist-Leninist ideology emerged and made the GDR a very special type of Soviet-style communist regime. The GDR, after a transitional phase in which the future of the new state structure remained in the balance, claimed to be a model and pillar of a future socialist order in the whole of Germany.

The West German state was founded as an antitotalitarian democratic order and as a 'well-fortified democracy.' The Federal Republic learned from the collapse of the Weimar Republic and the power of National Socialism and established a democratic order as a 'bulwark' against the claim to power of the Stalinist system in the Soviet Union and its German derivative in the GDR. This opposition made it easier to adapt to the new facts without dealing much with the burdens of the past. Only a generation later would the demand for a process of coming to terms with the past be clearly formulated during the political and cultural crises of the 1960s. The GDR understood itself as an antifascist answer to a 'country gone astray' and as a social order which was determined to fight the legacy of the capitalistic and bourgeois (pseudo)democracy.

This confrontational situation shaped more than two decades of domestic politics and foreign relations. In West Germany, communism was seen not only as a danger from outside, but also as a permanent threat to democracy from within. Totalitarianism was understood as the absolute counterimage of free democracy, as a (renewed) deviation from the path of human progress and politics defended by ethics. There was little room in this picture for shades of gray. This led to a permanent conflict in the early years of the Federal Republic between liberal-democratic principles and a political order understood as antitotalitarian, pugnacious and militant.

For more than a decade, the threat from internal and external political forces seemed to present a clear and present danger to democracy and the very existence of the West German polity. This also explains why provocation from the political left was often countered with excessive defense mechanisms. The 'militant democracy' of the 1950s and early 1960s quite often worked at the expense of liberal democracy. Even détente and the new *Ostpolitik*, introduced at the end of the 1960s, did not make this pattern fully obsolete. When, after the building of the Berlin Wall in 1961 and the Cuban Crisis of 1962, the chance for a *modus vivendi* between East and West did begin to form – which was finally accepted and sealed with the Treaty of Helsinki in 1975 at the final conference of the CSCE (Conference on Security and Co-operation in Europe) – the imminent threat of communist infiltration receded and a more liberal view vis-à-vis radical political ideas gained ground in West Germany.

In visible contrast, the GDR leadership, which had to accept détente because it was in the best interests of the Soviet Union, became more and more suspicious of Western political and cultural influence and developed a neurotic aversion to the West. The political regime answered with a policy of ideological and political 'demarcation' (*Abgrenzung*) as well as with the consolidation of a gigantic spying mechanism within the GDR.

The Second Foundation of the Federal Republic

The second founding of the state in 1989/90 took place under a luckier star than that of 1949. The revolution in the GDR and in other socialist states sounded the death knell of the Soviet Empire and the Soviet Union itself. The division of the world into two blocs, which was the logical if not intended result of the Yalta Conference, ended, and the division of Germany and the gap between the two parts of Europe was overcome. Ironically, the catalyst which triggered these developments came unintentionally from the Soviet Union itself under the leadership of Mikhail Gorbachev, who took over as head of the Communist Party in1985. The attempts to modernize the Soviet strand of socialism through a – belated – reform program stimulated political ideas that quickly forced themselves through the tight borders of the system. No other communist state was as dependent on the Soviet Union as East

Germany. As a 'front state' of the Soviet Empire and part of a divided nation, it had no identity as a national state, like for example Poland or Hungary.

Consequently, democratic revolution and regime change in the GDR would inevitably give rise to a new national question, which was not always clear to the actors and observers. Aside from the difficulty of tackling such an imposing political system, a lasting, democratic, independent GDR would only have been conceivable if growing societal agreement had been reached that it would be worthwhile to form out of the dictatorship a democratic political entity divided from the Federal Republic. In a political environment marked by nation states – even if these states formed supranational communities – this would have meant the need to uphold the exclusively political self-definition of the GDR, brought about by the circumstances after 1945. This proved to be unrealistic, even though a great many of the activists of fall 1989 wanted exactly that, a democratic GDR.

While in West Germany a positive identification with the political and social system and a de-facto national identity, labeled as 'constitutional patriotism,' had developed in the years of division, this type of positive understanding failed the society of the GDR. In this respect, the reestablishment of a united German national state was a logical consequence of the democratic revolution in the GDR and for the first time was made possible by the worldwide political constellation.

With reunification, the German political system underwent only minor changes. The basic features of the political and institutional order formulated for West Germany in 1949 could not only be maintained, but they also provided a solid basis for dealing with the unprecedented historical events during and after 1989. Even if German unification did not follow the 'script' which was written for it in the Basic Law and was met with varying misjudgments and problematic individual decisions, the results were remarkably clear. The democratic system of the Federal Republic had not only worked smoothly during the forty-year existence of the 'old' FRG, but also survived the accession of the GDR and German unification in 1990 almost untouched. The proven economic, social, and political order of the old Federal Republic, its constitution, the legal order, and its democratic institutions, became the basis for the united Germany.

To put it in a nutshell: the 'new' Federal Republic is, after the accession of the GDR, nearly identical with the 'old' Federal Republic founded in 1949; the 'Berlin Republic' is a geographically extended 'Bonn Republic.' The federal structure, the parliamentary and governmental system, public administration and the judicial system remained untouched and were simply extended to the east of Germany.

The same holds for Germany's role in Europe and the world. The political, economic, and cultural orientation toward the West was not put in question. The discussion concerning Germany's neutrality, keeping an equal distance between East and West or finding a 'special German way,' did not reemerge.

German unity was carried out harmoniously even with those neighbors, who were at first more than hesitant, such as France, Britain and Poland. However, for the first time in recent history, Germany no longer laid claim to its neighbors' lands. It did not come to a 'renationalization' of German politics, as many had feared, but instead, in the course of and as an indirect consequence of unification, the process of European integration was qualitatively raised to a new level at the Maastricht conference, followed by the Amsterdam conference and finally by EU extension into Central and Eastern Europe.

The Treaty of Maastricht paved the way for further European integration, which led to European Monetary Union and the foundation of a European Central Bank. Both were meant as institutional tools to check the future economic and political power of a state of eighty million people at the very center of Europe.

These developments, and the decisions connected with them, did not come about without conflict but were strongly disputed. Yet they provided the normative, institutional, and political foundations for the democracy of the Federal Republic and ultimately of a unified Germany. That the Federal Republic could serve as a model for a unified Germany can be credited to the decisions of the framers of the constitution. In 1949 they laid the foundations for a democratic political order based on human rights, the rule of law, and civil liberties. In addition, favorable political, economic, and social conditions enabled the Federal Republic to develop as a model for a democratic united Germany – despite the pressures of the Cold War and a divided nation state.

–2–

Constitutionalism and Constitutional Politics in Germany

Every political order requires legitimization. The settlers in North America who disassociated themselves from Britain legitimized themselves through the Declaration of Independence on July 4, 1776: 'We hold these truths to be self-evident, that all men are created equal, that they are endowed by their Creator with certain inalienable rights, that among these are Life, Liberty, and the pursuit of Happiness.' The Republicans of the French Revolution created the triad of Freedom, Equality, and Brotherhood. The constitution of the German Reich of 1871 stressed the sovereign rights of the German Knights, who had formed 'an everlasting bond' which would underpin the German Reich. The constitution of the Weimar Republic referred to the German people as united in ancestry and tradition, willing to renew their Reich, living in freedom and equality, committed to work for societal progress and to strengthen the idea of serving peace within society and between nations.

Every nation state requires a unified mandate. Debates over questions of principle are rare, but they are meaningful at historical turning points such as the critical turning points of German history in 1918, 1945, 1949, and 1989. Even if these debates are not public or fully inclusive, they shape future developments and greatly affect whether a stable political order will be formed.

Within the everyday life of a political community, many factors affect its legitimacy. In the years after 1945, the vast majority of German citizens were preoccupied with organizing their everyday lives under the harsh economic and social conditions of post-war Germany. Millions were left without homes and shelter. Nearly fifteen million people were refugees. Hundreds of thousands were 'displaced persons' of diverse national origins, liberated from Nazi concentration camps and stranded in post-war Germany. There were almost no newspapers, access to public radio was limited and, with the exception of the bigger cities, public life in general was virtually non-existent. These were not favorable conditions for the construction of a new political order based on democratic ideals and requiring the active participation of a people who, only a few years ago, had fervently applauded Nazi dictatorship. A second constraint upon the development of a future democratic order in West Germany was the active involvement of most of the political, economic, judicial, administrative, and scientific elite with the Nazis. Under these circumstances only former exiles and a small political elite from the days of the Weimar Republic could be called upon to play a decisive role in building what was to become the first stable German democracy.

This picture differs markedly from the one that faced Germany in 1989, when the people of the communist GDR, longing for their freedom and liberty, toppled their leadership in a peaceful revolution. As is usual in periods of revolutionary change, the masses played an important role in bringing down the old regime. But creating a new order is mainly the work of an elite. Here again the participants were small groups of former GDR dissidents (and some advisors from the Federal Republic), not those who took to the streets in fall 1989. However, the debate was extensively discussed in the media, and the public had a decisive influence on the process of German unification. The central question was: how and where should the line be drawn between the rules and principles binding for all and the many different opinions that competed within these rules?

The debate was that much more meaningful because German national history did not provide the requisite precedents to develop an uninterrupted historical and cultural self-consciousness and a consensus regarding the basic requirements of a democratic social and political order. Such favorable conditions as did exist were enshrined in the Basic Law of the constitution of the Federal Republic, which provided a solid basis for the constitutional order of a united Germany in 1990.

The Basic Law of West Germany

On May 8, 1945 the German Reich had capitulated. The Yalta formula of 'unconditional surrender,' agreed upon by the Allied forces of the United States of America, the Soviet Union and the United Kingdom at a conference on the Crimean peninsula in February 1945, had far-reaching consequences for Germany. Although the original plans for the 'dismemberment of Germany' were abandoned at the final meeting of the three powers in Potsdam in July/August 1945, all political power was taken over by Allied institutions and France was invited to join the three victorious powers. In Potsdam it was agreed that 'for the time being, no central German government shall be established.' Germany was, for the purpose of occupation, divided into four zones, allotted to the respective powers. These zones of occupation were administered by military governments. Berlin was established as a special political entity under the joint occupation of the four powers. An Inter-Allied Governing Authority (*Kommandantura*), consisting of the four commanders-in-chief, was created for the joint administration of the Berlin Area. Supreme power over Germany was handed to a civil, not a military, institution – the Allied Control Council, situated in Berlin.

This carefully drafted institutional framework collapsed only a few years later with the beginning of the Cold War. The first Berlin crisis of 1948/49 – when the Soviets cut off the supply routes to the Western sectors of Berlin – led to the breakdown of joint Allied institutions. With the creation of two German states in 1949, most of the power of the Allies transferred to the German political authorities. Nevertheless, crucial exceptions were made; despite growing hostility, the four powers maintained their joint responsibility for and reserve powers in Germany as a whole, mainly for any prospect of future reunification and for the administration of the four sectors of Berlin. The Soviets and the Western Allies also reserved special rights and powers both in their respective zones in case of emergency or military conflict, and in determining the future of Germany.

These reserve powers were expressed and documented on various occasions. In a letter to Konrad Adenauer, President of the Parliamentary Council – the body that drafted the West German constitution, the Basic Law – the Western military governors praised the new constitution, passed on May 8, 1949, as a document which combined German democratic tradition with the concepts of representative government and the rule of law. In approving the Basic Law, they made several reservations. The powers vested in the Federation, state (Länder) governments, and local governments were made subject to the provisions of an Occupation Statute. Police powers could not be exercised until approved by the occupation authorities. A third reservation concerned the participation of Berlin in the Federation. Following the approval of the Basic Law by the military governors, the new constitution was passed by the state legislatures (Landtage), not by a popular referendum, and was signed and proclaimed by the Parliamentary Council on May 23, 1949.

The architects of reconstruction were acutely aware that they needed to lay the groundwork for a new democracy that would be strong enough to deal with severe economic, social, and political conditions in a divided country. And they faced a unique problem in a time of constitutional history: where to find a trustworthy source of legitimacy? The founding of a state was only planned for one part of Germany. Germans lived under an occupation regime. The Allies held the highest legal and political power. Fundamental constitutional and political demands by the Western Allies set the course. Nonetheless, after a long and controversial debate, the Preamble to the Basic Law stated that 'the German people in the Länder ... desiring to give a new order to political life for a transitional period, have enacted, by virtue of their constituent power, this Basic Law for the Federal Republic of Germany.'

The Preamble presumed that the German people desired this new order. It also mentioned the fact that not all of the German people were given the chance to express their ideas in a democratic process of state and constitution building. It lay claim to acting on behalf of those Germans who could not take part and expressed the desire that they might have a chance to do so in the future. These statements brought about a series of new legal and political considerations. The writers of the constitution took the view that the founding of two new states did not constitute Germany as a new state. According to the majority opinion among the members of the Constitutional Council, with the unconditional surrender of May 8, 1945 the German Reich as a state had not gone down. In legal terms and as a subject of international law, it still existed but had been 'disorganized' and robbed of its legal competence. The concern now was to reorganize the state even if confined to its western regions. Reference was made in this context to the reconstruction of the fourth Republic in France after World War II and to the agreement in international law in 1919 on identifying the newly founded Poland with the old so-called 'Congress Poland.' A minority believed that, with the end of the armed conflict and unconditional surrender, Germany lost its statehood and became a territory or dependency of the four Allied powers. This legal argument meant that a German state not only had to be newly organized, but also newly constituted. To such a newly-to-be-formed state the Weimar Republic was not to be the legal predecessor. This position could not be sustained and made valid in law.

The assertion that the German Reich had not perished in terms of law, but was only suspended, brought about a series of difficult political and moral consequences. In 1945 a revolution did not take place as it had in 1918, after which the monarchical order was replaced by a republic. But, at the same time, a legal, continued existence of the German Reich had to make an explicit, clear and unambiguous break from the defeated National Socialist state. A connection to the democratic political order of the Weimar Republic was possible, if need be. Weimar's own inglorious decline during 1932 and 1933, however, could have contributed little to the legitimization of a new political order.

The dissent over the basics of the state order was stated very clearly in the proceedings of the Parliamentary Council, elected by the state parliaments in order to develop a constitution for the West German state. The question of the nature of the yet-to-be-founded state and its historical basis played a decisive role. The name 'German Reich' had to be *nolens volens* avoided. Psychological obstacles made the term 'Reich' unpalatable. As one of the most prominent members of the council, Carlo Schmid (SPD), put it, the term had 'been an aggressive accent all around us' and would be read as a 'claim to power.' Jakob Kaiser, the former CDU Chairman in the Soviet occupation zone, counterargued that, by giving up the term 'Reich,' a meaningful principle would be lost. It had a deep emotional meaning 'in this hopeless time.' His greatest worry was that if the term was given up and sober formulations were used, a movement could rise up in a few years that would 'again call for the Reich.' This objection was rejected by pointing to the provisional character of the constitution and the new state. Other members suggested the name 'German Republic' and in the end the later German President, Theodor Heuss (FDP), proposed the formulation 'Federal Republic of Germany.'

The uncertainty and the differences of opinion regarding the character of the state that was still to be formed are evident in the long, controversial debates over the Preamble to the Basic Law. What was the objective of the Basic Law? What should it aim to achieve? What were the normative principles governing the Basic Law? Would Germany continue to exist or must it be newly created? Where did the sources of the state's power lie: within its people or the federal states? Should the

Preamble emphasize the provisional state and transitional character of the Basic Law? Should reference be made to the historical factors that led to the emergence of the state? Should there be an all-German mandate and a guarantee of a right to representation for East Germans? What political outlook should be taken with regard to Germany's future? How should the question of future unification and the resulting constitutional consequences, namely the necessity of a constitution for all Germans, be approached?

The final version of the Preamble to the Basic Law of 1949 contains four basic normative principles. The formulation 'conscious of their responsibility before God and man' refers to Christian and natural rights for a state order, which precede the constitution and are viewed as constitutive for the democratic order. Second, the question of the sovereignty of the whole German people played a large role in the discussions. The Preamble does not refer to the German people in the newly founded Federal Republic but to the German people in the Länder, the federal states. This statement alludes to an empirical fact, namely the already existing democratically structured German states, but appeals also to the aspect of the federalist order.

The fact that the entire German population could not form the citizenship of the state was obvious. In order to make clear the validity of the constitution for all Germans, the Preamble awards the citizens in the West – only a part of the entire sovereign citizenship – the right to act on behalf of their fellow citizens in the East, and gives every German 'to whom participation was denied' the right to do so in the future. Acting on behalf of the East Germans in the Soviet zone and those Germans still living in parts of the former Reich now administered by Polish and Soviet authorities also meant granting citizenship to all Germans, regardless of their current residence.

The third basic principle was an emphasis on the temporary character of the constitution and the call upon the entire German population to achieve 'the unity and freedom of Germany in free self-determination.' Only with these qualifications could the new constitution claim its legitimacy. With regard to the future, the Preamble of the Basic Law refers to the will of the German people 'to promote world peace as an equal partner in a united Europe.' This commitment could be perceived as a fourth normative cornerstone of the new democratic political order in West Germany. The question of the legitimacy of the new political order was highly explosive given the fact that two separate states existed and in the light of the crimes of the National Socialist German Reich, whose legal consequences the Federal Republic inherited. All those who participated in the constitutional process were in agreement that a political order could only claim legitimacy if founded upon the principles of sovereignty of the people, respect for and protection of the dignity of man, and civil rights. This became even more critical as only a segment of the population could participate in this process, and only indirectly.

It was, of course, more than a question of legal theory. Could a political order that came about under the tutelage of and the legal terms set by the occupying forces make this claim of participation? Much was at stake in attempting to place the democratic order upon a secure foundation. This required more than an understanding of the formal organization of political institutions. A basic consensus was needed upon which the new order could be constructed. Because of this, the Basic Law formulated more than a mere legal framework for the allocation of authority and responsibility for each state institution – it defined essential elements of parliament, government, and the judiciary.

It described, and still does describe, a political program. This program lays down the idea that a democratic community can only exist if common basic principles are agreed upon and if institutions are formed that limit the powers of the state and bind them legally. This idea of modern constitutionalism allows for different concrete forms of organizing these basic principles – in the form of basic rights – as well as diverse institutional arrangements.

The Socialist Constitution of East Germany

Immediately after the war, most Germans assumed that Germany, after a short period of Allied occupation, would continue to be a united national state. Within three years of the war's end the division of Germany had become a central fact of Great Power politics. The foundation of two German states, closely associated with the now alien former Allies, was a logical consequence of the growing tension between East and West.

After the collapse of four-power control in 1948 and the Berlin Blockade, the Western powers and the Soviet Union sponsored German politicians to prepare for the foundation of separate states in the West and the East of Germany. In the Soviet zone of occupation, a quasi-parliamentary body, the German People's Congress, was established, as a counterpart to the West German Parliamentary Council, to write a constitution for East Germany. In response to the foundation of the Federal Republic in May 1949, the Congress elected a provisional parliament, which later became the People's Chamber (*Volkskammer*) of the GDR.

When the German Democratic Republic was proclaimed on October 7, 1949, a constitution came into being which did not reflect the Soviet Union's aim of establishing a Soviet-style socialist state but pretended to found a democratic republic that was meant to be a role model for Germany as a whole.

It was not a 'socialist' constitution in that it did not draw on the Soviet constitution of 1936 as a model. However, it left the door open to a socialist system and made the transformation of the GDR into a Soviet-style system possible. In many of its stipulations, the constitution was tied closely to notions of democratic socialism as well as the Weimar constitution. This was clear through the emphasis placed on social basic rights. Like the Weimar constitution, economic life would be regulated on the foundations of social equality. The introduction of economic planning in Article 21, the authorization to expropriate without compensation according to Articles 23 and 24, and the authorization of the state to socialization of private property in Article 27, as well as the obligation of the coal and steel and energy industries to convert to state-owned status, provided the constitutional instruments for the transformation to a centrally administered economy in the Soviet style.

The denunciation of the principle of separation of powers also revealed elements of a Marxist-Leninist progression. There was no provision for constitutional jurisdiction controlled by a supreme court, and the power to test the constitutionality of laws was transferred to the constitutional committee of the GDR's parliament, the *Volkskammer* (Article 66). As there was no general legal protection clause such as could be found in the Federal Republic's Basic Law, constitutional jurisdiction was restricted from the very beginning of the GDR. The implementation of a so-called 'bloc-system' in Article 92 was of great importance in the formation of the political order. All parliamentary groups were to participate in the government proportionately to their number of seats, and no provisions were made for a parliamentary opposition.

The first two decades of the GDR's existence were characterized by contradictions. While the political reality in the early 1950s was dominated by the almost complete adoption of the Soviet model, the constitution of 1949 gave the impression that the GDR was adopting political traditions stemming from the Weimar Republic. Over the years, constitutional norms and reality diverged ever more. The constitution included clauses on basic civil rights, freedom of association and freedom of expression, although in reality the implementation of these rights was never seriously considered.

In 1968 a new, 'socialist' constitution was passed unanimously by parliament. It described the SED (*Sozialistische Einheitspartei Deutschlands*, the Socialist Unity Party of Germany) as the leading force of socialist society, which, in 'eternal brotherhood' with the Soviet Union, intended to pave the way for a communist society. The constitution of 1968 put into law the societal changes that had taken place since the GDR's founding. It abolished a series of basic rights of the constitution of 1949. These included the right to opposition, the freedom to strike, the election of workers' councils, and the right to emigrate. The same thing happened for the regulation of the economic order. The rules regarding the building of the state, jurisprudence, and representative bodies of the people were adjusted as well.

The constitution of 1974, drawn up on the twenty-fifth anniversary of the GDR, guaranteed extensive basic rights and duties for each citizen: religious freedom, freedom of thought, freedom of opinion, freedom of assembly, freedom of association, freedom of movement (within the boundaries of the GDR), and equal opportunities for men and women. Social rights, such as the right to education, work, leisure time and recreation, health, public welfare, living space and the protection of family, and special support for the youth were all formally granted but never secured in practice. The fact that basic rights complied with basic duties was characteristic of the constitutional understanding of the GDR. For example, the right to a profession was coupled with the duty to work. Basic rights and basic duties not only determined the status of the individual citizen, but the GDR constitution also regulated 'collective' basic rights and duties, which were observed by businesses, cities, and municipalities or community organizations.

Herein can the concepts of Marxist-Leninist constitutional theory be found: individual and collective, personal and social basic rights build an indivisible unity. This meant that individual basic rights remained politically bound. In actual fact, these basic rights were subordinate to the interests of the political community. Individual civil liberties were denied in order to serve the greater good – as formulated by the Marxist-Leninist Party, not by the people. This interpretation of basic rights forbade legal enforcement of individual rights, be it through the administrative jurisdiction or with the help of a constitutional court.

Constitutional Basics of the Federal Republic's Political Order

In 1949 the constitutional legislators decided upon a representative parliamentary democracy for West Germany. At first sight, what the Basic Law means by 'democratic' seems straightforward enough. Thus the Basic Law asserts that: 'All state authority is derived from the people' (Article 20.2). The phrase 'is derived from the people' does not mean 'is conducted by the people.' The process takes place 'through elections and other votes and through specific legislative, executive, and judicial bodies' (Article 20.2). The Basic Law provides for state authority to be exercised directly by the people only in the case of Article 29 on redrawing the territorial boundaries of the Länder. The constitutions of the various Länder contain different and generally more extensive arrangements for citizens to participate directly.

The emphasis laid on the representative character of the new democracy was due to the political elite's distrust of the supposedly easily manipulated, unorganized will of the people. The prominence given to the representative principle at the expense of the direct participation of citizens was the result of a lesson learned from the negative impact of the masses and mass movements in the Weimar Republic and the experience of National Socialism, which was initially supported by the majority of the population. An aversion toward including elements of a plebiscite existed in the Basic Law. The founding fathers of the constitution were skeptical about direct participation in politics by the citizenry.

Until now that view has made it difficult to develop forms of political decision making based on popular participation and consultation. After the positive experiences of the citizens' rights movement in the GDR in 1989–90, many had expected that constitutional reform would lead to the introduction of elements of direct democracy, especially in relation to public petitions, citizens' action groups and referenda. This has not happened, mainly because the CDU–CSU and, to a lesser extent, the Liberals raised objections, and thus the two-thirds majority necessary to amend the constitution was not forthcoming.

Democracy as a political principle asks for the conversion of the political will of the citizens into political decisions and laws. Here the Basic Law allocates considerable authority to organized and institutionalized popular opinion: through the freedom of association and coalition-building which is anchored into the basic rights in Article 9, and the special emphasis upon the role of political parties – the so-called party privileges in Article 21 of the Basic Law. The tension between the, in principle, unlimited sovereignty of the people with a decision-making majority and the constitutional and legal limitation of this power in order to make democracy institutionally possible cannot structurally be abolished. All precautions are fragile and – at least during societal crises – at risk.

This fragility of the post-war political situation and the experiences drawn from the Weimar Republic caused several precautions to be added to the Basic Law. It puts a strong emphasis on clear-cut structural principles of the political order. These include popular democracy, federalism, separation of powers, the rule of law, party competition, and certain principles of self-defense of the democratic order. Democracy manifests itself in representative institutions, federalism in strong Länder governments and local self-government, separation of powers in the division of authority between the constitutional organs of the national government, the rule of law in a judiciary that is independent of the executive and the legislature, party competition in open, free, and direct elections, and principles of a self-defensive political order in the prohibition of activities that aggressively combat the values and principles of the constitutional order, the so-called free democratic basic order.

Safeguards were built into the constitution in order to immunize the political system against fundamental changes imposed by the political majority of the day or populist leaders:

- The decision for a parliamentary system instead of a presidential or semi-presidential system as in the Weimar Republic
- The installation of assurances against 'negative majorities' in Article 67 of the Basic Law – the vote of no confidence which allows for the replacement of the chancellor as head of government only if the majority of parliament is able to vote a successor into office
- The emphasis on the principle of representation in place of participation and especially elements of direct democracy
- The partial revision of this principle through the establishment of political parties as constitutionally privileged political actors
- The commitment (as demanded by the Allies) to a federal system instead of a unitary state.

The programmatic dimension of the Basic Law is expressed especially through certain important principles captured in Articles 20, 24, and 28. Article 20.1 of the

Basic Law defines the Federal Republic as 'a democratic and social federal state,' while Article 28.1 discusses the constitutional order of the Länder, which must 'conform to the principles of a republican, democratic, and social state governed by the rule of law, within the meaning of this Basic Law.' Article 20.2 anchors the separation of powers, and 20.3 the principle of the rule of law.

Article 24 is of particular importance. It gives the Federation the right to transfer sovereign powers to international organizations: 'With a view to maintaining peace, the Federation may enter into a system of mutual collective security; in doing so it shall consent to such limitations upon its sovereign powers as will bring about and secure a lasting peace in Europe and among the nations of the world.' These formulations were written at a time when the German authorities had almost no sovereign powers. They were, however, meant as a signal to the outside world that the new Germany would never try 'to go it alone' but be constrained by international law and mutual agreements of democratic states.

To add to these, the new Article 23, inserted after German unification, allows the transfer of sovereignty to the European Union. The involvement of the Federal Republic in the development of the EU is bound to one specific normative framework: the Union must be 'committed to democratic, social, and federal principles, to the rule of law, and to the principle of subsidiarity,' and ensure 'a level of protection of basic rights essentially comparable to that afforded by this Basic Law.' Hereby, six constitutive leading principles are formulated in the Basic Law: the republican principle, the principle of a federal state, the principle of the rule of law, the social state principle, the democratic principle, and the principle of loss of partial sovereignty.

Basic Rights and the System of Values (*Werteordnung*) of the Basic Law

In formulating the Basic Law, the Parliamentary Council debated the nature of human and citizens' rights. Should, for example, elements of the political order be secured within the basic rights, along with the rights of individuals? Should there be a catalog of basic rights? Given the proposed provisional nature of the document, some legislators determined that it would be sufficient to concentrate their efforts on developing legal norms for state organization. Taking into account the conditions and restraints demanded by the occupying powers, German politicians, especially those involved in the SPD, were in favor of omitting basic rights completely from the Basic Law.

Yet a catalog of basic rights was nevertheless formulated – sparked not only by constitutional-theoretical debates but by direct political causes. Within the competition between the political systems of Western democracies and communism, the question of securing freedom and the dignity of man played a significant role.

From the point of view of the liberal democracies of the West, Bolshevism seemed as dangerous and as inimical in principle to the freedom and dignity of the people as National Socialism had been until 1945. Countering Bolshevism meant emphasizing liberal ideas and values in order to allow democracy to flourish and to develop the strength to defend itself.

To achieve this, the Basic Law would enshrine an extensive catalog of basic rights in order to anchor the principles of democracy. This would also serve as a defensive line against counterattacks from those intent on destroying the democratic order. However, the Parliamentary Council did not allow for the inclusion of extensive social and economic civil rights. The incompatibility of the various positions of the political parties in the Council made clear that a considerable expansion of the list of basic rights would make agreement impossible. This moved the CDU/CSU as well as the SPD representatives to plead for the inclusion only of classical fundamental rights.

This 'minimalist' position could not be sustained, partly because the politicians were unable to ignore societal demands or to standardize certain basic elements of a political and social order within the basic rights section of the constitution. Article 6 of the Basic Law places marriage and the family under special constitutional protection. Article 7 states the rights of parents and establishes religion as a formal subject in public schools, while prohibiting preparatory schools. Article 14 protects property and inheritance rights, defines property as imposing duties and requires that 'its use should also serve the public good.' Expropriation shall only be permissible in the public good and is tied to an appropriate compensation. Article 15 allows under certain conditions the socialization of 'land, natural resources, and means of production' and the transfer of private property to public ownership or other forms of public enterprise. But in general, principles of individual freedom and civil liberties take precedence in the basic rights section of the constitution. The restriction of personal freedoms can only be justified if a judge rules that it is in the interest of the public good.

The founders of the constitution insisted upon drafting a coherent set of rights that included individual freedoms, civil liberties, restrictions on state powers, and legal tools to put a curb on unconstitutional and antidemocratic movements and activities. German history spoke heavily against the restriction of basic rights to individual rights of freedom, especially when parliament could override constitutional provisions with a simple majority, as had often been the case in the Weimar Republic. That is why changes to the provisions of the Basic Law need a two-thirds majority in both houses of parliament, the Bundestag and the Bundesrat.

And last but not least, they put basic rights and constitutional law above all other legal norms. All legislation, as well as every act of government, must be measured against constitutional norms. This was meant to avoid the extensive use of state authority, as widely exercised by governments and the President of the Weimar Republic. The President, in particular, had far-reaching legal options in a state of emergency, which derived from Article 48.2 of the Weimar Constitution. The President could suspend basic rights by stepping in 'with the help of the armed forces, if necessary.' This was the legal basis for the so-called Enabling Act of February 28, 1933, delivered by the President of the German Reich without the consent of parliament. This decree suspended the most crucial basic rights 'for the time being' and shifted all state power to the president and the government, led by the Nazi Party. The Act paved the way for the National Socialist dictatorship. National Socialism then annulled all basic rights, as its ideology was founded on the denial of personal and civil rights and of a civilized society.

Against this background, the vast majority of the Parliamentary Council was convinced that, after the excesses of Nazi power, securing fundamental basic rights had absolute priority over other considerations. Therefore, these rights were formulated as standing above all other laws. In addition, initial experiences with the extensive catalog of basic rights enshrined in state constitutions drafted immediately after the war revealed the danger of a gap between constitutional rhetoric and constitutional reality which might threaten the consolidation of a democratic order after the end of a dictatorship.

After more than fifty years of constitutional practice, today there is no controversy about the vital role of the catalog of basic rights formulated in the Basic Law. This is especially thanks to the guardian of the Constitution, the Federal Constitutional Court. In many fundamental judgments, the court developed the position that the Basic Law does indeed represent a normative order, but in its basic rights section 'also sets up an objective system of values.' The Basic Law binds not only the state but also its citizens and influences civil rights.

When basic rights are understood as an expression of a value system and their legal and factual forces are secured, then the question arises if and to what extent they are at the legislator's disposal. The Basic Law explicitly binds all state powers, as well as the legislator, to respect basic rights. Basic rights take immediate effect and the general laws must be in line with the special status of the basic laws: 'The following basic rights shall bind the legislature, the executive and the judiciary as directly applicable law' (Article 1.3). Any amendment to the Basic Law can only be made through a law that 'expressly' amends or supplements the text (Article 79.1 Basic Law).

A legal annulment of basic rights through laws passed by a two-thirds majority – as required in order to change the constitution – is possible only in limited cases. "In no case may the essence of a basic right be affected" states Article 19.2 of the Basic Law. Some basic rights are protected against any change or annulment. One of the most important provisions of the constitution is the so-called 'eternal guarantee' in Article 79.3: 'Amendments to this Basic Law affecting the division of the Federation into Länder, their participation on principle in the legislative process, or the principles laid down in Articles 1 and 20 shall be inadmissible.' Article 20 defines the institutional principles of the Federal Republic, and Article 1 refers to the inviolability of human dignity: 'To respect and protect it shall be the duty of all state authority.'

The rights enshrined in the Basic Law demonstrate the extent to which Nazism influenced the new political order. Standard individual rights were enlarged substantially and stated more precisely than they had been in the Weimar Constitution. Article 2.1, for instance, secures the right of every person to develop his personality freely as long as he 'does not violate the rights of others or offend against the constitutional order or the moral law.' Other provisions directly rooted in the Nazi experience are evident in Article 6.3, whereby it is unlawful to separate children from their parents against the will of the persons entitled to bring them up, and Article 12.3, which bans forced labor.

New basic rights were also established in Germany. Article 1.1 anchors the dignity of man and its protection by the state. Reacting against the torture, euthanasia and forced sterilization under National Socialism, Article 2.2 recognizes the right to life and the inviolability of each person. Article 16.2 guarantees the right of asylum. The example of the right of asylum, whose original meaning was annulled in 1993 with the addition of Article 16a of the Basic Law, demonstrates the importance of changing political frameworks in shaping legal norms. Another new right considered was the right of individual resistance against state authority. The Parliamentary Council initially dismissed a right of resistance. Only in conjunction with legislation in times of emergency was a right of resistance introduced in 1968 in Article 20.4 of the Basic Law, which gives all Germans the right to resist anyone who tries to 'abolish this constitutional order.'

The Basic Law contains no explicit statements regarding whether, and to what degree and with which means, the state acts not only as the addressee of individual rights, but also as the agent that protects its citizens against threats and intrusion into their rights by others. The old, classic-liberal dichotomy of citizen versus state was no longer in evidence. In modern societies personal freedom is at risk not only from the government; the rights of an individual are no longer threatened only by the state, but also by societal forces. In democracies, the state is given the task of protecting the citizen's range of freedoms through legislation against any threat. The state can, and must, in some cases, protect citizens against non-state powers and step in as the guarantor and protector of basic rights: life, freedom, security, and property. These are duties of the state that traditionally belonged to the list of tasks assumed by state authorities, but were handled exclusively within the civil, criminal, and procedural law.

Because of serious inequalities within society and basic changes in the economic and social structure, people in modern societies are prevented in many ways from fully developing their skills and gaining opportunities. The task of the political community is to give people the chance to live free and unchallenged. These freedoms are, however, endangered not only by state involvement. Increasingly, these freedoms are endangered through economic and social groups with power over the means of production or human capital, internationally operated economic interests or through criminal activities. Non-state powers are becoming the force against which individual rights must be protected. This problem escalates as powerful groups and interests build across international networks beyond the control of nation states.

Here the previous situation is turned on its head: the state must build a corrective against these claims to power since individual and social groups are too weak to protect their rights effectively. The endangerment of the freedoms of the people does not originate exclusively from the state. The democratic state functions more often as a protector against private powers; in other words, it takes over in a new way functions that were pertinent at the beginning of modern state development after the religious civil wars of the seventeenth century.

To conclude from this that society has become omnipotent and developed into a danger to the individual would be an overstatement. Some authors, like the former Federal President Roman Herzog, who is also an eminent lawyer, argue this case. However, following this argument, the state is not the only addressee of distrust, but society also becomes a source of threat to basic rights. The fear of a 'society that is turning totalitarian' can develop into the call for a strong state which can put an end to these developments. This leads to the belief that only an independent and strong state can secure and push through basic rights against these bearers of social power.

The members of the Parliamentary Council, as previously mentioned, declined to embrace such far-reaching theoretical and political-programmatic ideas and to add matching statements to the catalog of basic rights. They concentrated much more on the anchoring of individual basic rights and on their protection in ways that were unambiguous and free from loopholes. This does not mean, however, that they acted in a value-free fashion, as is shown by the debate surrounding the Preamble and individual basic rights. On the contrary, the relativity of the values of the Weimar Constitution and of legal thought during the years between the World Wars was sharply criticized and deemed responsible for the fact that the first German democracy had failed. For the constitution of the second German democracy, legislators wanted a more explicit value reference system.

Since the Basic Law does not provide this directly and could not, the Federal Constitutional Court was called upon to act as the 'guardian of the constitution.' In many verdicts the court justified a 'duty of protection' for the state with regard not only to the individual, but to all citizens as a whole. The state, with its responsibility for the protection of the individual, has the power to decide whether considerations for the public good, however understood, should take precedence over individual interests in certain situations. Such an interpretation in favor of the public good over the specific rights of the individual is not without danger. This can lead to a suspension of basic rights, as seen in the debate about the right to asylum in Article 16 of the Basic Law and its new version in Article 16a, dated June 28, 1993.

Modern constitutions, like the Basic Law, often include in their basic rights section, alongside subjective basic rights, other rights that do not formulate primary rights but instead contain fundamental elements of a given society and the political order, like property rights or the freedom of assembly. These elements of the political order are anchored in basic rights in order to remove the chance of quick action and possible easy manipulation of the legislator and a ruling majority. In the Basic Law, legislators added a series of elements to the usual regulations regarding freedom of expression, freedom of assembly, and freedom of association; these were once again motivated by history. They include, for example, the state supervision of the education system (Article 7.1 Basic Law), the teaching of religion in schools (Article 7.3 Basic Law), the autonomy of tariffs (Article 9.3 Basic Law), the social obligation of private property (Article 14.3 Basic Law), and the forfeiture and restriction of basic rights (Article 18 and 19 Basic Law) to protect the constitutional order.

The Basic Law purposely does not formulate basic rights that can be interpreted as individual claims on state performance. This means, for example, that in Article 12 all Germans are given the right to choose freely their trade, occupation, or profession, their place of work and their place of training, but there is no right to a certain profession or certain training. With the formulation that the Federal Republic is a 'social federal state' in Article 20.1 and a 'republican, democratic, and social state governed by the rule of law', in Article 28.1, the term 'social' became a keyword of German constitutional and political thinking. Legislators and the Supreme Court referred to the social obligation of the state in order to legitimize the extension of the social welfare state. The meaning of the social state shifted from the entitlement of people to support if needed to an understanding of all-encompassing provision of social welfare by the state. Nevertheless, attempts in the aftermath of German unification to add social basic rights and state goals to the Basic Law failed. It is left to the legislator to interpret and fill in the general statements regarding the social welfare state as mentioned in the Basic Law.

The Basic Law influenced later legislation, in particular the highly contested verdicts of the Supreme Court, such that a kind of canon of values developed. This canon goes beyond liberal ideas in defense of individual citizens in opposition to the sate and establishes certain principles that are binding not only on the state and its institutions, but also on social and political actors. The canon includes, to give just a few examples, the idea of a social market economy, the basis of the German welfare state, the special protection of the family, and the principle of freedom of research and teaching.

The 'Free Democratic Basic Order'

As previously mentioned, the Basic Law is not only a statute book formulating rules for the functioning of state institutions, but also a document that lays down the very basis of fundamental norms for a liberal and democratic political order. In forming the Basic Law, legislators drew heavily from the lessons learned from the failed

Weimar Republic and the rise of National Socialism. This historical context helps explain why a particular vision of liberal democracy was formulated in the Basic Law. The Basic Law formulates binding normative positions – in particular in the basic rights section – and defines in the Preamble and in Article 20 the unchanging basic requirements for such a free and democratic political order: a republican democratic order and social state, governed by the rule of law.

These principles constitute what the Basic Law labels as the 'free democratic basic order,' which is basically the constitutional order of the Federal Republic. The protection of this order allows for the abolition of the secrecy of post and telecommunications (Article 10.2), the restriction of the freedom of movement (Article 11.2), the forfeiture of basic rights (Article 18), and the unconstitutionality of political parties (Article 21.2). The term is also mentioned in the context of internal emergency (*innerer Notstand*) and 'any imminent danger to the existence or free democratic basic order of the Federation or of a Land' (Article 91), and the use of armed forces within the country's borders to support the police 'in protecting civilian property and combating organized armed insurgents' (Article 87a.4). The term is used in the Basic Law whenever the protection of the political and social order and the associated restriction or forfeiture of basic rights are concerned. The term does not encompass the entire set of constitutional regulations regarding the political order, but refers to the inalienable values and basics of the constitution. Against disturbance or endangering of the free democratic basic order the Basic Law provides for many drastic measures, up to and including the forfeiture of citizens' rights. This makes it all the more astonishing that the legislators did not provide a legal definition of this order.

Despite the constant questioning of the Basic Law's positive, coherent, and systematic value system, the fact that it is a declaration of a political order which rests on specific basic principles and that only an ex negativo definition of this order exists is rarely discussed. This means that the Basic Law itself, as mentioned, does not positively define the free democratic basic order. However, it imposes sanctions on any attempt to disrupt this order, for example by providing regulations declaring certain political parties unconstitutional and outlawing them.

At first sight, it appears completely reasonable and unquestionable that a core of the political community must be protected. Therefore, sanctions must be available. The threat of sanctions, however, equals a restriction of freedom. The question is whether democratic freedom can be restricted – and if yes, under which circumstances and with which resources – in order to protect democracy against enemies of freedom. The concern here is to protect not only the state and its institutions, but the republican and the constitutional order.

Based on past experience, which showed that a democracy can be weakened or even eliminated by its own devices, the idea of a 'militant democracy' originated. This idea, originally proposed during the war when the Western powers were fighting the Nazi empire in collaboration with the Soviet Union, gained new prominence during the Cold War. Against the background of National Socialism, the heightening of the Cold War, and the threat to democracy coming from an aggressive communist system in the Soviet Union, restrictions on civil rights and participatory democracy seemed justifiable. It was clear to both society and state that it was worth protecting the democratic order even at a high political price. This protection had to be guaranteed by extraordinary means that, in more peaceful times, would be considered antiliberal but were now essential in stabilizing and protecting democracy against its enemies.

In light of the significance which Article 21 of the Basic Law assigns to political parties as bearers of informed political opinions, it is not surprising that the Constitutional Court only defined the term 'free democratic basic order' more specifically with regard to the banning of the neo-Nazi *'Sozialistische Reichspartei'* (SRP) in 1952 and the 'Communist Party of Germany' (KPD) in 1956. The two parties were banned because they jeopardized the liberal democratic order. A similar attempt made by the government and the two chambers of parliament to outlaw the right-wing 'National Democratic Party' (NPD) failed in 2003 not because the court ruled on the democratic credentials of that particular party but because of procedural deficiencies. The court had not been informed by the authorities that nearly one third of the leading members of the state and federal boards of the NPD were informers of the *Verfassungsschutz*, the German agency for the protection of the constitution.

The starting point of the Constitutional Court was the legitimacy of the Federal Republic's political order and the determination, based on experience, of the framers of the constitution not to fall into the arms of the enemy of democratic order. If parties are given such a prominent role as they are in the Basic Law, where political parties were raised to the level of constitutional institutions, they have to comply with basic democratic norms and rules. In its judgment against the SRP, the court defines the free democratic basic order as a political order which refrains from arbitrary rule and despotism and is based on the right of self-determination of the people, as well as liberty and equality among its citizens. The guidelines of such an order are human rights as articulated in the Basic Law, the basic principle of separation of powers, responsibility of the government to parliament, public administration bound to the rule of law, independence of the judiciary, a multiparty system and the right of the opposition to express its view in parliament and in public.

Based on this idea, the Constitutional Court later decided upon questions of political extremism and the rights and duties of civil servants. Civil servants are not only expected to accept the basic principles of the democratic order, but also to keep a clear distance from groups and movements which offend, defame and fight against the constitutional order.

Interestingly enough, the meaning of the term 'free democratic basic order' was broadened in the course of German unification. In the treaties signed by the GDR and the Federal Republic, which provided the constitutional framework for unification, the term 'social market economy,' never before mentioned in the Basic

Law, was added. The social market economy was a term of central meaning to the political understanding within society in the Federal Republic and the aspirations of the people of the GDR.

Article 1.3 of the Treaty on Monetary, Economic and Social Union states: 'The basis of the currency union is a social market economy'; Article 2.1 states: 'The parties of the contract avow to a free, democratic, federal, constitutional, and social basic order.' The Preamble to the Unification Treaty speaks of a 'constitutionally oriented democratic and social federal state.'

These formulations – even if no more than verbal concessions to the mentality of the East German contractual partner – shift the weight of the term "free democratic basic order" from a political defense mechanism in its original use to a broader meaning. This order not only includes political norms and regulations but also encompasses the social basis of the political order.

The Basic Law, originally intended to be a provisional constitutional foundation, survived the forty years of the Federal Republic and in 1990, with only slight changes, was transformed into the constitution of the reunified Germany. What is more, the Basic Law served in the decades after 1949 as a plausible model constitution for many countries which had shaken off dictatorship and were searching for a foundation for their new democratic order. Out of a provisional legal arrangement, a constitution was formed over the decades which not only proved itself as a solid foundation of German post-war democracy, but could also serve, without significant amendments, as the constitution of the reunified Germany.

–3–

The Constitution of the United Germany

In 1989 both German states planned their fortieth anniversaries. While the Federal Republic could look back proudly on forty years of democracy and freedom, the GDR observed its anniversary in a shattered political state in which the accustomed autocratic rule of the Communist Party was deeply questioned.

The fortieth anniversary of the Federal Republic was marked by pride in what had been achieved: the solid foundations of the second German democracy and hope for the future. Simultaneously, positive signs were emerging from the communist bloc. The rise of non-communist governments in the spring of 1989 and the leadership of the Soviet Union under Mikhail Gorbachev led to hopes of reunifying the 'European house' and improving German–German relations. Still, the political situation of early 1989 did not suggest that a reunified Germany was on the cards in the foreseeable future. Within months this scenario changed dramatically as the borders in Hungary opened and growing unrest in East Germany began to spread to other states in Eastern Europe. However, when the question first arose in fall 1989 of how the two German states might one day be unified, it seemed more or less hypothetical.

The two German states had become accustomed to the division of Germany and Europe. In the 1960s the leadership of the GDR had already given up its claim to represent the 'better' Germany and therefore serve as a model for a unified Germany. By the mid-1970s hints of future unification were no longer on the table. Article 1 of the 1949 constitution of the GDR had called Germany a 'non-divisible democratic republic,' built upon the German states. At that time, the GDR, like the Federal Republic, saw itself as a provisional state and part of a divided nation. The 1968 constitution described the GDR as a 'socialist state of German nationality.' This formulation was dropped in an amendment to the constitution in 1974. The new formulation reads as follows: 'The German Democratic Republic is a socialist state of workers and peasants. It is the political organization of the working people ... under the leadership of the working class and its Marxist-Leninist Party.'

This change was an indication of the state's altered self-image. It signals the central problem of a state that sees itself as part of a divided nation, established within a particular political-historical situation in which no final answer to its national question existed. In sharp contrast to the leaders of all other socialist states, the GDR leadership could never claim to act as representative of the nation pursuing national interests. The constitution of 1968 and the altered version of 1974 formulated the basic elements of a socialist state based on the Soviet model. They caused a change in the self-image of the GDR, which until then had stressed its role as forerunner of a socialist future for the whole of Germany.

In the Federal Republic the aspiration to attain German unification was never officially given up. The Basic Law in its preamble even claimed the right of the German people in the West to act not only on their own behalf but also on behalf of those Germans in the East. Over the years, it became obvious that this goal might only be achieved in the distant future. Even the idea of a single German nation state took a back seat to the goal of European-wide peace, which seemingly provided an answer to the German question.

The Quest for Reunification in the Basic Law

In the event of future unification, the Basic Law contained a special concluding article (Article 146 Basic Law), and the Preamble to the Basic Law expressed the desire to achieve "the unity and freedom of Germany" in free self-determination. Therefore, a restriction was included in Article 146 of the Basic Law regarding the duration of its own validity, which would end when a new constitution was 'freely adopted by the German people.'

Another provision of the Basic Law, the old version of Article 23, provided 'other parts of Germany' with the chance to join the Federal Republic. This was meant primarily for the Saarland, but also for the Soviet occupation zone and those areas which after 1945 were put under Polish rule. Politically, this provision became obsolete after the accession of the Saarland to the Federal Republic in 1957, the recognition of the current European borders as stated in treaties with the Soviet Union and Poland in 1971 (*Ostverträge*), the so-called Basic Treaty (*Grundlagenvertrag*) between the Federal Republic and the GDR in 1972, and the Final Act of the Conference on Security and Co-operation in Europe (CSCE) in Helsinki in 1975.

These developments led to a heated debate about whether these provisions of the Basic Law had become legally obsolete because there were no other parts of Germany left which could join the Federal Republic. The *Ostverträge* put (not in legal but in political terms) an end to the discussion about whether those former parts of Germany that were now part of Poland would, in the case of unification, be subsumed into Germany. With the Basic Treaty, the Federal Republic for the first time accepted the statehood of the GDR. According to the Preamble to the Basic Law, 'the entire German people' were called upon to achieve the "unity and freedom of Germany in free self-determination". In actuality, only West German democratic institutions had the chance to determine a new constitution for this part of Germany. However, they claimed by virtue of 'their constituent power' that they had also, as the Preamble put it, 'acted on behalf of those Germans to whom participation was denied,' i.e. the East Germans in the Soviet zone of occupation.

It is from this phrasing that the Federal Republic asserted its right as the legal representative of German statehood after the defeat of the Nazis and the division of Germany following World War II. These legal claims made a *modus vivendi* with the GDR extremely complicated because, in terms of international law, the Federal Republic could not acknowledge the statehood of the GDR like that of any other state. Under the constitution, the GDR was nothing more than an integral part of the German state, only temporarily separated from the rest of Germany. In addition, it must be said, the Germans had only very limited room for maneuver as to the future of Germany and Berlin, due to the Allied reserve powers stemming from the end of the war – powers which were finally used by the four former Allies, the USA, Soviet Union, Britain, and France, through the Two-Plus-Four Treaty to accomplish German unification in 1990.

Legally, two elements of the Basic Law (Article 23 and Article 146) allowed for the unification of the two states in 1990. The passionate and partly ideologically determined debate regarding whether Article 23 or Article 146 would be the ideal way to unify Germany did not change the fact that constitutionally both were options. The Basic Law could become the constitution for all of Germany through the accession of the GDR, or unification could result from the forming of a new constitution for all of Germany.

Article 23 of the Basic Law offered a useful instrument within an unusual historical constellation. It allowed for a quick and uncomplicated accession of the GDR to the Federal Republic. A relevant statement by the GDR would have been enough to trigger the responsibility of the Federal Republic to take the GDR into its political association. This sort of accession would also have meant that the Basic Law would have automatically become valid for the acceding part of Germany, just as in the case of the Saarland in 1957.

This position was strengthened by the Constitutional Court's decision of July 31, 1973 regarding the Basic Treaty between the Federal Republic and the GDR. Article 23 of the Basic Law was closely connected to the 'unification commandment' of the Preamble and belonged among the central regulations that gave the Basic Law its particular character. The court stated that the Federal Republic understood itself as part of a bigger geographical entity and that, if conditions were favorable, it had the duty to do everything possible to make these 'other parts' join it. Only then would the Federal Republic be 'complete.' The Constitutional Court was realistic enough to admit that this legal position was influenced politically and factually by the existence of those parts of Germany 'which, in the meantime, were organized as a state,' i.e. the GDR. This, however, did not cause the legal position to become outdated.

Those who supported the Article 23 option of the Basic Law brought a political argument as opposed to a purely legal argument to the table, noting that it would only be possible to control the process politically using a proven constitutional order as a basis. The Basic Law and the decision of the Constitutional Court were underpinned by powerful legal arguments based on Article 23. The stability of the

Federal Republic was correctly attributed to the Basic Law. Its continued validity was secured by virtue of the fact that the Basic Law offered a functional federal state order and that the expected economic and social problems would be easier to manage with a proven constitution as a basis, instead of having to construct a new legal foundation for a united Germany.

Article 146 of the Basic Law laid out the original plan for reunification. It put the GDR as well as the Federal Republic at the disposal of the all-German constituency. A constituent assembly, or comparable institution, would have had to construct a new constitution for all of Germany and to decide whether the order established by the Basic Law should remain for all of Germany or whether it should be replaced by a new constitutional order. In this case, the representatives of the Federal Republic in the constituent assembly would no longer be bound by the Basic Law, only by the principle of self-determination. According to general understanding, the new constitution would have to have been ratified by the entire citizenry. The united German political system would have had to newly construct itself legally and politically.

Those who supported unification through Article 146 of the Basic Law added that only in this way could the interests of the GDR citizens be protected. At the core was the question: would the future nation state be founded on the unity of the nation or on the democratic self-constitution of a political community of citizens? Based on its provisional character, the Basic Law never had to answer the still open question of reconciliation between the constitutional concept of the sovereignty of the people and the fact that it came into being in 1949 without having asked the people in a constitutional referendum.

The situation in 1989–90 was quite different from that in the post-war period. West Germans had accepted the Basic Law as the very foundation of their political community and state order for over forty years. The oft-used phrase 'constitutional patriotism' (*Verfassungspatriotismus*) meant exactly that. The situation in the GDR, however, was quite different. East Germans had revolted against their oppressors and, in a revolutionary upheaval, gained freedom and democracy. On March 18, 1990, in a free and fair election, a majority had voted those parties into office that wanted a quick accession to the Federal Republic. Nevertheless, the argument went that, only by a public referendum on the final constitutional settlement could this process be brought to a conclusion. The argument that only in this way could the citizens of the GDR be given a chance to participate in the building of the future state order weighed heavily on the supporters of a unification process based on Article 146.

There were also arguments in favor of combining both articles of the Basic Law. Whether or not this was legally possible depended on how the phrase 'freely adopted by the German people' used in Article 146 was interpreted. The many variations on how to utilize Articles 23 and 146 led to fierce debate. Critics argued – and events proved them right – that, if Article 23 was adopted, neither a broad constitutional debate nor real participation of the people would take place. In hindsight, the procedural debates surrounding the reunification of Germany seem strangely artificial. While legal experts, political scientists, politicians, and civil rights activists in the GDR argued over basic constitutional and politically normative questions, thousands of citizens were fleeing the GDR daily, the economy fell apart and public administration came to a standstill. The GDR state was not swept away by the political revolution of 1989 but instead imploded in the spring of 1990 through the pressure of these events.

The government voted into office during the first and last free parliamentary elections of the GDR on March 18, 1990 was left no choice but to seek a quick and regulated 'liquidation' of the GDR and its unification with the Federal Republic. But even after the accession of the GDR, the discussion about the constitutional consequences of German unification did not cease.

Constitutional Reform or Continuation of the Basic Law?

The conditions for unification along the lines of Article 23 of the Basic Law were laid down in the decision by the democratically elected GDR parliament in June 1990 to join the Federal Republic of Germany and in two treaties negotiated by the two German governments: the 'State Treaty on Monetary, Economic and Social Union' of May 18, 1990 and the 'Unification Treaty' of August 31, 1990. In the Unification Treaty, the question of the possible amendment or revision of the Basic Law was raised but not finally answered. At the heart of the conflict was the question as to whether it was appropriate at that point in time to modify, renew, or even replace the Basic Law.

In the debate about whether to continue with the Basic Law or construct an entirely new constitution for the whole of Germany, two camps stood diametrically opposed to one another. The one side refused to enter a political debate and argued in purely juridical terms. They wanted to avoid deeper constitutional discussion, especially with reference to new state goals and far reaching participatory rights for citizens, goals which had already been discussed in the 'old' Federal Republic of the 1980s – to the growing displeasure of conservative lawyers and politicians.

The proponents of a principled constitutional debate, including a former president of the Federal Constitutional Court, Ernst Benda, and other distinguished law professors, argued not only in legal terms, but also politically and normatively, that, with the as yet unfulfilled precept 'in free self-determination' of the whole of the sovereign German people, a public debate over constitutional matters was necessary if not unavoidable. They argued that there was a general perception that the Basic Law had been forced upon West Germans by the victorious powers of the Second World War. There had been no public plebiscite over the Basic Law; instead, the parliaments of the West German states had ratified the constitution in 1949. Now, after a democratic revolution in East Germany which had led to German unification, there was a widespread feeling among the citizenry and legal experts that the people should finally decide about their future.

For many observers, the GDR constitution written in the early weeks of 1990 by the Round Table, which was established after the revolutionary events of the fall of 1989 to serve as an intermediary force between the old regime and the new democratic groups, could serve as a model for a revised and modernized Basic Law. This idea gained widespread publicity because it, once again, underlined what was lacking in the discussion about an all-German constitution: the people. The people, bearer of sovereign rights, were not involved and, as understood by many observers, were sidelined.

Furthermore, the draft constitution for a democratic GDR invoked the experiences of a free democracy in West Germany and the democratic revolution in the East. 'State goal agreements,' such as the right to a profession, social security and the protection of the natural fundamentals of life, were included in the new constitution and new forms of democratic citizen participation were suggested.

This draft, which was ultimately not passed by the GDR parliament (*Volkskammer*), and other pleas for comprehensive constitutional reforms focused on two arguments. First, they questioned whether politics based only on the principle of representation made sense in modern society. The experiences of the former socialist countries – the peaceful upheavals in Poland, Czechoslovakia, Hungry, and the GDR – offered proof that the people are more mature than politicians usually acknowledge. Only a comprehensive democratization could solve the problems that faced the states and societies of Europe.

This question of whether the Basic Law – valid in all of Germany from October 3, 1990 – should be revised or replaced by a new constitution for the whole country was the source of sharp political controversy not only between East and West, but also within political groups in the old Federal Republic. Members of the conservative camp feared that a constitutional debate would only be used to subvert tried and tested constitutional fundamentals and to establish a 'different republic.' An article entitled 'The Threat of Article 146' in the influential *Frankfurter Allgemeine Zeitung* of September 24, 1990 highlights the political key to this controversy. The writer suggests that the Basic Law had masterfully survived its trial period and qualified as a constitution for all of Germany. Some powers in the West who had imagined not an accession of the GDR but a convergent unification were, the author concludes, in favor of ideas contained in the draft constitution of 'Modrow's GDR.' Hans Modrow was the last communist prime minister of the GDR before democratic elections took place. The message of this argument was clear: everyone who supported further discussion on constitutional matters was playing into the hands of post-communist politicians and parties who would take advantage of the complicated situation.

Volker Rühe, the then General Secretary of the CDU, wrote in the *Welt am Sonntag* of May 19, 1991 that those who wished to have a new constitution should ask themselves if their true goal was in fact the creation of a different social order and a different type of state. It was suggested that the goal of those eagerly arguing for a constitutional revision was a 'left shift' of the Basic Law. Those on the left and left-leaning Liberals were demanding that the opportunity be used to address long-postponed constitutional reforms, which meant in particular the inclusion of state goals and citizens' expanded participatory opportunities.

This view demonstrates that the process of unification was about far more than solely procedural questions. Behind it stood the fear that the democracy of the Federal Republic, with its tried and tested forms and procedures of pluralistic democracy, could be endangered. As Alfred Dregger, then Chairman of the CDU/CSU, argued in an article in the *Frankfurter Allgemeine Zeitung* of September 24, 1990, those who advocated a plebiscite on a constitution for all of Germany were essentially agitating for 'another republic.'

Generally speaking, the public debate demonstrated a strange mix of admiration for the political and constitutional order of the Federal Republic and, at the same time, a deep-rooted suspicion about whether or not East Germans were really 'ripe' for democracy.

Constitutional Provisions of the Unification Treaty

The Unification Treaty between the Federal Republic and the GDR offered a third way, one that would combine the regulatory benefits of both solutions – accession plus constitutional amendments. The treaty deferred the (domestic and societal) political disagreements about constitutional changes to a time after the legal state unification. Articles 4 and 5 of the Unification Treaty explicitly paved the way for later consideration of constitutional questions. In this way the legal controversy surrounding Article 146 of the Basic Law, which became obsolete after the GDR had joined the Federal Republic under Article 23, was superseded. Representing a compromise in reformulating Article 146 of the Basic Law, Article 4.6 of the Unification Treaty stated that, after the achievement of the unity of Germany and the freedom of all the German people, the Basic Law 'shall cease to apply on the day on which a constitution freely adopted by the German people takes effect.' This wording was later adopted in the reformulation of Article 146 of the Basic Law.

Materially, the debate about the Basic Law hinged on two aspects: (1) should state goal agreements such as those on environmental protection, the right to a profession, etc., which lawmakers had consciously avoided, be taken up, and (2) should the Basic Law be opened to a plebiscite?

The Unification Treaty was hardly precise on the matter of necessary and desired constitutional changes. Articles 4 and 5 of the treaty were formulated first and foremost as gestures to the East Germans that their interests would not be obviated in the further stages of the process. As a result of massive conflicts during the negotiation of the treaty, only one recommendation to the 'lawmaking bodies' emerged – that 'they should deal with the questions concerning amendment or extension of the Basic Law raised in connection with German reunification within two years' (Article 5). In particular, the following points, which should 'especially' be dealt with, were mentioned:

- dealing with the topics that were formulated in the joint agreement of the minister presidents of July 5, 1990, the so-called 'key points' of the Länder for the federal states order in a reunified Germany. These included far-reaching demands, especially regarding the financial constitution, the lawmaking powers of the Länder (Article 72 Basic Law) and their participation in establishing international organizations (Article 24 Basic Law);
- the new regulation of the Berlin-Brandenburg region through an agreement of the participating Länder – an attempt that was rejected by the populations of Brandenburg and East Berlin in a referendum in 1996;
- deliberations on the inclusion of state goal regulations in the Basic Law, which represented one of the main demands from the GDR side;
- the question of implementing Article 146 of the Basic Law and, in conjunction therewith, the holding of a plebiscite about a constitution, as demanded by the parliamentary opposition and the GDR citizens' movement.

The word 'especially' in the Unification Treaty did not exclude dealing with other matters. Nevertheless, it had already become clear during the negotiations with the GDR that the governing coalition wished to keep changes to a minimum and thus charged the commission accordingly, whereas the SPD and Alliance90/Greens conceived of the Unification Treaty's regulations more broadly. As with the material questions about the goal and breadth of future constitutional changes, the differences on the normative aspects of the process of the treaty were left unclarified. The result was a long-term debate about the designation and membership of the planned commission, which the Unification Treaty had not addressed.

The political parties' different positions became clear to a broader public during the meeting of the Bundestag on May 14, 1991, when they dealt for the first time with the planned constitutional reform. The governing coalition's point of view was crystal clear: there was no need to debate a new constitution because the Basic Law served that purpose. The only thing to debate were the guidelines of the Unification Treaty. Along with this position went the coalition's demand to establish a 'Joint Constitutional Committee,' made up of only 16 members each from the Bundestag and the Bundesrat.

The Social Democrats originally wanted to establish a 'Constitutional Council' that would deliberate about the 'further development of the Basic Law into a constitution for the unified Germany.' It was to have 120 members, half women and half men, and to be elected by the *Bundesversammlung*, or full federal assembly, which otherwise only meets to elect the president of the Federal Republic. This Constitutional Council would have been a mixture of parliamentary council and constitutional assembly.

Alliance 90/Greens, a new party formed by the West German Greens and a coalition of citizens' movements in the GDR, also demanded the establishment of a constitutional council, which would consist of 160 members, half of them women, and be elected in equal parts by the Bundestag and the Länder parliaments. Like the SPD, they argued for the participation of non-parliamentarians and demanded the election of national representatives through the state parliaments. The main justification for their position was, not surprisingly given the failure of the western Greens in the parliamentary elections of 1990 and their absence from the Bundestag, to include the East Germans in the process.

In the main, the PDS, successor party of the SED, the state party of the communist GDR, supported the suggestions put forth by the SPD and Alliance 90/Greens, but went further in demanding the removal of the emergency constitution and the anchoring of community property and economy in the Basic Law.

After a long and controversial discussion, the Bundestag agreed to establish a 'Joint Constitutional Commission' of the Bundestag and the Bundesrat with 64 members. The members of the Bundestag were represented according to the strength of their party: the CDU/CSU sent 15 members, the SPD 11 members, the FDP 4 members, and Alliance 90/Greens and the PDS one each. The 32 members from the Länder were not decided upon by the Bundesrat but instead by the state governments.

Having been called into being by resolutions of both the Bundestag and Bundesrat, the Joint Constitutional Commission was an institutional innovation and simultaneously an expression of the Federal Republic's cooperative federalism, in which important political decisions cannot be made without the *Länder*. According to Article 53a of the Basic Law, in addition to the Mediation Committee (established to resolve disputes over concurrent legislation) and the Joint Committee (established to deal with emergencies), the Joint Constitutional Commission was a third committee in which the representation of the legislature and the Länder – in contrast to the Bundesrat – did not reflect the population census. In comparison to the other two committees, the Länder had a stronger presence in the Joint Constitutional Commission because they had the same number of members as the Bundestag (in the Joint Committee the ratio was 2:1) and the Lord Mayor of Hamburg, Henning Voscherau, was one of the chairpersons (in the Mediation Committee, this position shifted every three months). Its position was also strong because its consultations were not bound by the agenda developed by the Bundestag. It was sovereign in focusing on topics chosen by itself.

Constitutional Amendments after Unification

The Joint Constitutional Commission had a complicated mission. Its instructions were terse and not sufficiently precise in dealing with the extremely divergent ideals of the actors. The various divisions can be simplified in the following manner.

First, there was the opposition between those who wanted to protect and secure the Basic Law, on the one hand, and the proponents of a fundamentally new constitution on the other. The first group's position resulted from two different issues: fear of operating from an insecure constitutional base, given the unknowable territory of the transformation and integration processes. This argument was plausible given the developments in Eastern and Central Europe. The other issue, which was frequently but not always interwoven with the first, was the fear of readdressing questions that had been successfully resisted in the old Federal Republic of the 1980s. Among these were the possibility of including a plebiscite clause in the Basic Law and the addition of certain state goals to the constitution itself. Among the advocates of a new constitution there were also two driving concerns. One group argued normatively and demanded the realization of the original intentions of the constitution's writers. In the case of unification, this included the approval of the constitution (which could materially also be the Basic Law) by all the German people. The other group focused on fundamental material changes to the constitution.

Second, the divisions between the actors ran neither along the usual left–right political split, nor between East and West Germans. The representatives of the governing coalition tended to assume a more conservative, status-quo oriented perspective, while the opposition demanded far-reaching changes. But Eastern parliamentarians in the governing coalition also tended toward the idea of qualitative amendments and material changes, while the Westerners of all political parties favored the Basic Law as a touchstone even when they proposed changes.

The influence of the Länder also complicated matters. During the negotiations leading up to the Unification Treaty they had used their power and strengthened their position. The same process occurred in connection with the Maastricht Treaty. Through the combination of the constitutional discussion with the ratification of the Maastricht Treaty, they again saw an opportunity to better their position, which they successfully did especially in regard to the Basic Law's new Article 23, dealing with European integration and changes to the federal structure. They found their position confirmed in the Constitutional Court's later decision about the Maastricht Treaty. The court had rejected the claim that the new Article 23 was 'anticonstitutional constitutional law', i.e. conflicted with the 'essence of a basic right' (Article 19.2 Basic Law).

The homogeneous interests of the Länder, which had been successfully pursued in determining the article relating to Europe (the new Article 23 of the Basic Law) and in strengthening the Länder's position by improving their legislative competence in concurrent and framework legislation of the Federation (Articles 72, 74 and 75 Basic Law), were not to be replicated in regard to the most pressing problem of German federalism – the financial structure. Once again, this area remained unregulated. The interests diverged: between the eastern and western Länder and between the most productive Länder and those which depended on the provisions for financial redistribution. The positions of the Länder were also determined by varying coalitions.

Most importantly, the collaboration of the Bundesrat in the Constitutional Commission meant the participation of the Länder governments. The Länder parliaments were broadly denied influence.

Lastly, according to the procedural regulations of the Commission, a quorum of two-thirds of members was required for all decisions. This rule secured a significant opportunity for the Commission to achieve the necessary majorities in the parliamentary consultation and voting.

At the same time, this quorum – in which neither the large parties nor the Länder nor the federal government had the majority necessary to override the other sides – required a large degree of compromise during the debates. Comparing the topics for discussion that preoccupied the Commission with the final recommendations, it is clear that four aspects were broadly discussed but led to no results:

1. Most important was the debate about state goals. From a comprehensive list that stretched from the right to a profession to social security and from the right to shelter to animal rights, only the goal of environmental protection remained. This goal was not, as originally requested by the CDU/CSU, implemented with legal reservations, but was bound to the 'constitutional order' (Article 31 Basic Law).
2. A further aspect, demanded to differing degrees and with differing intensity by the SPD and Alliance 90/Greens, was the expansion of citizens' collaborative rights, especially the people's initiative or petition for referenda and referenda themselves. Here the majority maintained a strict representative order and confirmed the Basic Law's plebiscitary abstinence.
3. The Commission suggested the introduction of an Article 20b with the following text: 'The state recognizes the identity of ethnic, cultural, and linguistic minorities.' This item only became part of the Commission's recommendations through a shift in party positions (some eastern CDU deputies voted with the opposition), but it was rejected both by the CDU/CSU in the Bundestag and by the Mediation Committee.
4. Heated controversies in the Commission and in the public realm erupted over the issue of a possible right of the Bundestag to dissolve itself, which for a short time seemed to have the necessary support for passage. Not without good reason, this was seen as an attack on the Federal Republic's constitutional structure. Negative public reaction contributed to finally thwarting this suggestion.

In two areas the consultations did bring about important changes: in the partially new regulation of the relationship between federal government and the Länder in lawmaking, and in the new Article 23 of the Basic Law, concerning future European integration.

In the document 'Legislative powers and the legislative process in the federal state,' the Commission suggested a number of procedural changes and reauthorizations of responsibility. As the report noted, the basis for these changes was a demand of the Länder minister presidents in a joint agreement of July 5, 1990, which formulated the Länder's claims in regard to Article 5 of the Unification Treaty and clearly demanded strengthened legislative power for them. The Länder demanded heightened barriers to the federal government's concurrent legislation, a new boundary for the competency catalog of federal government and Länder, the enhancement of the Bundesrat's authority of approval (especially in regard to federal laws with financial consequences for the Länder), and longer consultation periods in the Bundesrat.

The most significant problem was the renewed failure to adjust the regulation of the financial constitution. Clearly the changes that were implemented were shifts in competence to the benefit of the Länder, because their approval was required for changes and amendments to the Basic Law. This related to the concurrent and framework legislation of the federal government in Articles 72, 74 and 75 of the Basic Law, the regulation of procedural questions in the Bundesrat's lawmaking and rights (Articles 76, 77 and 80 Basic Law) and the participation, cooperation and co-decision-making of the Bundesrat in dealings with the European Union (Article 23 Basic Law).

The Länder attempted successfully to expand their responsibilities, but had in mind those of the governments, not the Länder parliaments. According to Article 50 of the Basic Law, the Länder have an effect 'on lawmaking and the Federal administration' through the Bundesrat, and Article 77.1 of the Basic Law states without reservation that federal laws 'shall be adopted by the Bundestag.' The factual revaluation and status enhancement of the Bundesrat to an equal 'second chamber' manifests a constitutional shift in the relationship between the 'legislative bodies,' as the problematic formulation in Article 5 of the Unification Treaty reads. This represents a shift in the weight of the constitutional bodies, in particular given that the process of European unification pulls power away from national decision-making committees, especially parliaments.

The possible gain from such a strengthened observance of the subsidiarity principle through a strengthening of the Länder powers is, however, obviated by the shift strengthening the Länder governments, which does not benefit the representational bodies with direct mandates from citizens, namely Länder parliaments. This results in the further exclusion of the Länder parliaments from decisive questions and contributes to the development of quasi-intergovernmental relations between federal government and Länder.

The Commission regarded the new version of Article 23 of the Basic Law as 'its child.' It formulates the state goal of European unity and holds the Federal Republic responsible for the realization of a unified Europe 'committed to democratic, social and federal principles, to the rule of law, and to the principle of subsidiarity, and ... guarantees a level of protection of basic rights essentially comparable to that afforded by this Basic Law.' This new formulation contributed fundamentally to the Constitutional Court's allowance of the Maastricht Treaty in that version. The new Article 23 of the Basic Law allows a transfer of sovereignty to the European

Union; but, in regard to constitutional rights, only within the limits set forth in Article 79.2 and 79.3 of the Basic Law, which prohibit a repeal of fundamental, basic elements of the constitutional order, such as the principle of the constitutional state or federalism.

In summary, the Joint Constitutional Commission's work led to remarkable changes only in one area: that of the federal structure of the Federal Republic, especially through the new Article 23 of the Basic Law, which enables the participation of the Länder in foreign affairs if these affect their legislative powers. Traditionally, this was only the responsibility of national governments.

The failures of the Constitutional Commission are evident in mistakes such as those made in the handling of 'the question of changing or amending the Basic Law as a result of and in conjunction with German unity.' Essentially, the problems of modernizing the constitution were dealt with in the context of the old Federal Republic. This meant that 'East German interests' played no role in the debates of the Commission, although they did have a strong influence on the general political agenda since they were in many ways connected to Western actors. However, a dominant will did not exist to use the revolution in the GDR as an excuse to create something new but instead to secure something that had proven the test of time.

Critical was the fact that among the participants no basic consensus regarding the aims and goal of the process could be reached. In the dispute between the minimalist position of the government coalition, which was supported by powerful voices in constitutional law circles and represented the opinion that the Basic Law was in fact the all-German constitution, and the maximalist position of the SPD and especially Alliance 90/Greens, who wanted to achieve wide-reaching political goals, especially the anchoring of state goals, the lowest common denominator finally won. Neither the structural reforms suggested by a Special Commission on constitutional reform founded as early as the 1970s nor the possibility, newly rooted in the 1980s, of a participatory – but not necessarily plebiscitary – opening of the Basic Law found a place in the reformed Basic Law.

This would have been easy to justify if the legislators had had the same reserves as in the United States, whereby constitutional amendments were only passed in exceptional cases. However, this was not the case in the Federal Republic. In the history of the Federal Republic, several constitutional changes and amendments have been made, although most have been of a technical nature. Deep encroachments into the basic normative framework of the constitution are rare: the constitutional regulations for the armed forces of 1956, the emergency laws of 1968 and the elimination of the general and non-restrictive right to asylum for political refugees in Article 16 of the Basic Law in 1993 all represent exceptions.

For the supporters of a fundamental constitutional debate on the occasion of German unity, the results of the Joint Commission proved to be 'constitutionally immobile.' The chance for a modern Basic Law was lost and 'the constitutional reform ship had run aground,' as one constitutional lawyer put it.

According to the supporters of the constitutional status quo, the Federal Republic came away from the constitutional debate with only a 'flesh wound.' The political initiators of a thoroughgoing constitutional discussion were not after minor reform, they wanted more; their expectations were targeted at reform of the fundamentals of the constitution and a complete overturning of the old constitution.

Beyond the necessity for practical compromises, politicians did not make real movements from their starting positions. To this extent a constitutional debate can only be spoken of in a limited sense; there was an exchange of familiar arguments, which were well known from discussions about the constitution in the old Federal Republic. The attention and dignity supposedly accorded to the 'East German experience' by all sides served simply as support and proof for each position. The results of the constitutional debate meant in political practice that the new Federal Republic would continue to live with the constitution established in 1949.

The abandonment of the idea of a new all-German constitution meant also that the constitutional discussion in the years between 1990 and 1994 had little to do with the development of an all-German consensus about the basic fundamentals which could contribute to the collective political and social order. The search for consensus was something that in all other post-communist states, regardless of how chaotically their constitutional discussion proceeded, played a very important role.

The Joint Commission had to act 'on the occasion of German unification,' but one could cast doubt on whether it acted to enhance the spiritual and constitutional dimensions of German unity. More could not have been done, since the Commission's remit was not only formal but also, through its majority relationships, politically limited. This meant, however, that unified Germany found itself in a similar situation to that of the Federal Republic after 1949; the Basic Law still has to prove itself as an all-German constitution. But, while the Federal Republic in 1949 had to be built upon the spiritual and tangible ruins left by National Socialism, the new Federal Republic was founded on a secure democratic order in the West and a revolutionary turnaround in the East – seen together, good starting conditions for the future.

–4–

West and East

Germany in Europe

The two German states of the Federal Republic and GDR were outposts of two alien political systems and social orders. Both could be regarded as classic examples of a 'penetrated system' – a country regulated and controlled by external actors. After the unconditional surrender of Nazi Germany, all power lay with the four Allied powers, the Soviet Union, the United States of America, the United Kingdom, and, since it had been invited to join the three states in 1945, France. With the foundation of the two German states in 1949, some of the Allied powers were transferred to German authorities.

While the GDR never gained a significant degree of independence from the Soviet Union, the Federal Republic did from its masters – step by step. There were four phases of German foreign and security policy during the Cold War:

1. From the founding of the Federal Republic in 1949 until 1955, when it gained (almost) full sovereignty over its own affairs, the Allied High Commissioners had complete power over foreign and security affairs. The Occupation Statute of 1949, which was revised in 1952, did not allow for a sovereign and independent German foreign policy but did, however, leave some room for German politicians to act in a more informal way. The first federal chancellor used these opportunities in a sovereign manner mixed with a good deal of chutzpah. In addition, the Basic Law deliberately renounced some of the rights of a sovereign state, rights that the Federal Republic did not acquire in this period. This was meant as a signal to the outside world that West Germany, if granted more or full sovereignty, would not go it alone but anchor the new Germany into a wider community of democratic states. In stark contrast, the GDR remained until 1955 an entity at the full disposal of Soviet foreign and security interests without any political capacity of its own.

2. In the decade between the accession to NATO and achievement of full sovereignty in 1955 and the inauguration of a new government formed by Social Democrats and Liberals in 1969, West German foreign and security policy was basically aimed at securing and consolidating the Federal Republic's integration into the Western alliances and at improving Franco-German cooperation. As time went by, it became obvious that the conservative governments lacked a vision of how to make any progress on the German question. If, as it were,

unification was not on the agenda for the foreseeable future, the question of whether and how relations with the GDR should be shaped became more and more urgent. This issue became even more urgent when the GDR managed to gain some international backing in the 1960s, mainly from former colonies and new states that did not belong to one of the two main political blocs. The federal government tried to fend off these threats to its claim to represent all of Germany. But when it transpired that even by threatening to break diplomatic ties it could not prevent states from 'normalizing' their relations with the GDR, a redefinition of foreign policy was unavoidable.

3. Foreign policy under CDU/CSU governments had concentrated on integration into Western and European organizations. After the Cuban crisis of 1962, the Western powers started to consider a policy of détente, however, and suspicions grew stronger in the German government that the Federal Republic could be sidelined. The CDU/CSU proved incapable of developing new ideas for an active policy vis-à-vis the East, especially the Soviet Union and the GDR. It was the Liberals and Social Democrats who reformulated foreign and security policy concepts in the 1960s. When they agreed on forming a government in 1969, a new foreign policy with respect to the East in general and the GDR in particular came to prominence. What followed was *Ostpolitik* as a trademark of that government and a long period of détente which led to treaties with the Soviet Union, Poland, Czechoslovakia and the GDR, Allied agreements over Berlin, the accession of both German states to the United Nations in 1973, the Conference for Security and Cooperation in Europe with its final document signed in Helsinki in 1975, and dozens of agreements with the GDR over trade, commerce, science and education, culture, etc.

4. Against all odds and despite a revitalized Cold War in the early 1980s, relations with the GDR proved to be quite robust. Partial stabilization of the GDR was a central goal of Western policy. Stabilization meant laying the ground for the improvement of German–German relations and, hopefully, a partial liberalization of the GDR regime. Until the end of 1989 it seemed inconceivable and (dangerously) utopian to try to undermine a regime which was part and parcel of an alien socio-economic and political system protected by Soviet bayonets.

The Question of Sovereignty

In its early years, before the attainment of sovereignty in 1955, the Federal Republic was only a 'semi-sovereign state' on which the Western Allies had a major influence in the field of policy, especially foreign and security policy. The last remnants of these Allied rights – concerning Berlin and a solution to the German question – remained in force right up to German unification in 1990 and the arrangements made in the 'Two-Plus-Four Treaty' between the two German states and the four wartime Allies.

What could sovereignty mean for a state that only represented one part of a divided country which had started an all-out war against all of its European neighbors and the entire world? A country that had unconditionally surrendered and been put under absolute control of the victorious powers? Clearly, it could not mean national sovereignty as traditionally understood because the nation was divided into two state entities, and some parts of it were put under foreign control. Full sovereignty was also an impossibility because the four Allies of World War II were, whatever their other differences, not willing to give up their claims on Germany, especially their exclusive right to decide finally on Germany's future. And, last but not least, full sovereignty was neither in the interest of the Federal Republic's Western neighbors and future partners nor in its own interest.

When established in 1949, the Federal Republic was endowed with only a limited and revocable degree of sovereignty and only gradually were the reins of the occupying forces relaxed. Until 1951 it had no foreign policy of its own, and it was only in 1955 that the first Minister of Foreign affairs was inaugurated. The external representation of the new state lay in the hands of the High Commissioners of France, the United Kingdom and the United States. Negotiations with the Western Allies were conducted by the federal chancellor, mostly without consulting the cabinet, which explains his extraordinary authority in foreign affairs.

The Allies also had far-reaching powers to intervene in domestic German affairs. Even after the Occupation Statute was replaced by a General Agreement or *Deutschlandvertrag* in 1955, residual powers remained in the hands of the Allies. With the coming into force of this agreement, the Allies' powers of intervention in the domestic affairs of the Federal Republic had been revoked, and the Allied institutions, the Allied High Commission and the Offices of the Land Commissioners in the federal *Länder*, were abolished. The three powers (the USA, Britain and France), nevertheless, retained special rights as to a final peace treaty for Germany. These rights related to the stationing and the security of the Allied forces in Germany, to Berlin as a separate entity governed by the four powers and to 'questions concerning Germany as a whole.' The Federal Republic and the three powers agreed that an essential aim of their common policy should be a peace settlement for the whole of Germany freely negotiated between Germany and its former enemies. They also agreed that the final settlement of the borders of Germany, which mainly concerned those parts 'temporarily' under Polish administration, should await such a peace settlement. Even after the Federal Republic had gained 'full sovereignty' in 1955, restrictions concerning the future of Germany and German unification remained.

Yet this limited sovereignty was not only the result of external compulsion. At its foundation in 1949 the Federal Republic's temporary constitution, the Basic Law, deliberately renounced some of the rights of a sovereign state. The Basic Law came into force at a time when cooperation between defeated Germany and its victorious Western neighbors seemed scarcely conceivable. Nevertheless, it showed the Federal Republic's constitutional readiness to learn from the consequences of the belligerence and aggressiveness of the German Empire and National Socialism and to develop a future political order for Germany as part of the European order which was yet to be created.

The special quality about the development of the Federal Republic is that it has changed from being a 'penetrated system' into an 'integrated system.' Since the time when Germany joined the European Communities (the European Coal and Steel Community in 1952, the European Economic Community and EURATOM in 1957), national rights of sovereignty have gradually been handed over to supranational institutions. From being a restriction imposed from outside, semi-sovereignty became part of Germany's deliberate policy of curtailing its own freedom of action, not only in the field of foreign policy.

The Politics of Integration

Against strong criticism Konrad Adenauer, the first Federal Chancellor from 1949 to 1963, broke with traditional German anti-Western politics and embedded the Federal Republic into the Western liberal democracies. For him European unity was meant to overcome old hatred between the 'arch rivals' France and Germany. The GDR, in contrast, became an integral part of the Soviet empire, the first 'workers' and farmers' state on German soil.' As West Germany became a member of NATO and East Germany joined the Warsaw Pact, the prospect of reuniting these two wrecked states seemed more remote than ever.

The decision to create a democratic order in the western part of a *de facto* occupied Germany originated from a vision of incorporating the new state as part of 'the West' in opposition to the Soviet-dominated East. The Western Allies, especially the United States, were motivated to embrace West Germany by a Wilsonian vision of democracy, and by the new foreign policy doctrine formulated by President Harry S. Truman on March 12, 1947. The 'Truman Doctrine,' as it was called, worked on the assumption that the world was divided into two disparate camps – Western democracies on the one hand, and the Soviet Union with its 'satellite states' threatening world peace on the other. It was the duty of the United States not to withdraw from the European continent, as it did after World War I, but to stay in order to 'contain' Soviet expansionism and to support the European countries by economic and military means. The 'European Recovery Program' (ERP) of 1947, known as the 'Marshall Plan,' was the most visible expression of this policy.

Germany played a vital role in Allied strategic considerations. The war and post-war conferences of the four powers had left Allied and German politicians with three unanswered questions. First, the national question: how long would 'temporary' division last and what were the future prospects for a reunited Germany? The second question was centered on what kind of economic, social and political order would develop in either a united Germany or the separate German states. And the third, most urgent, issue was the question of security.

The answer to the second question was relatively easy – the Allies settled on establishing a democratic order and market economy in West Germany. The other two questions were more problematic because they contradicted each other. If German reunification was the first priority, any idea of including the Federal Republic in the evolving Western security system seemed counterproductive. However, it was hardly conceivable that German reunification could be achieved on democratic terms without a firm and robust security component, given the dictatorial nature of the Soviet system. In suppressing all democratic intentions and holding Eastern Europe hostage for its world revolutionary ideology, the Soviet Union pursued its construction of a 'Soviet Camp.'

For the Allies, the alternatives seemed clear: either pursue a 'national' policy by giving absolute priority to reuniting Germany – a policy advocated by Kurt Schumacher of the Social Democrats and Jakob Kaiser of the CDU – or promote a policy that would reintegrate West Germany into the community of democratic nations step-by-step. Such a process would ensure that the Federal Republic became a firm component of the Western system of collective security and would contribute to the policy of containment vis-à-vis the Soviet Union, which would ultimately lead to the collapse of the communist system. It was Konrad Adenauer who, against all the odds, stood for this strategic policy, which had no popular support in West Germany at the time. Adenauer's foreign policy was bitterly opposed by the Social Democrats. His opponents argued that participation in Western institutions would destroy any chance of reunification.

There was also fierce opposition to the idea of rearming Germany. 'Never again' and 'without me' were views generally held by the German public. The issue of rearming Germany sparked heated debates at home and abroad. Propaganda in the Soviet realm charged 'West German revanchism' with desiring to start a Third World War. The new German democracy had to confront a bitter debate on the issue of rearmament. When the leader of the opposition, Kurt Schumacher, denounced Adenauer as the 'Chancellor of the Allies,' he went so far as to evoke memories of the Weimar Republic and the buildup to World War II.

At the beginning of the Korean War in the 1950s, it became clear to everyone that the security situation had changed dramatically. Defending Western Europe would mean strengthening the structures already in place and answering the question as to whether a German contribution of whatever sort was necessary and acceptable. An independent German army was as inconceivable at that time as membership of NATO. The question was how to make German rearmament palatable to the other European states and, first of all, to the public.

The French idea of a European Defence Community (EDC) seemed to present a resolution to the problem of how to integrate the Federal Republic of Germany into the emerging security structures. The proposal led to the signature, in May 1952, of the EDC Treaty, in which Belgium, France, Italy, Luxembourg, the Netherlands, and the Federal Republic of Germany were due to participate. The plan, which aimed at an integrated European army under a French supreme commander, could be interpreted as an attempt to make German rearmament less threatening in a political situation in which, due to the Korean War, German rearmament as part of Western defenze was unavoidable. The realization of the EDC would have meant German soldiers without a German army. These plans finally failed in 1954 because of the resistance of the French parliament.

The failure of the EDC put considerable pressure on the political actors to find another way to integrate the Federal Republic of Germany into the Western security system. The only acceptable solution was for the Federal Republic to become a member of the Western European Union (WEU) and NATO. The WEU was created by the Treaty on Economic, Social and Cultural Collaboration and Collective Self-Defense signed in Brussels on March 17, 1948 (the Brussels Treaty), as amended by the Protocol signed in Paris on October 23, 1954, which modified and completed it. The Brussels Treaty was signed by Belgium, France, Luxembourg, the Netherlands, and the United Kingdom. Its main feature was a commitment to mutual defense should any of the signatories be the victim of an armed attack in Europe. By demonstrating their resolve to work together, the Brussels Treaty powers helped to overcome the reluctance of the United States to participate in the nascent European security arrangements.

Talks between these powers and the United States and Canada led to the signature in Washington on April 4, 1949 of the treaty that founded the North Atlantic Treaty Organization (NATO) Denmark, Iceland, Italy, Norway, and Portugal were invited and agreed to accede to the Treaty. The most important aspect of this new type of collective security was Article 5 of the Treaty, which states that an armed attack against one of the signatories shall be considered an attack against all of them and that each party will then take such action as it deems necessary to restore and maintain the security of the North Atlantic area. From the point of view of the European members, the formalized commitment by the United States and Canada to the defense of Europe was the core of the Treaty. At a special conference in London in the fall of 1954, attended by the Brussels Treaty powers and the United States, Canada, the Federal Republic of Germany and Italy, it was decided to invite the latter two countries to join the Brussels Treaty. The conclusions of the conference were formalized by the Paris Agreements, signed in October of that year, which amended the Brussels Treaty, created the Western European Union (WEU) as a new international organization, and provided for the membership of the Federal Republic of Germany and Italy.

In the final declaration of that conference the Federal Republic officially agreed to conduct its policy in accordance with the principles of the Charter of the United Nations. Upon her accession to NATO, she declared that 'she will refrain from any action inconsistent with the strictly defensive character' of the alliance. In particular the Federal Republic committed herself never to use force in order to achieve the reunification of Germany or the modification of her present borders and to resolve by peaceful means any disputes with other states.

The three Western powers declared that they considered the federal government as the only German government 'freely and legitimately constituted and therefore entitled to speak for Germany as the representative of the German people in international affairs.' They also committed themselves to a peace settlement and the reunification of Germany, to the maintenance of the security and welfare of Berlin, and to maintaining armed forces in Berlin, and they finally stated that they would treat any attack against Berlin as an attack upon their forces and themselves. Despite widespread public opposition to the accession to NATO and to German rearmament, the Bundestag ratified the 'Paris Treaties,' which were the result of the decisions of the London conference on February 27, 1955. With the Paris Treaties the General Agreement between the Federal Republic and the former Western occupation forces came into being. Adenauer's idea of a quid pro quo had succeeded; the Federal Republic had gained sovereignty.

Konrad Adenauer was the dominant figure in German politics for more than a decade. It was he who negotiated with the representatives of the Western Allies, and it was he who personally conducted German foreign policy until 1955. Adenauer used the prospect of a German army and NATO membership as a bargaining chip for a formal treaty with the Western powers, the so-called General Agreement or *Deutschlandvertrag*. This removed most of the restrictions on German politics, mainly in the field of foreign policy, which had remained even after the foundation of the Federal Republic in 1949. Adenauer traded sovereignty against a German contribution to a system of mutual security. This could be legitimated by the provision of the Basic Law of 1949 that the Federation, with a view to maintaining peace, 'may enter into a system of mutual collective security' (Article 24).

Integrating the Federal Republic into Western security structures was the first pillar of Adenauer's foreign policy; the second pillar was reconciliation between Germany and France, who had fought three wars in seventy years, and European integration generally. Adenauer was a firm supporter of the idea of supranational integration, a vision shared by his French counterparts. He held the view that the primary need for West Germany was security, and this could only be provided by the United States. Everything must be done to keep the Americans committed to European security. A combination of attempts to overcome traditional conflicts among European states with a European component of mutual security was intended to serve this goal.

Exactly five years after the end of World War II, the French Minister of Foreign Affairs, Robert Schuman, announced his vision of a joint Franco-German administration for coal and steel production. After long discussion, this vision was transformed into the European Coal and Steel Community (ECSC) of 1952. It was significant for being the first decisive step in the direction of European integration, marking a new era of cooperation rather than the competition between nation states that had previously dominated the region.

Robert Schuman and his *spiritus rector*, Jean Monnet, put an end to the French policy regarding Germany that had prevailed for decades – attempting to control

Germany by isolating it and making alliances with anti-German states. The new dominant concept was control by integration. Germany's membership of the Council of Europe (founded in 1949) was the first step in reintegrating Germany into the international community of states. The ECSC ended the post-war control of the German Ruhr coal and steel industry and was advocated by France as compensation for the foundation of the Federal Republic. With the ECSC, the first European institution with a supranational character had been established. In March 1957 the Federal Republic was one of the six founding members of the European Economic Community (EEC), which later developed into the European Community (EC) and ultimately into the European Union (EU).

In the years to come Germany proved to be a reliable partner in European affairs and a strong supporter of a future European federal state. Until unification this seemed the only way to pursue German national interests. As reunification remained a distant dream, the only realistic way of achieving a better future for the divided German people seemed to be progress in European integration and intensified cooperation between East and West as envisaged in the 'Helsinki process.'

Deutschlandpolitik and *Ostpolitik*

The longer the division of Germany into two states and socio-economic orders lasted, the less likely German reunification seemed. The reunited Germany was to be a democratic Germany based on the model of the Federal Republic. This aim was legally binding not only because of the provisions of the Basic Law but also by the General Agreement of 1955 signed by the Federal Republic and the three Western powers.

As the years of division accumulated, it became more and more obvious that the final goal of West German politics would be severely endangered if no attempt was made to improve relations with the other part of Germany. Families had been divided for decades. The Korean War had caused conflict. East–West communication was at an all-time low. After the erection of the Berlin Wall on August 13, 1961, nearly all contact was cut off by the GDR authorities. It took years of complicated negotiations before West Berliners were allowed, under certain extremely restricted conditions, to visit their relatives in the East.

In order to negotiate improvements, the federal government and the authorities in West Berlin had to accept the GDR government as their partner in negotiations – even if they still doubted its legitimacy. Coming to terms with this reality caused quite a lot of hardship among political actors and government officials. It also had legal and constitutional implications. Would the international position of the Federal Republic be seriously undermined? Would the government thereby send a signal to the outside world that it no longer insisted on representing all Germans (*Alleinvertr etungsanspruch*)? Would it mean the *de facto* recognition of the GDR? And last but not least, would there be constitutional constraints in the Basic Law's Preamble that did not allow for negotiations with East Germany because this would hamper the goal of achieving 'the unity and freedom of Germany in free self-determination'?

Those in favor of a new policy argued that, given the international situation, unification was not likely to be achieved for a very long time. Under these circumstances, the main duty for responsible politicians was to protect the two German communities from further estrangement. Those opposing any policy change were not only driven by mistrust of the communist regime but also feared that negotiations would mean enhancing the status (i.e. lead to a reevaluation or *Aufwertung*) of an illegitimate regime and lethally hamper any further attempts to achieve a single united state. There was also a suspicion that the Western partners would give up their unconditional support of West-German demands concerning the German question. The first steps toward détente after the Cuban crisis were thus viewed with some misgivings, especially in the conservative circles of the CDU/CSU. The policy vis-à-vis the GDR (*Deutschlandpolitik*) and the Soviet Union and its satellite states (*Ostpolitik*) became a battleground of German politics for more than a decade, and can only be compared with the controversies over rearmament and Western orientation in the 1950s.

The new *Ostpolitik* inaugurated by Chancellor Willy Brandt in 1969 tried to establish structures of cooperation with the GDR which would help to keep the 'unity of the nation,' not in political terms as a united political entity, but in cultural and historic terms as a community with a common destiny (*Schicksalsgemeinschaft*). The opportunities for overcoming the division of Germany had not improved since the foundation of the two German states, notably because the GDR, in agreement with its controlling power, rejected the notion of any future national unity. The old concepts seemed to have led into a cul-de-sac.

The new policy aimed at step-by-step improvements. It had three pillars:

1. The renunciation of any threat of the use of force;
2. The inviolability of the existing frontiers and territorial integrity and sovereignty of all states in Europe, including the 'inner-German' borders;
3. Peaceful coexistence and the development of normal and good relations between East and West.

These goals could only be achieved if and when the Soviet Union was ready to subscribe to these principles. Accordingly, *Ostpolitik* meant establishing a network of bilateral treaties with all relevant countries in the East, first and foremost the Soviet Union, since it was seen as the ultimate repository of power in Eastern Europe. On the basis of such treaties, German–German relations could be improved. And last but not least, the permanent center of crisis, Berlin, had to be included in any attempt to consolidate the situation for a longer period of time. Only after the Quadripartite Agreement of September 1971, signed by the Soviet Union, the USA, the United Kingdom and France, was serious progress made in inner-German affairs.

The new *Ostpolitik* started with a dramatic overture. At the end of 1969, in his first address to parliament as federal chancellor, Willy Brandt referred to 'two states of one German nation,' stopping short of full international recognition of the GDR. This statement by implication ruled out reunification as a realistic option for the foreseeable future. Brandt even went further; his government declaration was also the first not to mention 'reunification' at all.

Insisting on a policy based on the primacy of reunification – as the former governments had done – was not a realistic option for the future because it would only strengthen the hard-line elements in the GDR leadership. Accepting that reunification was not an option in the near future would, it was hoped, ease the pressure on the GDR leadership, allowing them to be more flexible and to feel free enough to liberalize the contacts between the two states and thus strengthen the 'feeling of belonging together' (*Zusammengehörigkeitsgefühl*). Even if the pursuit of one nation state (*Staatsnation*) seemed unrealistic for the time being, they would still be a nation culturally and mentally (*Kulturnation*), as the Poles had been for more than a century when the Polish state had been destroyed by Russia, Austria and Prussia.

For the new government, normalization of relations with the Soviet Union and Eastern Europe was of paramount importance because normal relations first and foremost with the Soviet Union were seen as a precondition for progress in German–German relations. The underlying argument was that the GDR had only very limited room for maneuver, if any, without the acceptance of the Soviets. Second, normalization with Poland was of high symbolic and political importance. Poland had been the first victim of World War II – the aggression against Czechoslovakia in 1938 had been accepted by Britain and France when they signed the notorious 'Munich Agreement.' Moreover, relations with Poland were severely strained because the new Polish state had been shifted to the West by agreements reached between the three Allied powers at the Yalta conference in 1945 and had been compensated with former German territories for its territorial losses to the Soviet Union.

As no peace treaty had been signed with Germany, this 'temporary administration' of parts of Germany was not definitely decided, a final solution still requiring to be reached in terms of international law. No German government could legally accept the western borders of Poland (as the GDR government pretended to do in a friendship treaty with Poland in the early 1950s) but – and this is what the new government did in a treaty with Poland signed on December 7, 1970 – could accept the situation politically for now and in the future and agree that there should not be any attempt to change the borders by force.

The Federal Republic and Poland agreed that 'the existing boundary ... shall constitute the western state frontier of the People's Republic of Poland' and went on to reaffirm 'the inviolability of their existing frontiers now and in the future and undertake to respect each other's territorial integrity without restriction.' A similar statement concerning the Western borders of Poland was made in a West

German–Soviet treaty signed on August 12, 1970, where in addition the territorial integrity of all European states was secured, including the Oder–Neiße line and the boundaries between the Federal Republic and the GDR.

One of the most amazing aspects of these treaties was that two states, the Soviet Union and Poland, signed agreements in which the other partner, the Federal Republic, agreed to accept borders that were not its own. There was a good reason for that absurdity: as the Federal Republic claimed to represent German statehood per se and because no peace agreement had yet been reached, no German government could legally give up the quest for a final regulation of the German question, including the final boundaries of a united Germany. But what a government could do, and former German governments did not dare to do because of stiff resistance by organized and highly influential groups of refugees, was to accept the status quo politically and to confirm that no future German government would put into question the existing borders in Europe.

Despite the lasting division between East and West, the federal government's *Ostpolitik* proved to be a success. The accession of both German states to the United Nations and the results of the CSCE in Helsinki in 1975 were direct consequences of the policy of détente. Both *Ostpolitik* and the Helsinki Final Act were founded on the mutual agreement of the two power blocs that a change to the status quo could only be achieved by force and was therefore impossible. At the same time, they offered new opportunities for cooperation. These were the parameters in which the two German states tried to regulate their relations.

The GDR availed itself of every opportunity to prove its sovereignty. It insisted on the principles of territorial integrity and the maintenance of the status quo as laid down in Helsinki. The Federal Republic appealed for the respect for human rights to which the signatories had committed themselves. All the political forces in the Federal Republic invested their energies in securing the most favorable conditions which would make the division of Germany as tolerable as possible, whilst undertaking to improve the lot of the people in the GDR. Both the SPD–FDP coalition (1969–82) and its CDU–FDP successors (1982–90) failed, however, to resolve the ambiguities inherent in such a policy. The adherence to legal positions and the respective social and political orders, on the one hand, and the goal of unification on the other were mutually exclusive in the context of an *Ostpolitik* which did not really constitute an end to the Cold War.

This policy was based on a shared analysis of world political circumstances which foresaw the end of the division into opposing blocs as at best a remote objective – at least, that is, until 1989.

The Aims of *Deutschlandpolitik*

The thirty years of *Ostpolitik* and *Deutschlandpolitik* pursued by the Federal Republic adhered to the following criteria:

1. The primary objective was not reunification but the right of self-determination for all Germans. Observers never seriously doubted that the people of the GDR would, if offered, opt for the Western system.
2. *Deutschlandpolitik* was subordinate to *Ostpolitik*. The primary objective lay in establishing a *modus vivendi* and a reconciliation with the neighboring countries of Eastern Europe. Only lasting success in this area could offer any opportunity for a general improvement of the situation in Germany.
3. *Deutschlandpolitik* was subordinate to the policy of the Western alliance. The resolution of the division of Germany was conceivable only within the framework of a European peace order. An independent German line was seen as neither propitious nor desirable. The Federal Republic has never seriously challenged its position in the West.
4. *Ostpolitik* and *Deutschlandpolitik* were possible only if the political situation in the socialist states was accepted in its existing form. The Helsinki Conference which vouchsafed the opposition in Central and Eastern Europe the right to dissent (consider Charter 77 in Czechoslovakia) produced a conflict of objectives in this policy since the new opposition groups subscribed to the very democratic order which *Ostpolitik* set out to achieve. Dissidents in these countries were not unjustified in accusing politicians and intellectuals in the West of bias toward the ruling political class. Circumstances in the GDR were different, since it was only in 1989 that an identifiably structured political opposition emerged.
5. The *Deutschlandpolitik* of the federal government and the opposition failed to recognize the gravity of developments after Gorbachev assumed power. Observers only realized the ramifications that the concept of a 'European home' would have for a divided nation as late as 1989.

Despite hopes of a new political order in Europe kindled by Soviet policy after 1985, there remained no signs of change in the objectives of *Deutschlandpolitik* until mid-1989. Thinking was still very much long term. The former federal chancellor Helmut Schmidt expressed a widely held view in an article published in the weekly *Die Zeit* on September 22, 1989: 'An eruption in the GDR would jeopardize the reform process in Eastern Europe.' He felt that there was no prospect of a panacea for the German question, and he reminded the German people of Poland, which had been divided for over a century and again been truncated in the twentieth century but nevertheless had emerged as a nation state. 'I am confident that in the course of the next century the German nation will have a common roof under which freedom can shelter.'

There was broad consensus in the Federal Republic that it would be a long time before reunification could be achieved. This was the background to Willy Brandt's view of 1988 that, in its quest for unification, the Federal Republic was living a lie.

Even in conservative circles, which accused the Social Democratic–Liberal government of being too soft on communism, a discussion started in the late 1980s as to whether German unification was still a goal to be aimed at. The following statement in the *Frankfurter Rundschau* of January 2, 1985 by the Chairman of the right-wing-conservative CSU, Franz Josef Strauss, illustrates this point: 'Are we truly impelled, tortured, burdened and driven by reunification? It is not so much a matter of reunification in the sense of a recovery of the state unity of Germany as a longing for the restoration of democracy and conditions under which people can live in dignity in that part of Germany.'

Even for the CDU/CSU and the federal government they had led since 1982, unification of the two German states was not a pressing issue. Indeed, at the beginning of 1988 consideration was given, in a draft of the CDU's new party program, to the possibility of dropping reunification as the aim of *Deutschlandpolitik*. The CDU's draft program focused on the European dimension of the German question. The aim of unity could only be achieved 'with the agreement and support' of neighboring states in East and West. This implicitly meant that the legal position that had always been invoked, particularly as regards the Oder–Neiße border with Poland, was no longer tenable. An end to the division of Europe, and therefore of Germany, presupposed an end to the East–West conflict: 'A solution to the German question therefore cannot be achieved at present.' The responsibility of the Germans consisted in doing whatever was currently possible to temper the East–West conflict in Germany and in Europe.

The CDU/CSU's *Deutschlandpolitik* had long been characterized by a growing contradiction between its official program and the realities of practical politics. This stretched back to the 1960s. The *Ostpolitik* and *Deutschlandpolitik* of the social–liberal coalition pursued by the SPD and FDP from 1969 to 1982 brought a lasting improvement in Germany's relations with her eastern neighbors, but was vehemently opposed by the CDU/CSU. The CSCE, which in 1975 concluded in Helsinki with a final accord which became a kind of 'Magna Carta' for the opposition movements in communist countries, had also been rejected by the opposition.

The prospects for a policy based on conciliation and cooperation in practical matters in Germany were anything but favorable at the beginning of the 1980s. The great expectations accompanying the implementation of the Helsinki Final Act of 1975 had not been realized. After Helsinki, Europe was preoccupied with the Soviet invasion of Afghanistan in December 1979 and, in the same month, NATO's 'Twin-Track Decision' to locate a new atomic short-range missile program in Europe in the hope that this would bring the Soviet Union to the negotiating table.

The GDR leadership, nonetheless, displayed a willingness to negotiate. Despite the strains in external policy imposed by the worsening of East–West relations, the following years clearly illustrated that the SED had no interest in witnessing a deterioration in its relations with the Federal Republic. Although it insisted on West German acceptance of far-reaching demands, and continued to do so until the end of its rule in 1989, the GDR was genuinely interested in negotiation.

The governments of the Federal Republic and the GDR aimed not to heighten tensions but rather to contribute to détente by further developing treaty relations between two states on the fault line of the two world systems. Neither government nor opposition had a strategy for dealing with the process of emancipation of GDR society from the party state which would not presuppose an end to the *modus vivendi* with the authorities. The parties of the government and the SPD opposition failed to grasp that a curious contradiction ran through their policies that would become even more acute in the years to come. The search for a consensus of interests with the East was bringing improvements for the people, while, at the same time, further consolidating orthodox regimes in Central and Eastern Europe.

Even after Helsinki both *Ostpolitik* and *Deutschlandpolitik* remained the exclusive preserve of government policy. The human rights principles contained in 'Basket 3' of the Helsinki Final Act of the CSCE were continually invoked but this stopped short of demonstrating solidarity with those in the GDR who fought for civil rights, as laid down in the Helsinki charter. (The situation was different in the East-Central European countries.) The reason for this was that the opposition in the GDR was extremely small and marginal and raised issues that would cause discomfort for politicians in Western societies, namely radical disarmament, environmental protection, grassroots democracy, solidarity with the 'Third World.' The Honecker government shrewdly played on this contradiction.

However, the contradiction only became clear when the Soviet Union under Gorbachev changed its political course and the SED leadership started to shield itself from glasnost and perestroika by deploying more repressive measures. The changes in the Soviet Union not only upset the old political structures and those of the socialist alliance; they also had a far-reaching impact on the sensitivities of socialist societies. Hitherto marginalized dissident and opposition groups gained influence deep in the ranks of the governing communist parties and paved the way for new thinking, new forms for the representation of political and social interests, and growing national independence. All this posed a grave threat to the monopoly of power of the party leadership.

The Path to German Unity

No one in 1987/88 could have predicted the collapse of the communist system within less than half a year. The fact that the communist system was in (latent) crisis could not be overlooked, but until 1989 no serious observer had the fantasy to imagine that a world power like the Soviet Union would give up its authority over a vast empire stretching from the Elbe River to Wladiwostok. However, the framework of *Deutschlandpolitik* clearly began to change after Gorbachev's accession to power in 1985 and, with it, the prospect of a fundamental improvement of East–West relations. The federal government and the largest opposition party reacted to the new situation to the extent that they declared their support for Gorbachev's policy.

The upheaval in the GDR in fall 1989 elicited only predictable responses from the West German government and opposition: on the one hand, they appealed for greater freedoms but, on the other, they were prepared to sit down with the various party and state leaderships 'in the interests of the people.' Even in November 1989 the federal government welcomed with stunning reluctance the announcement of the new SED leadership that it would open the Wall. It greeted this historical event and offered immediate talks to the GDR authorities.

The reasons were obvious. Nobody in Europe could be interested in allowing events to get out of hand, and it was not yet clear how the Soviet Union, which had not been asked in advance by the GDR government, would react to the new situation. It took some time before it became obvious that the fall of the Berlin Wall was the direct catalyst for the implosion of the political system. It did not solve the political crisis in the GDR but brought discontent to boiling point. This left the party leadership, as it judged the situation, with only one set of alternatives: either to capitulate or to start negotiations with the opposition over regime change and the Federal Republic over financial support.

Both the GDR authorities and the West German government were caught unawares by the dynamics of what had turned into a revolutionary situation. The day before the Wall fell, the Chancellor of the Federal Republic had declared in his report on the state of the nation: 'However difficult it may be for us and above all for our compatriots in the GDR, let us continue with patient perseverance to trust in the path of evolutionary change at the end of which must stand full respect for human rights and the free self-determination of all Germans.' On November 28, 1989 the Chancellor had drawn up a long-term 'Ten Point Program' which provided for contractual and confederative structures between the two German states as a first step and was intended ultimately to lead via a federation to the unification of Germany. No timetable was attached to these proposals: 'No one knows today what a unified Germany will finally look like.'

It took the visit by the federal chancellor to Dresden on December 19, 1989 to finally and dramatically make it clear to everyone that the GDR had no future and that a cautious step-by-step approach to the question of unification, as pursued only days before in the Ten Point Program, was now obsolete. Hundreds of thousands of people, waving the (West) German flag, shouted 'Germany united fatherland.' The dam had broken and only force could have stopped the process that led to the final end of the GDR and to unification within a mere month.

The GDR government tried very hard to get Soviet support, but it failed. On January 30, 1990 Hans Modrow, then prime minister of the GDR, traveled to Moscow to consult the Soviet government on the future of the GDR. It could be seen by them that the unification of the two German states would inevitably take place in a relatively short time; people were on the streets categorically demanding nothing less. After his visit to Moscow, Modrow suggested, to the evident discomfort of his own party (now renamed the SED-PDS), that Germany should again become, in the words of the GDR's own national anthem, the united fatherland (*einig Vaterland*) of all citizens of the German nation. In so doing, he took up the demand that had been voiced with increasing fervor at the weekly mass demonstrations that the SED-PDS still rejected as an expression of growing nationalistic and chauvinistic tendencies. Thus Modrow was ahead of his party in bidding farewell to one of the greatest illusions of the Honecker era, the idea that a socialist nation could be artificially created in the GDR.

In the following weeks and months, the question of urgent unification came to predominate over all others. All the politicians were trying, with varying degrees of success, to catch up with events. Modrow returned with the Soviet Union's agreement that it would not oppose such a development. What only two months before had appeared a distant possibility on the horizon was now the pressing issue of the day. However, the Soviet Union still appeared set on the neutralization of Germany.

Developments received a push from the results of the elections to the People's Chamber (*Volkskammer*) on March 18,1990. These demonstrated that the population did not share with the citizens' movements and many intellectuals the dream of a renewed, human socialism in the GDR. The majority wanted the rapid unification of Germany, in the hope that this would bring the solution to their problems.

Still undecided was the future status of Germany in the alliances. The federal government had left no doubt that it did not support neutrality, indeed regarded it in the long term as highly problematic and even dangerous. However, this hurdle too was surmounted during the Chancellor's visit to the Soviet Union in the summer of 1990. The stage was now set for a successful conclusion of the German question.

The New Germany and the European Order

For forty years the Western Allies had supported the Federal Republic's claim for a peaceful reunification of Germany as a democratic state. Now they had to prove whether they would keep their promise to actively support a unification policy when the time came. The popular upheaval in East Germany was only the prelude to a fundamental change in the whole framework of European politics. In the fall of 1989 the West Germans and the three Western Allies were united in their fear of destabilization in Europe. It was in this context that their first priority was to avoid anything that could make things even more complicated. This meant first of all stabilizing the GDR by negotiating with the current leadership and trying to win them over to a strict reform course. Secondly, it meant helping with whatever means, especially financial support. When mass demonstrations demanded immediate and decisive steps toward unification, a policy change was unavoidable.

This was the moment when different views and divergent ideas put a great strain on relations between the governments of some of the Western countries and the federal government in Bonn. Chancellor Kohl had proposed his 'Ten Point Program' of November 28 without consulting the Western Allies (and with his own foreign minister). This was interpreted as an indication of a new political pattern: even though unification was still only a distant possibility 'the Germans' were suspected of a tendency to want to go it alone once again. Additional suspicion was raised by the fact that (until early summer 1990) no word was uttered on the crucial question of the final borders of a united Germany. Last but not least, this program was seen as an attempt to fix the terms of unification before those who had the final say, the four victorious powers of the Second World War, and above all the Western Allies of the Federal Republic of Germany had made up their minds. That was especially true for France, despite the cordial relationship between Chancellor Helmut Kohl and President François Mitterand. The British prime minister, Margaret Thatcher, was openly opposed to any progress that could speed up developments in the direction of German unity. She considered a united Germany a threat to stability in Europe and a 'loose cannon' potentially aiming at neutrality.

To calm these suspicions, which were also held in other European countries, a special summit of the European Community was convened in Paris on November 18, 1989, and a second one in Strasbourg – where the way was paved for a process that ended in the Maastricht Treaty. Ironically enough, the fear of a new German nationalism – triggered by the prospect of German unification and the reemergence of a German national state – proved to be the decisive driving force behind further European integration. The hidden agenda could be described as containment by integration, paralleling the situation at the very beginning of the European integration process in the early 1950s.

Only the American administration unequivocally supported the German longing for unification and proved in the months to come to be the only unambiguous ally of the Kohl government. The Bush administration was, however, cautiously aware that everything had to be done to avoid alienating the Soviet Union, whose final position was not yet clear. At a summit on a warship near Malta in early December 1989, Presidents George Bush and Mikhail Gorbachev agreed not to speed things up and to keep in close contact in the time ahead.

At a special NATO summit in Brussels on December 4, the American president expressed four guiding principles:

1. The right to self-determination had to be respected. That meant that it was for the Germans to decide on their future. A closer look at this formulation reveals that it put a curb on any intention to say farewell to NATO and European integration.
2. Unification could only proceed in the context of the Federal Republic's responsibilities within NATO and the European Community regarding the responsibilities and powers of the Allied powers with respect to Germany.
3. In the interest of stability and peace in Europe, unification should be a step-by-step process.

4. As to the final borders of a united Germany, the principles laid down in the Helsinki accord of 1975 were binding.

The Soviet Union reacted with extreme caution to the developments that followed the fall of the Berlin Wall. In early December Mikhail Gorbachev, at a meeting of the Central Committee of the CPSU, expressed the Soviet leadership's determination to categorically support the GDR as a befriended nation and a close ally in the Warsaw Pact. That position did not hold for long and the Soviet Union played an important historical role by not vetoing a final solution of the German question which could only be achieved by its giving up a part of its post-war empire. It paid a heavy price for that, as others perceived this decision as a sign of weakness and they too demanded sovereignty and self-determination. The empire began to crumble.

When in January 1990 it became clear that the reunification of Germany was imminent – whether or not some actors liked it – a way had to be found to conclude a process that had stalled when the four victorious powers in 1945 decided to leave the final settlement of the German question open. After some discussion on whether the former Allies alone should agree upon the conditions of unification without German participation, the American administration came forward with the idea of calling for a conference of the four powers and the two German states. After personal interventions by the American president with François Mitterand and Margaret Thatcher and after intensive consultations with the Soviet leadership, an agreement was reached during the Open Skies Conference in Ottawa on February 12–13, 1990. The two German states, the Soviet Union, the United States of America, the United Kingdom, and France were to negotiate the conditions and procedures under which a united Germany could regain full sovereignty.

The idea of a Two-Plus-Four conference was born; it started on May 5 in Bonn, continued on June 17 in Paris and held its final meeting on September 12, 1990 in Moscow. The treaty granted full sovereignty to united Germany. In its first article, the treaty prescribed the conditions under which this final settlement of the German question had to take place. The 'Treaty on the Final Settlement with Respect to Germany' contained ten articles and some supplements, including a letter by the German foreign minister that confirmed agreements negotiated with the Soviet Union concerning financial compensations.

The preamble referred once again and for the last time to the powers and responsibilities of the four Allies for Germany and Berlin and the decisions made by the Yalta and Potsdam conferences. The 'recent historic changes in Europe' had made it possible 'to overcome the division of the continent.' The Germans, by freely exercising their right of self-determination, were willing 'to bring about the unity of Germany as a state so that they will be able to serve the peace of the world as an equal and sovereign partner in a united Europe.'

The most decisive provision of the Two-Plus-Four Treaty was Article 1, which included these paragraphs:

(1) The united Germany shall comprise the territory of the Federal Republic of Germany, the German Democratic Republic and the whole of Berlin. Its external borders shall be the borders of the Federal Republic of Germany and the German Democratic Republic and shall be definitive from the date on which the present Treaty comes into force. The confirmation of the definitive nature of the borders of the united Germany is an essential element of the peaceful order in Europe.

(2) The united Germany and the Republic of Poland shall confirm the existing border between them in a treaty that is binding under international law.

(3) The united Germany has no territorial claims whatsoever against other states and shall not assert any in the future.

After some hesitation the Soviet Union had accepted, under certain conditions, full membership of the united Germany in NATO. Article 6 of the treaty accepts that the 'right of the united Germany to belong to alliances, with all the rights and responsibilities arising therefrom, shall not be affected by the present Treaty.' This formulation paved the way for full membership of the united Germany in NATO.

The formula with which the former Allies definitely ended their responsibilities for Germany is stated in Article 7 of the Treaty:

(1) The French Republic, the Union of Soviet Socialist Republics, the United Kingdom of Great Britain and Northern Ireland and the United States of America hereby terminate their rights and responsibilities relating to Berlin and to Germany as a whole...

(2) The united Germany shall have accordingly full sovereignty over its internal and external affairs.

In addition to the Two-Plus-Four Treaty, the Soviet Union and the Federal Republic of Germany agreed upon a treaty to solve the problem of sending back nearly one million Soviet soldiers stationed in the GDR. The delicacy of this issue became evident to all when in summer 1991 a putsch was launched against Mikhail Gorbachev and the real danger of a military rollback nearly became reality.

The dramatic events triggered by the upheaval of 1989 and German reunification altered what for decades had seemed permanent – the Yalta order. It also meant a farewell to the cosy certainties on which the previous decades of foreign and security policy had been based. High-flying visions of a new world based on human and citizens' rights, economic freedom, and social justice, as formulated in the CSCE Charter of Paris in November 1990, however, did not come to pass. They only became a reality for some of the states formerly under communist rule. Many former Soviet republics and new independent states are still run by authoritarian regimes, unlike the countries of Central and Eastern Europe, which became market-economy democracies within a few years and are now members of the European Union, which today encompasses nearly all European states and nations.

But there are still legacies of history to be overcome. One is a subcutaneous fear of German dominance in Europe. The reasons are complex. Underlying them is the historical experience with 'the Germans' – an experience itself intimately related to the question of the German nation state and its role in the center of Europe. In addition, the old fear of German romanticism, irrationalism and nationalism plays a role. Western reactions to the events of 1989 and 1990 demonstrate that, despite the official pronouncements, attitudes toward the German people remain reserved, cautious and sometimes colored by suspicion. Occasionally, sentiment verged on the bizarre, as when united Germany was described as the 'Fourth Reich.'

Nevertheless, a nation of 80 million people is too great a country to fail to emerge as a dominating force within European politics. Zbigniev Brzezinski was quite open about his expectations. In an interview with *Le Figaro* (July 18, 1990) he stated that the end of the Cold War would leave two victors: the United States and Germany, and two losers: the USSR and France. Despite the positive attitude that Germany's neighbors in East and West expressed toward reunification, doubts remained about the resolve and political reliability of the German people. A reunified Germany had still to prove that it was in a position to preserve the Federal Republic's forty-year-old democratic tradition despite its increased size and the threat of social and political conflict. In 1990 Thomas Mann's vision of a European Germany has been frequently invoked in an attempt to allay fears abroad. This kind of appeasement strategy has proved to be as antiquated as the fears it addressed. The problem does not lie in a German Europe of disreputable intentions but in the political geography of Europe in which Germany has to take her place.

The basic decision in favor of adherence to a Western-liberal political and social order was taken on October 3, 1990. The decision to adopt a political order that the old communist system had consigned to the trash can as obsolete is now a common feature of nearly all the states in Eastern Europe. The peculiarity of the German revolution derives from the fact that the GDR was able to become part of a political order of some forty years' standing – in marked contrast to the painful transition anticipated in Poland, Czechoslovakia and Hungary, not to mention the former Soviet Union. The problem is that the merging in the heart of Europe of two states that had hitherto belonged to two opposing ideological systems and alliances has, apart from internal difficulties, shifted the balance in Europe.

German reunification, accompanied by its membership of NATO and the EC, on the one hand, and the collapse of the Warsaw Pact and COMECON on the other, required the creation of a new European equilibrium. The new equilibrium would affect the political, economic, military, and cultural spheres. This also presupposes an analysis of the consequences of an eastward shift in Europe's center of gravity. The Poles, Czechs, Slovaks, and Hungarians have left the periphery of the Soviet empire and rejoined the center of Europe.

The Germans in East and West had been the respective outposts of two opposing systems. At the end of the twentieth century, they found themselves as an economic power in a radically altered political constellation right in the heart of Europe. It is not necessary to be a devotee of the romantic ideal of some *Mitteleuropa* (Central Europe) between East and West to understand that the geopolitical coordinates have shifted eastward. Europe is coming together and Germany has still to find its role in the new Europe.

–5–

The System of Government

Among German politicians in 1949, there was a basic consensus on three guiding principles of the political order and system of government for West Germany: the new German state was to be a democratic republic, based on federal structures and the rule of law as a general maxim of political and social activity, and a state which should guarantee the social welfare of its citizens. The Basic Law speaks of a democratic and social federal state and of the principles of republican, democratic, and social government based on the rule of law.

Guiding Principles of the System of Government

The constitution of the Weimar Republic of 1919 contained this short, sharp statement in Article 1: 'The German Reich is a republic. All state power emanates from the people.' The Basic Law employs no such wording. It refers to the republican principle indirectly (in Article 28.1), where there is mention of the 'principles of a republican, democratic, and social state governed by the rule of law,' and in Article 20.I it is implicitly assumed that the Federation should take the form of a republic and other types of democratic state are precluded, such as a constitutional monarchy. This principle is also constitutionally anchored in the term chosen by the Parliamentary Council: 'The Federal Republic of Germany.'

The initial decision in favor of a republic still permitted various options as to how the state would be organized – it could be constituted as a centralized state or as a federal structure. However, Germany had no tradition of centralization and there was no doubt that it would be a federal state, in the light of both German traditions and the clear instructions of the Allies, who would not have permitted a centralized state. Another factor was the reconstitution of the Länder, which had already taken place. The fact that the Länder existed before the Federal Republic came into being is an historical element that continues to have its effect today. The federal order and the autonomy of the Länder became the central structural principles of the Federal Republic.

The idea of the *Rechtsstaat* (a state based on the rule of law) has a long tradition in German political and popular thinking. National Socialism had destroyed the validity of law, so it was therefore understandable that restoration of the rule of law became a vital condition for the political order of the Federal Republic. The essential elements of the principle of the *Rechtsstaat* are: 'the right to due process,' confidence in legal norms, the preeminence of the constitution over all other legal norms, and the commitment of all state authorities to the law and the separation of powers.

The separation of powers, the commitment of the legislature to constitutional order (as set out in Article 20.3 of the Basic Law), and the commitment of the executive and judiciary to the law are taken for granted in established democracies. But in Germany after the Second World War, this represented a new constitutional statement that had never before been formulated so unambiguously. This helps to explain the great importance attached to formal legalistic procedures in German political culture. How well the separation of powers has been effected has to be assessed more cautiously.

The classic idea of the separation of powers in the Basic Law has given way to a system of functional relationships. The political system of the Federal Republic is characterized by a horizontal separation of powers between the legislature, the executive, and the judiciary, and by a vertical separation of powers between the Federation, the Länder, and the local authorities (*Gebietskörperschaften*). But at the same time the necessary cooperation between these different levels in a federal system leads to an intermeshing of the rights and control of these powers. The basic idea of German constitutionalism, as laid down in the Basic Law, is of limited government, checks and balances, and a dispersion of decision-making authority through the principle of federalism.

The Basic Law treats the *Rechtsstaat* not only as a formal principle, as was the case with the conservative German doctrine of constitutional law, but also as one containing basic elements of a material kind. (The phrase 'a social *Rechtsstaat*' in Article 28.1 of the Basic Law is an illustration.) But opinions vary widely as to which specific elements are involved, and in particular what the 'social dimension' is and how far it should be taken. This poses a direct question about the social content of the *Rechtsstaat* and about the political actors who interpret it. It is a question of how widely the principle of the social or welfare state and that of democracy should be extended.

The principle of the welfare state (*Sozialstaat*) is one of the entrenched constitutional clauses. The welfare state is of vital importance to the legitimacy of the political and social system, an importance that has increased since reunification because East Germans regard social welfare as a service provided by the state as a matter of course. For a long time its extent, significance, and content were matters of controversy. Whereas conservative theories of constitutional law interpreted the welfare state only as correcting the existing situation to make it 'more social,' others saw the clause as a compromise formula, since those framing the constitution had been unable to agree on moral concepts.

Eventually, after extensive discussion and several legal judgments, particularly those of the Federal Constitutional Court, a degree of consensus emerged about the meaning of the 'welfare state' in the sense of the Basic Law: it was interpreted more as a broad set of targets than an agreement on its concrete shaping. There is still a general consensus that the principle of the welfare state places an obligation on the state to establish social justice, that is, a constitutional obligation to secure social justice in the sense of promoting equal opportunities and individual freedom. The inherent conflict between social rights and individual freedom has led to detailed discussions on German constitutional theory.

A purely technocratic or authoritarian and paternalistic understanding of the welfare state would be incompatible with the Basic Law. The former President of the Federal Constitutional Court and later Federal President, Roman Herzog, emphasized the connection between the principle of the welfare state and basic rights. In his view the welfare state in its widest sense not only requires a respect for and the implementation of basic rights, but also implies a strong social component.

The two main parties, the CDU–CSU and the SPD, have always pledged themselves to the idea of the welfare state and the state's responsibility for social welfare, both in the era of the social–liberal coalition (1969–82) and during the conservative–liberal coalition (1982–98). Expenditure on social welfare has amounted to around 50 percent of all public expenditure. Only the liberal FDP has consistently argued against excessive state activity in the social field, but as a mere partner in the coalition the FDP has been unable to make major policy changes. However, since the beginning of the 1990s, as is the case in other industrialized Western countries, the social security system has reached its financial limits due to demographic developments, and the problem has been exacerbated by immense transfer payments to eastern Germany since the early 1990s. The new debate on 'reconstructing' the welfare state is in reality a discussion about 'cutting it back.' This will have far-reaching consequences for the political self-perception of the Federal Republic, since it owes its political stability very largely to the way in which it has been able to maintain a high level of social welfare.

The Federal Structure

The main characteristic of the German political system is its federal structure. The Federation now comprises sixteen states or Länder and the independent local authorities, which join in governing and administering Germany.

The federal system creates a highly complex network of institutions, with specific rights and duties for each of the three levels of government, and a range of interwoven powers and a variety of checks and balances. This is why the functioning of the German political system could be described using terms such as division and fusion of powers, which contradict the classical concept of the separation of powers developed by Montesquieu in the mid-eighteenth century. His distinction between the autonomous rights and powers of the executive, the legislature and the judiciary – the result of a misconception of the English system – provides a normative tool for modern democratic systems insofar as it underlines the necessity of avoiding the monopolization of power in one hand, but it could not serve as a blueprint for the basic structure of a modern, democratic system of government. There is, however, no doubt about the importance of the independence of the judiciary and the principle of the separation of powers. Quite the contrary, it is considered as a cornerstone of a modern state under the rule of law. But the relationship between the legislature and the executive is considerably more blurred.

The traditional liberal idea that parliament as a whole controls and checks the government is simply incompatible with modern democratic rule, where political parties dominate the political scene and where it is inconceivable that the majority parliamentary parties should oppose the government. This observation has led some political scientists and legal experts to conclude that it would be more realistic to distinguish between the classic normative idea of separation of powers and a more functional approach. A more functional approach would look at what precisely political institutions are doing, whether and how they cooperate, and consider their respective powers and authority.

This approach is particularly helpful in describing and analyzing the German federal system. Here the horizontal separation of powers (executive, legislature, judiciary) is complemented by a vertical division of powers, i.e. the rights and duties of the Federation, the Länder, and the local authorities in a federal system of government. All three levels of government are by the same token bound to cooperate, because decisive political decisions can only be made if and when the Federation and the federal states find a basis of common understanding. The federal order of the Federal Republic is characterized by three elements: legislative powers are allocated to both the federal parliament and to the Länder, administrative tasks are divided between the federal government and the Länder, but mainly rest with the latter, and financial resources are shared between the three levels of government, Federation, Länder, and, to a lesser extent, local authorities.

The federal system provides not only for a sharing of tasks and responsibilities between the federal government and parliament, Länder and the local authorities, but also for a corresponding division of financial resources. The Basic Law precisely regulates the division of tax revenues between Federation and Länder (right down to the 'Beer Tax') and the allocation of financial resources to the local authorities. The idea developed in the Basic Law of a 'democratic and social federal state' and 'joint tasks,' which are 'important for society as a whole' and where 'federal participation is necessary for the improvement of living conditions' (Article 91a.1), require the sharing of revenues between the corporate bodies. The financial relations between the federal government, the Länder and the local authorities involve the following principles:

- vertical equalization, that is, federal payments to poorer Länder
- the sharing of common tax revenues by the federal government and the Länder

- federal payments to the Länder to cover the cost of administering federal law
- horizontal equalization between the Länder, where federal legislation 'shall ensure a reasonable equalization between financially strong and financially weak Länder, with due account being taken of the financial capacity and financial requirements of local authorities and local authority associations' (Article 107.2)
- intergovernmental grants for joint tasks, for example improvement of regional, economic, or agricultural structures.

This system, combined with special infrastructure programs for structurally weak regions, has led to a considerable reduction in regional disparities in West Germany. When the GDR joined the Federal Republic there was a shift in the balance of influence among the Länder, shown above all in their relative financial status. The accession of the five new states meant that the system for allocating financial resources, which had been carefully balanced over a period of decades, was thrown into confusion. For a long time to come Brandenburg, Mecklenburg-West Pomerania, Saxony-Anhalt, Saxony, Thuringia and Berlin will require considerable financial support. This has turned states such as the Saarland, which previously received funds through the financial equalization mechanism, into states that now have to pay considerable sums in financial equalization to *Länder* in the east.

For this reason, the introduction of the West German financial arrangements, according to Article 7 of the Unification Treaty, was delayed until December 31,1995. A final date had to be set, since prolonged special treatment of the eastern states would not only have endangered social peace in the unified Germany but would also have been impossible to reconcile with the basic rules of the federal political system. The eastern Länder were reestablished in 1990 more out of feelings of nostalgia than with an eye to economic and political rationality, and they will be dependent on financial help from the federal government and the western Länder for much longer than originally anticipated. Since, as with the eastern Bundestag representatives, they are in a minority position, they need to find allies among the western Länder, but they too are experiencing increasing financial constraints and are coming under political pressure.

Even though the basic structure of German federalism has not been fundamentaly affected by reunification, the delicate balance of influence among the eleven states has been altered through the accession of five new, smaller Länder and Berlin. However, the influence of individual Länder and the balance of voting in the Bundesrat after unification have caused problems for the western states. Before 1990 each of the large Länder – Bavaria, Baden-Württemberg, North-Rhine Westphalia and Lower Saxony – had five seats and together these four held a blocking majority. This strategic advantage would have been lost through the accession of the five new Länder and Berlin, even though in total the latter only have the same number of inhabitants as North-Rhine Westphalia, the largest of the Länder. To preserve their strategic position, in 1990 the large Länder agreed to sign the Unification Treaty only if the voting ratio in the Bundesrat was changed in their favor. Finally, the accession of the new Länder, and above all the different development of the party system and voter behavior in East and West Germany, has led to new differences between the Länder and new problems in the relationship between Bundestag and Bundesrat.

The most decisive challenge to German federalism, however, does not stem from German unification but from the process of European integration. The transfer of sovereign rights to the European Union has had a considerable effect on the German federal system. The criterion of 'subsidiarity' developed in the Maastricht Treaty and later the Amsterdam Treaty means, according to the Basic Law, that the principles of federalism have to be respected and the agreement of the Bundesrat (the upper house of the federal parliament and representative of the federal states) has to be obtained; in other words, the Länder have a say in European affairs.

This required an amendment to the constitution (Article 24), which *inter alia* provides for the Bundesrat to be expressly included in the 'formation of political will' in the affairs of the European Union. Furthermore, within the EU framework the responsibility for decision-making in matters that affect the exclusive legislative authority of the Länder (for example, questions of education) isto be transferred from the federal level to a Länder Committee appointed by the Bundesrat. The increasing regulatory activity of the EU is restricting the rights and authority of national parliaments, but these rights are not being transferred to the European parliament. This democratic deficit is becoming all the more serious in federal systems, where the authority of the elected assemblies of the constituent states is being undermined.

The Federal Constitutional Court, in its ruling on the Maastricht Treaty, produced a series of clarifications in its judgment of October 12, 1993. It declared: 'The democratic principle does not hinder the Federal Republic from membership in supranational international communities, provided that legitimation and influence emanating from the people, the validity of basic rights and the principles of the "democratic and social federal state" of Article 20.1 of the Basic Law are not affected.' When all these internal and external factors are taken together, it is clear that Germany's federal system is facing a severe test from the further advance of European integration and quasi-state building.

The Constitutional Bodies

The Basic Law provides a differentiated description of the institutional order of German democracy. To a British or American reader, the provisions of the constitution would appear extremely formalistic and much too detailed. Given the German legal tradition and historical experience, formal legal arrangements that describe the rights, powers, and duties of political institutions and provide carefully regulated procedures for dealing with political issues were meant as a safeguard against any autocratic or dictatorial tendencies and another failure of democracy. The institutional order established by the Parliamentary Council in 1949 is the basic framework for German politics. The Basic Law describes at length and in detail the role of parliament, the chancellor, the president, the government and the Federal Constitutional Court.

Germany is a parliamentary democracy. The German Bundestag is the parliamentary assembly representing the German people. The second chamber, the Bundesrat, represents the sixteen federal states. The Bundestag is elected every four years. It can only be dissolved under exceptional circumstances, which has only happened twice – in 1972 and 1982. In 1972, after the government formed by the Social Democrats and Liberals had lost their majority in parliament, the opposition CDU/CSU tried to oust Chancellor Willy Brandt by a vote of no confidence, but failed. In 1982 Chancellor Helmut Schmidt was replaced by the leader of the opposition, Helmut Kohl, by a majority in parliament resulting from a change of allegiance by the smaller coalition partner, the FDP.

The chancellor cannot call early elections, as the British prime minister can. The main functions and objectives of the Bundestag are – as with any other modern democratic parliament – legislation, electing the head of government (the federal chancellor), and keeping a check on the government. The Bundestag is a 'working parliament,' which means that most of the work is done in parliamentary committees that correspond with the government's departments. Generally speaking, these committees are not open to the public. It is mainly in these committees, and not in plenary discussions, that parliament controls and scrutinizes government activities and policies.

Most of the more than 6,000 bills passed by parliament since 1949 were initiated by the government. A growing number of legislative measures – more than 50 percent – these days are acts to implement European Union legislation in German law. Laws receive three readings in parliament and are usually referred to one or more appropriate committees, which then do the fine-tuning. The final vote is taken after the third reading. A law is passed if it gains the majority of votes cast. In the case of constitutional amendments, a two-thirds majority of the members of the house is necessary. Legislation which affects the interests of the Länder also needs the approval of the Bundesrat.

The Bundesrat is, in legal terms, not a second chamber like the United States Senate or the House of Lords in the United Kingdom, but an assembly representing the sixteen states or Länder. It is a federal institution and participates in the legislative process and administration. Unlike a senate in other federal states, the Bundesrat does not consist of elected representatives of the people of the respective Land, but of members of the state governments or their representatives. Depending on the size of the population, the states have between three and six votes that can only be cast as a block. This regulation, which was severely tested during a heated debate over a new immigration law in 2002, has recently been upheld by the Constitutional Court.

The Bundesrat plays an important role in German political life, because many bills require its formal approval and cannot pass into law without its consent. This applies especially to laws that concern vital interests of the Länder, such as their financial affairs or administrative powers. The Bundesrat must also agree to amendments to the constitution and international treaties, including EU treaties.

In general there are two types of legislation: laws for which the consent of the Bundesrat is not required but where the first chamber is nevertheless involved in the legislative process, and those laws for which the consent of both chambers is necessary. In the first case, decisions of the Länder chamber can be overruled by the Bundestag. If the consent of the Bundesrat is required, the upper house maintains veto power. If the two houses of parliament cannot reach an agreement, a mediation committee (*Vermittlungsausschuss*), composed of members of both chambers, must be convened, which in the majority of cases is able to work out an acceptable compromise. If there is no compromise, the legislation fails.

It is often the case that the majority of Länder representatives are of a different political color from the federal government. This gives the opposition in parliament a tool to influence government policies. The parliamentary opposition can then be effective in making waves for the federal government and pursue its own political agenda in the Bundesrat. The opposition might be tempted to use the upper house, which should represent the interests of the federal states, to counterbalance its weakness in the Bundestag. The result could be a blockade of the legislation and reform projects of the government and its majority in the Bundestag. This is clearly against the intentions of the drafters of the Basic Law, but nevertheless over recent years the Bundesrat has often been used as an instrument of the opposition. To give only two examples: in 1999 a far-reaching tax reform proposed by the government of CDU/CSU and FDP did not pass the Bundesrat because of the decision of the opposition SPD to block it all together. After the 2002 elections, which were won by the Social Democrats, the CDU/CSU blocked new immigration laws, which were even supported by the Liberals, who were also in opposition to the government of the day. However, this does not mean that the Bundesrat has evolved into an opposition house. In most cases, voting in the Bundesrat is driven by state interests, which could – especially when it comes to money and taxes – contravene the policies of the opposition in the Bundestag.

The federal government consists of the federal chancellor and the chancellor's ministers in the cabinet. The chancellor is the only member of government elected by parliament, and he or she alone is accountable to it. The chancellor is the head of government and chairs meetings of the cabinet. The federal ministers are legally chosen only by the chancellor and proposed to the president for appointment. As all the governments since 1949, except for one, have been coalition governments, the chancellor has had no *de facto* say in choosing individuals for ministries given to a coalition partner. Furthermore, it has become a convention since the grand coalition of 1966 that the (smaller) coalition partner has the right to propose the minister for foreign affairs, who is also vice-chancellor, an office not mentioned in the Basic Law.

The chancellor is constitutionally entitled to lay down the guidelines of government policies. Within these limits, ministers have the right to conduct the affairs of their department independently and under their own responsibility. Differences within the cabinet are resolved by the chancellor. Ministers are bound by what is called 'cabinet discipline.' If they are inclined to be too independent, create conflicts within the cabinet or with the chancellor, or become a liability for the government, they can be fired by the chancellor – Helmut Kohl and Gerhard Schröder have used this power extensively.

The Federal Constitutional Court, which came into being only in 1951, is the guardian of the constitution. It plays a very prominent role in German political life, mainly due to its capacity to control the compatibility of legal norms with the constitution and its role as mediator in conflicts between constitutional bodies. The powers of the various constitutional bodies and the system of the division and fusion of powers as construed by the Basic Law are shown in Figure 1.

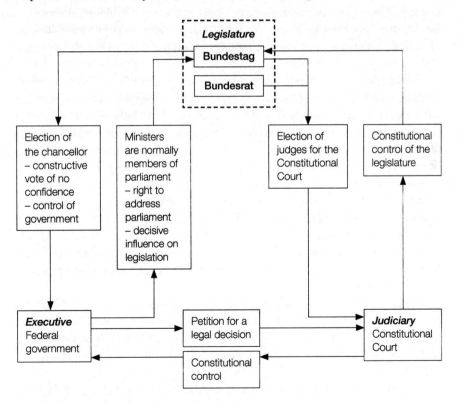

Figure 1 Division and fusion of powers

The Central Role of Parliament

Two fundamental structural decisions shaped the two-chamber governmental system of the Federal Republic. First, unlike the semi-presidential system of the Weimar Republic, a parliamentary system was established that stressed representation rather than direct democracy and provided a strong position for the government and the chancellor. Second, the representation of Länder interests was not entrusted to a second chamber whose membership would be decided by popular vote, but to the Bundesrat, which is composed of representatives of the Länder governments and where seats are allocated according to the population size of the Länder. By contrast, the Bundestag is directly elected by universal suffrage for a maximum four-year term.

The German version of the parliamentary system is based on a historically understandable but problematic analysis of the Weimar constitution, which despite its institutional weaknesses (emergency decrees, the strong position of the president and so on) was a modern constitution for a parliamentary republic. Some peculiarities of the post-war German parliamentary system can be explained with reference to the 'modern' constitution of the Weimar Republic, which, despite the provision of various safeguards in the constitution, did not prevent the overthrow of the democratic system by the Nazis.

In institutional terms, the Bundestag is the leading legislative organ. In practical, everyday politics, 'classic' legislation – that is, laws dealing with basic questions of the political, social, and judicial order – comes second to bills that adapt existing regulations to changing conditions. By and large, the civil service initiates this type of legislation. Thus the Bundestag, as well as the Länder parliaments *de facto*, have been reduced to a control function rather than having an initiating role.

In principle, the Basic Law proceeds from the assumption of the responsibility of the *Länder*: 'The *Länder* shall have the right to legislate insofar as this Basic Law does not confer legislative power on the Federation' (Article 70.1). In practice, however, an ever greater shift of legislative activity has taken place from the *Länder* to the federal parliament, which was achieved by the latter's exploitation of the authority of the general provisions of the Federation and extension of the provision for 'joint tasks' (see Figure 2).

The Basic Law sets out the areas of exclusive and concurrent legislation of the Federation, in which the Bundesrat participates. The various areas are specified in a detailed catalog (Articles 70–74). In addition, the federal government can make general provisions in particular fields, such as public sector pay and nature conservation.

Legislation at the Länder level is limited. Exclusive responsibility is given to them over education, including universities, cultural matters, policing, provision of social services, and the system of local government. In some cases the Länder can

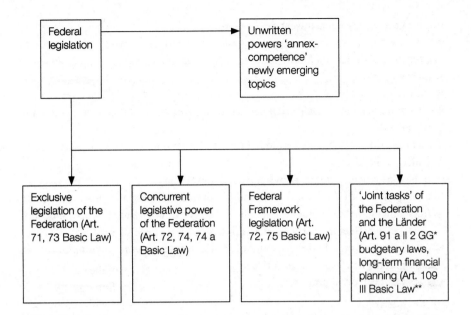

Notes:

In certain areas the Länder have the power to legislate as long as the Federation does not exercise its own power to legislate

*Building of institution of higher education, improvement of regional economic and agricultural structures, coastal preservation.

**Principles applicable to the Federation and the Länder governing budgetary law, the responsiveness of budgetary management to economic trends, and long-term financial planning.

Figure 2 Legislative powers of the Federation

legislate within the parameters laid down by so-called federal framework laws under Article 75 of the Basic law.

The distinction between exclusive and concurrent legislation in the Basic Law allows the denomination of those topics of federal legislation where the Federation has sole power and the Länder are only entitled to act if they are expressly authorized to do so by a federal law (Article 71). In contrast, concurrent legislation marks those fields where the federal states can legislate 'so long as and to the extent that the Federation has not exercised its legislative powers by enacting a law' (Article 72.1).

The Federation has exclusive rights to legislate with respect to:

- foreign affairs and defense, including the protection of civilians
- citizenship in the Federation
- freedom of movement, passports, immigration, emigration, and extradition

- currency, money, measures and other standards
- treaties respecting trade, commerce, and navigation, the free movement and exchange of goods, including customs and border protection
- air transport
- railways
- telecommunications, and postal services (to the extent that these are not already privatized)
- legal relations of persons employed by the Federation or in federal corporations under public law
- industrial property rights, copyrights, and publishing
- cooperation with the Länder concerning criminal police work, protection of the free democratic basic order, protection of the constitution, and protection against activities which endanger the external interests of the Federal Republic
- establishment of a Federal Criminal Police Office (*Bundeskriminalamt*) and international action to combat crime
- statistics for federal purposes.

Some of the most important subjects of concurrent legislation, mentioned in Article 74 of the Basic Law, are:

- civil law, criminal law, corrections, court organization and procedures, the legal profession, notaries, and provision of legal advice
- the law of association and assembly
- the law relating to residence and establishment of aliens
- matters concerning refugees and expellees
- weapons and explosives
- public welfare
- production and utilization of nuclear energy
- labor law
- waste disposal, air pollution control, and noise abatement
- state liability.

Concurrent legislation concerns matters listed in the Basic Law (Article 74) where the Federation has the right to legislate. However, as long as and to the extent that the Federation does not exercise its rights in this respect, the Länder too may legislate. The Basic Law originally gave the Federation the right to legislate 'to the extent that a need for regulation by federal legislation exists' because a matter could not be effectively regulated by the individual Länder and a law of a particular federal state may prejudice the interests of other Länder or the people as a whole, or where the 'maintenance of legal or economic unity, especially the maintenance of uniformity of living conditions beyond the territory of any one Land, necessitates such regulation' (Article 72.2). The original formulation 'uniformity of living conditions' was replaced after unification in order to cope with the dramatic discrepancies between east and west. A slow paced adaptation, rather than uniformity, was and still is a realistic goal in German politics. Article 72.2 now reads: *A, 72.2*

> The Federation shall have the right to legislate on these matters if and to the extent that the establishment of equal living conditions throughout the federal territory or the maintenance of legal or economic unity renders federal regulation necessary in the national interest.

These provisions, intended as a tool to preserve the political, economic and social unity of the Federation and to provide help for those parts of Germany less well off and trailing economically and socially behind, opened the floodgates for intensive federal legislation. The Länder, which held a key position in legislating the necessary regulations leading to German unification, managed to establish new powers insofar as they are now given the right to supersede federal law by Länder law if federal law is no longer needed according to the regulations of Article 72 of the Basic Law.

Legislation is the central task of parliament. The second, equally important duty of parliament is to vote a government into office, to support and control the government, and, if the government loses the confidence of parliament, to replace it through parliamentary procedures. In contrast to the Weimar Republic and constitutional regulations in some of the Länder, the federal parliament has the right to vote for the head of government, the federal chancellor, but not for individual ministers or the government as a whole.

Once elected, the position of the head of government is very strong. The opportunity to remove a serving chancellor (and the government) is severely restricted and can only be achieved through a 'constructive' vote of no confidence. Under Article 67, one of the most important provisions of the Basic Law, the legislature can express its lack of confidence only by electing a successor by the vote of a majority of its members and requiring the federal president to dismiss the chancellor. The president has no choice of his own and has to comply with the decision of parliament and appoint the person elected. Nevertheless, the governing majority has a decisive influence over appointments to ministerial posts, and it can even force a chancellor to quit, as happened in 1974, when Willy Brandt, after an espionage affair and dwindling support from his own parliamentary groups, gave up and resigned.

Furthermore, as bodies such as the national executive, Land associations and special working groups enjoy growing influence, conflicts increasingly arise over the respective roles of the national party and the parliamentary party on the one hand, and the power of the head of government on the other. The Basic Law (Article 65) is very explicit on this subject: the chancellor, not parliamentary parties or party organizations outside parliament, 'shall determine and be responsible for the general guidelines of policy.' These legal regulations and the strong and determined leadership of the first chancellor of the Federal Republic from 1949 until 1963,

Konrad Adenauer, constituted the German version of prime-ministerial government or 'chancellor's democracy.' Since then the system of government has undergone significant changes as to the role and position of the head of government. The chancellor is, depending on his capacity as political leader, the state of the coalition and the level of support from his own parliamentary group, often more a moderator and *primus inter pares* than an authoritarian leader such as Adenauer used to be in his prime.

A vital element of liberal democratic systems of government is the responsibility of government to parliament and the control of government by parliament. The brief provisions of the Basic Law allocate only secondary importance to parliamentary control of the legislative process. The Bundestag's most important control instrument is the right to advise on and to control the budget. The Bundestag and each of its committees can demand the presence of a member of the government (Article 43.1), set up committees of inquiry (mostly with only moderate results), and as a last resort vote the chancellor out of office. In controlling the general political direction taken by the cabinet, the executive government and the majority parties of the coalition in the Bundestag are dependent on one another; they can only succeed by sticking together. This has led to government deputies exercising their control function only internally, within the governing parties, if indeed at all. Thus it is left to the opposition to try to embarrass the government and gain as much publicity as possible in the process. The opposition can also look for support from Land governments of the same party in the Bundesrat, an important aspect of opposition in the context of German federalism. Control of public administration allows deputies from the government and the opposition parties to act together, and, because of the federal structure of the administration, they play a greater role in the Land parliaments than in the Bundestag. In practice, government and parliament, Federation and Länder very often work closely together so that the relevant literature refers to 'cooperative federalism' and the 'governmental functions of parliament' rather than a strict dichotomy between government and opposition.

The legitimacy of parliamentary opposition is recognized, and is mentioned in some new Land constitutions, but is not separately identified in the Basic Law itself. It is questionable whether the idea of an 'alternative government' power, borrowed from the British model, really conforms to the intentions of the Basic Law. The fundamental decision to adopt a federal system, together with the nature of the relationship between government and parliament, have produced structural elements that have led to the contemporary system of 'political intertwining' (*Politikverflechtung*) – the complex process of negotiation involved in policy-making. It has also led to cooperative methods of conflict solving as an opposition strategy. However, bringing all parliamentary parties, including the opposition, into the political decision-making process has had a considerable effect on the ideal model of the 'dual system,' in which political outcome is fashioned through a contest between the government majority and the opposition. Since – via the Bundesrat – the opposition actually participates in the process of government, the system may be described as one of 'shared leadership of the state.'

The Bundesrat is in an extremely strong position with regard to legislation planned by the central government. Since its members are mandated delegates of the Land governments, acting on instructions from them, the direct participation of the Land governments in federal legislation is secure. Thus, in addition to their functions in public administration, the Länder also play an important legislative role at the federal level.

The Executive and Public Administration

The federal system not only allocates concrete and clearly differentiated legislative powers to the federal government and the Länder. It also allows administrative tasks to be distributed, on the basis of subsidiarity, to the individual corporate bodies – the Federation government, the Länder, and the local communities and their

Table 1 Administrative structure of the Federal Republic

Federal administration with its own administrative substructure (Article 87 Basic Law)	Foreign Office Federal financial administration Federal railways and post office (before privatization) Federal waterways Federal security authorities 'Indirect' federal administration (social insurance organizations)
Länder administration on behalf of the Federation (Article 85 Basic Law)	Executing federal laws on behalf of the Federation Supervising the Federation (for legality and effectiveness). Responding to the Federation's right to issue directives
The carrying out of federal legislation as the Länder's own responsibility	The Federation has no right to issue directives, except in special cases with the agreement of the Bundesrat. Federal supervision (for legality only). Administration costs are borne by the Länder
Joint tasks (Article 91a Basic Law)	Participation of the Federation in Land responsibilities through 'joint framework planning' (e.g. new university buildings, regional economic structure). Costs are shared by the Federation and the Länder. Participation in Land administration to carry out federal laws
Local authority administration	Tied to instructions of the Land supervisory organizations

associations. The essential characteristic of the German administrative system is that while the federal government has an administration of its own in just a few – though important – areas, most administrative tasks are conducted at the Länder level or by local authorities in the towns, districts, and regions.

Exclusively federal administration exists in only a few areas, such as the Foreign Office, financial administration, the army, the federal border guards, and other security bodies. These institutions, where necessary, have offices of their own at the Land and local authority level (for example, the army has administrative offices in the Länder and with local authorities). Apart from these few exceptions, the Länder are solely responsible for applying federal law. This provides the main autonomous function of the Länder, along with the exclusive legislative authority accorded to them, although this is limited to a few spheres.

Checks and Balances: the Federal Constitutional Court

The Basic Law implemented a carefully drafted system of checks and balances. It provided the government, and especially the federal chancellor, with a strong mandate to govern without the interference of 'negative coalitions' in parliament. On the one hand, this was meant to avoid weak governments, always on the brink of defeat in parliament, as seen in the Weimar Republic. On the other hand, it constructed heavy counterweights to check the government: the second chamber of parliament, the highly influential Bundesrat, representing the Länder governments which can and often do pursue their own interests during the process of legislation; the independent Central Bank (*Bundesbank*), now a national branch of the European Central Bank (ECB), and, most importantly, the Federal Constitutional Court (*Bund esverfassungsgericht*).

The Federal Constitutional Court was created by the Basic Law as a guardian of the constitution and as an integral element of the system of government, controlling both government and parliament. The framers of the constitution wanted the court to be a *pouvoir neutre* and, as such, to play a role that in the Weimar Republic had been assigned to the president – with catastrophic results. The Federal Constitutional Court has been given the authority to rule on the conformity of legislation with the constitution, to ensure that basic rights are guaranteed and maintained, to interpret the Basic Law, and to decide whether federal law is compatible with international law.

One of the most innovative features of the new system of checks and balances as implemented by the Basic Law was the power given to the court to render binding decisions on the constitutional legitimacy of acts of government and laws passed by a democratically elected chamber. This feature has quite often been reproduced by constitution-makers in Europe in the following decades. By the same token, endowing judges on a supreme court with such wide-ranging powers imposed unprecedented judicial constraints on both executive and legislature. Its decisions are binding, which means that the Constitutional Court also possesses a *de facto* right to amend legislation. But above all, the Constitutional Court is the guarantor of the constitution, and particularly of the basic rights laid down in Articles 1–20. In this respect it has proved an effective brake on attempts to restrict or alter basic rights for purely political reasons.

The Basic Law provided the Federal Constitutional Court (and to a lesser extent the Constitutional Courts of the Länder) with a range of jurisdictions. It has original jurisdiction in constitutional disputes between constitutional bodies. In conflicts concerning the federal structure and the extent of the rights and duties of a supreme federal body or of other parties vested with rights of their own, the court serves, at the request of one of the parties involved, as mediator (*Organstreit*). It decides over the rules and procedures of a supreme federal body, as happened in 2002 when the court had to decide on the voting procedures in the Bundesrat.

The court also rules when disagreements or doubts arise respecting the formal or substantive compatibility of federal law or Land law (passed by state legislatures) with the Basic Law, or of Land law with other federal law. In these cases the federal government, a Land government or one-third of the members of the Bundestag can make an application to the Constitutional Court. In the case of concurrent legislation the Bundesrat, too, or the government or parliament of a Land can make such an application. Furthermore, the court decides on disagreements respecting the rights and duties of the Federation and the Länder, especially the execution of regulations of the Basic Law by the Länder and the exercise of federal oversight. Last but not least, municipal authorities can call for a court decision if their rights of self-government under Article 28 of the constitution are infringed by a law.

Most of the cases brought before the court, however, are not disagreements between institutions or over laws, but constitutional complaints by individuals, which may be filed by any person alleging – not necessarily proving – that one of his or her basic rights as protected by the constitution has been infringed upon by public authority. This sweeping degree of responsibility has also produced additional problems. Frequently the Constitutional Court is asked to mediate in cases of dispute between government and opposition, between federal and Land authorities, and even within the government coalition itself. Those who have been defeated in the decision-making process hope that the court will make a judgment in their favor. Thus in spite of its inclination to exercise judicial self-restraint, the court is provided with an authority that forces it into the role of a referee. This role was not intended by the constitution. The court was established to be the final arbiter in conflicts between constitutional bodies or competing interests but not to replace parliamentary powers and decisions.

Political reality, however, has put the court quite often in the position of *de facto* 'counterweight' to the government of the day. This results from the institutional device of abstract norm review, which means that the court can review acts of parliament or decisions of government in the light of constitutional norms and, if they do not fit, declare a law null and void, or provide an authoritative interpretation of an act, or stop the government doing something unconstitutional.

The Constitutional Court has, over the years, become something like a last resort for the opposition in parliament when it is trying to stop on constitutional grounds an act passed by parliament. The threat to invoke the court is one of the most powerful weapons in the armory of any opposition in the Bundestag. Combined with the necessity for any ruling coalition to win over the Bundesrat in order to pass important legislation, it gives the opposition an important tool to pursue its own political agenda.

Constitutional courts are, whatever their particular rights and duties, factors of political power. Their judgments have a political impact. The Federal Constitutional Court has come to be a central pillar in the political system. It is no wonder that it has been severely criticized from time to time, mainly because of alleged political activism. This interpretation is only partly true. Unlike their American counterparts in the Supreme Court of the United States, the judges are not allowed to refuse to deal with contentious political issues on the grounds of a 'political-question-doctrine.' This gives the court, as has been argued, more constitutional responsibility than the United States Supreme Court – the judges cannot shy away from a decision. That might explain why in some cases judges are unable to withstand the temptation of judicial activism. Examples include the relationship with the GDR in the early 1970s, the progress of the EU, the role of the European Court of Justice, and various abortion laws.

In the case of the 'Basic Treaty' with the GDR in 1972, the court intervened in a spectacular way in the affairs of government and parliament. It delivered an explicit judgment and, for the first time, insisted that every single phrase of that particular judgment should be binding on the government. In the case of abortion, it rejected a first version of a bill legalizing abortion under certain restricted conditions, and in a later opinion in 1993 presented an extremely narrow interpretation of the legal limits of abortion, clearly challenging the decision of the majority in parliament. And in European matters the court has, until a decisive judgment in 2001, pursued its own political skepticism vis-à-vis European integration on the grounds of protecting the constitutional order.

A striking example of the court's political influence was its Maastricht decision of 1993. Here the court maintained the skepticism it had observed from the 1970s through to its last decision of 2001. On the other hand, it upheld the government's case that the treaty was in accord with the Basic Law. It is hard to envisage a court being ready to challenge and put into question the very rationale of German foreign policy since 1949 and its political commitment to European integration. Nevertheless, the Constitutional Court added an *obiter dictum* to its judgment which suggested that it was worried about the constitutional foundations of further European developments as agreed by the Treaty of Maastricht.

In order not to put the process of European integration in jeopardy, parliament passed an amendment to the Basic Law, the new Article 23.1, which repeated word for word the arguments of the court: 'the Federal Republic of Germany shall participate in the development of the European Union that is committed to democratic, social, and federal principles, to the rule of law, and to the principle of subsidiarity, and that guarantees a level of protection of basic rights essentially comparable to that afforded by this Basic Law.'

External Actors: Organized Interest Groups

The picture of the political order of the Federal Republic would not be complete without mentioning external actors that heavily influence the political decision-making process. First and foremost, this means pressure groups and the media. Political scientists often describe Germany as a prototype of a corporate system, where powerful organized interest groups conduct a decisive influence on political decisions and legislation. Especially in the realm of industrial relations, a tripartite structure is observed: government, parliament and organized interests cooperate in many ways in order to negotiate political decisions, to pursue vested interests of certain social groups, and, last but not least, to avoid political and social conflicts over decisions which are not accepted either by powerful political groups or the wider public.

The German system of a social market economy is based on the ability and willingness of social and economic actors to work together. The constitution provides specific regulations for this kind of cooperation: 'The right to form associations to safeguard and improve working and economic conditions shall be guaranteed to every individual and to every occupation or profession. Agreements that restrict or seek to impair this right shall be null and void; measures directed to this end shall be unlawful' (Article 9.3 Basic Law). Even in cases of emergency, the measures taken 'may not be directed against industrial disputes' (Article 9.3 Basic Law).

Industrial relations are regulated by a variety of measures, among which the right of trade unions and associations of entrepreneurs to negotiate freely – without interference by the state – about wages and working conditions, the principle of co-determination on the managerial level, and the right to form work councils on the shop floor are the most important. This gives trade unions and employers' associations an important say in matters of far-reaching economic and social consequences and leaves the political institutions quite often as bystanders. However, sometimes politicians act as mediators in conflicts that cannot be resolved by the two main actors.

Industrial relations are only one, though the most important, sector where organized interest groups play a decisive political role. The second largest sector is social welfare and security and the health service. Organized interest groups are also very active in cultural matters and education. Finally, mention must be made of the growing number of NGOs that try to put specific topics on the public agenda and to influence political decisions.

All these organizations are trying to get access to political decision-making bodies and political actors like parliamentarians, members of government or high-ranking civil servants. Special statutes of parliament and the government provide formal regulations concerning how and at what stage of the decision-making process representatives of important and influential interest groups shall be invited to consult the administration and, at a later stage, parliamentary committees.

Even more important are informal relations between interest groups lobbying for their cause and politicians and bureaucrats. Many members of the Bundestag (more than 60 percent) or Länder parliaments are members or functionaries of interest groups. Public administration, parliament and organized interests quite often form a policy network of experts in defense matters, social security, health policy, education, cultural policies, etc. These people, even if they are pursuing different institutional interests, know each other well; they share a certain expertise and trust each other to a certain extent.

This type of political system is sometimes called 'consociational democracy,' a political arrangement in which various groups, such as ethnic or racial populations, employers and trade unions, and other groups with conflicting interests within a country or region, share power according to an agreed formula or mechanism. It is firmly believed that, many political and social conflicts, which in an adversarial political system would have a negative impact on the economy or politics, can be avoided by negotiation and compromising beforehand.

The price is a lack of transparency because most of this takes place behind closed doors. When it comes to public debates, they are quite often ritualized and carefully directed by the main actors in order to demonstrate to their respective supporters or members that they mean business and are fighting forcefully for their just cause.

External Actors: the Media

As in all modern democracies and open societies, the media are very influential, often termed as the 'fourth estate' in addition to parliament, government and the judiciary. After twelve years of brutal dictatorship and political indoctrination, the framers of the constitution put special emphasis on guaranteeing the freedom of the press and of reporting. They ruled out any sort of censorship. Everyone has the right to obtain information from generally accessible sources.

Germany has one of the most flourishing media landscapes in the world. Daily papers sell more than 25 million copies per day. Besides the biggest tabloid, *Bild-Zeitung* (with a circulation of more than 4 million copies), the German equivalent to the British *Sun*, and local papers of that kind, a number of broadsheet papers are influential when it comes to political controversies and attempts to influence political decisions by government or parliament. These include the conservative *Frankfurter Allgemeine Zeitung* (FAZ), the liberal *Süddeutsche Zeitung* (SZ), the liberal-left *Frankfurter Rundschau* (FR), and the left-leaning *Tageszeitung* (taz). Even though the electronic media are seen as the principal mediator between political actors and the public, first and foremost television, these papers still have an influence not to be underestimated.

One of the special features of the German media is the variety of regional papers, like the biggest-selling subscription paper the *Westdeutsche Allgemeine Zeitung*, which sells nearly 1.5 million per day. There has been a process of concentration since the 1950s, but until now all important German papers have been owned by German media groups. After the war, radio, and later television, were dominated by public broadcasting corporations based in the respective Länder and co-ordinated by a federal Association of Public Broadcasting Corporations (ARD). Later, in the early 1960s, based on an agreement between all German states, a federal TV channel, the *Zweites Deutsches Fernsehen* (ZDF) based in the city of Mainz, was founded.

Public radio and television are controlled by so-called Broadcasting Councils, composed of all relevant political, social and cultural groups and institutions, like the churches, trade unions, employers' associations, and political parties, to mention only a few. Meant to act in the interest of the general public, to secure pluralism, and to avoid one-sided information, these boards are dominated *de facto* by political parties and their associates in other institutions and associations.

Public broadcasting corporations are obliged to ensure that their programs show no political bias to a particular party or political group and that the content of the program reflects a balanced view. That does not apply to private television and radio, which, since the 1980s, has gained more and more influence. However, the Federal Constitutional Court has ruled that private broadcasters, like the public corporations, may not influence public opinion to a significant extent. Advising voters who to vote for, as is a familiar pattern in the run-up to British elections, is unusual for the German media.

Private broadcasters are subject to legal supervision conducted by regional media authorities, which are responsible for licensing private broadcasters, monitoring programming, and ensuring a diversity of opinion. In 1993, after fierce criticism of the content of many TV productions, the private television broadcasters founded an organization for the voluntary self-regulation of television within the legal framework of protection for children and young people.

All these and a variety of other regulations are meant to secure plurality in the media, even if they are privately owned. In comparison to other countries, one could say that these mechanisms work. However, they also give political groups, especially political parties, a legal means of monitoring and conducting direct influence on the content of media reports and, even more so, on the appointment of personnel to leading positions in the media.

A fundamental shift has taken place over the last twenty years or so, regarding the question of whether the media or democratic political institutions and actors determine which topics are put on the public agenda, and the way problems and political conflicts are discussed in a modern society. In Germany one could say that, given the plurality of the media, all mainstream political views are represented and voiced. The system of public radio and television has contributed a great deal to the plurality of the most influential modern medium – television – and prevented Germany from being dominated by private media moguls exercising uncontrolled and unchecked political power, as is the case in some European countries.

–6–

Elections, Coalitions, and Coalition Governments

A noteworthy feature of the political system of the Federal Republic is the remarkable stability of government coalitions. From 1949 to 1966 a right-of-center coalition was in power, usually involving the liberal Free Democrats (FDP). From 1969 until the break-up of the coalition at the end of 1982, the Social Democrats formed an alliance with the FDP, but then the latter changed its coalition partner and brought the Kohl government to power. The effect of this unique political structure is that just two changes of government have come about through an election – the socialist–liberal coalition in 1969 and the red–green government in 1998. The others took place through the break-up of a coalition as a result of action taken by the FDP, or, in the case of Helmut Kohl in 1982, by a constructive vote of no confidence in which a partner in the earlier coalition participated. This situation, which is somewhat problematic when measured against the criteria of classic democratic theory, results from the constitutional features of the government, the strong institutional position of the chancellor and the *de facto* as well as *de jure* strength of the parties.

The Central Role of Political Parties

Political parties play the decisive role in German political life. The framers of the constitution constructed the political system of the Federal Republic of Germany as a strictly representative political order. The decision in favor of a representative system and a strong executive was rooted in the lessons learned from the Weimar experience of a weak parliament, a weak government and a strong president who had far-reaching emergency powers to override parliamentary decisions and to intervene in the business of the government. But the Basic Law did not stop there. It also responded to the fact that the parliament and government in the first half of the twentieth century had developed into institutions heavily influenced – and sometimes used as an instrument – by social movements, sometimes with disastrous consequences.

It was the experience with modern mass movements that left the drafters of the constitution highly suspicious of any attempt to grant more direct political power to the people. The people were seen as a disorganized social entity which could easily be influenced by populist and/or extremist ideas. In order to counteract this, political parties and organized interest groups were given a vital role in the new republic. with the hope that they would structure and organize the people. In stark contrast to conservative concepts of a strong state that assumes the role of the representative of the public good above and often against contradicting social interests, and in contrast also to traditional liberal ideas of representation, according to which free individuals act free from the influence of individual or collective interests, the Basic Law accepts that there are powerful and less powerful social, political and cultural interests, and that these interests should be articulated and considered when it comes to political decisions.

In over fifty years, only a very few parties have managed to play a role in German political life as parliamentary parties. For more than twenty-five years, two large parties, the CDU/CSU and the SPD, and one small party, the FDP, were the only parties represented in the federal parliament and most Länder parliaments. Due to the prominent role of the political parties as privileged political actors, the Bundestag has never been a place for exercising 'parliamentary sovereignty.' On the contrary, it is the party organizations rather than the parliamentary parties that have a decisive influence on the political constellations that lead to particular government coalitions. Party committees rather than parliamentary groups decide on coalitions. Once governments have been voted in, members of parliament are generally held to owe them their loyalty.

The Electoral System

The nature of the German electoral system inevitably tends toward coalitions rather than an outright majority in parliament. Coalitions are unavoidable and changes of allegiance during the term of parliament can lead to a new government. The German electoral system has two decisive elements. It is a system of proportional representation (PR) with elements of majority voting. Half the seats in parliament are filled by members from the party lists, and the other half are filled by those candidates who gain the majority of votes in the 299 constituencies. The total number of seats in the legislature is allocated according to the share of votes that each of the competing parties receives from the voters. Unlike in other countries with proportional representation, German voters have the opportunity to vote for candidates in their respective constituency and to cast a second vote for a party list of candidates.

This mixed or hybrid voting system is meant to avoid the 'injustices' and dispro-portionality of a first-past-the-post electoral system, where the winner 'takes all' and a minor share of votes can, under certain conditions lead to a big majority in parliament (as often happens in the United Kingdom or the United States). Combining PR and majority voting was meant to enhance the accountability and responsiveness of members of parliament to their home constituencies, while at the same time giving parties an opportunity to 'secure' seats on the party lists for those politicians seen as indispensable for political posts in parliament or government. Under the British system, former chancellor Helmut Kohl, like many other prominent politicians, would not have ascended to the position of head of government – he never gained a seat in his home constituency of Ludwigshafen, but was always voted into parliament on the party list of the CDU.

The second decisive feature of the German electoral system is that parties either have to pass a 5 percent threshold or have to win at least three constituencies in order to be entitled to gain seats and form a faction in parliament. It has been argued that such a regulation may be prohibitive for smaller parties – and indeed this is the case. The main argument in favor of such a regulation has been and still is that otherwise too many parties would be in parliament, which would lead to weak governments and perhaps foster 'negative coalitions,' as happened in the Weimar Republic. The 5 percent threshold has proved to be an effective means of reducing the number of parties represented in the Bundestag and most of the Länder parliaments. When this regulation was not in place in 1949, twelve parties managed to win seats in the first Bundestag. Once the regulation was established, the number of parliamentary parties fell to three: the Christian Democrats, Social Democrats, and Liberals from the mid-1950s until 1983, when the Green Party for the first time managed to jump over the 5 percent hurdle.

The concentration of the party system on only a few 'relevant' parties, in conjunction with the two-ballot system, leads many voters to think strategically when considering political priorities and future coalitions. The two-vote ballot facilitates what is called ticket-splitting. Ticket-splitting has become an increasingly popular voting strategy in recent years. This is especially true among younger and better educated voters, who award their first vote to a candidate from one of the two major parties while supporting a party-list from a smaller party with their second vote, mostly in order to improve the chances of a prospective coalition partner. Supporters of the liberal FDP, for example, have frequently voted for CDU district candidates when their party of choice was committed to forming a coalition with the Christian Democrats. The same holds true for Green voters who support SPD candidates. In the 2002 federal elections, 3 percent of the voters of the Green Party voted for an SPD candidate and 1.6 percent of the liberal FDP voters favored a CDU/CSU candidate; four years earlier, when the FDP had made it very clear that the only political option was a coalition with the CDU/CSU, 3,2 percent choose to split their votes. There are two preconditions for such strategic voting: there must be a real chance of and a firm commitment to a coalition, as in the 1990s with the CDU/CSU and FDP or in 2002 with the SPD and the Greens, and the programmatic and ideological positions of the parties must be (at least partly) compatible.

Many democratic systems, such as those in France and Italy, have seen dramatic shifts within the party system. In comparison to these and other countries, the

Federal Republic has seen a remarkable continuity of the party system that came into being under the dramatic circumstances of the years immediately after the Second World War. Astonishingly enough, the great majority of German voters have shied away from experiments with radical and populist parties. In general, voting patterns show great continuity over more than fifty years of democratic elections, and even most East Germans, with the exception of the 15 to 20 percent voting for the post-communist PDS, have fallen into line with their West German brethren.

Federal Elections 1949–2002

A close look at the election results since 1949 (see Figure 3 and Table 2) shows three trends that have had an impact on the formation of governments:

1. From the first elections in 1949 until 1957, when the CDU/CSU gained an absolute majority of the seats in parliament, a process of concentration within the party system is to be observed. In 1949 some indicators suggested that the party system would be as fragmented as in the Weimar Republic – eleven parties managed to obtain seats in the Bundestag and only the CDU/CSU gained more than 30 percent of the popular votes. Four years later six parties made it, and in 1957 only three parties, the CDU/CSU, the SPD and the FDP, were left. From the mid-1950s until 1983 a three party system – some analysts talk of a two-and-a-half party system – set the conditions for governments and coalitions. The smallest party, the FDP, gained a strategic position and could decide on which of the two parties could govern.
2. With the emergence of the Green Party in the early 1980s, the picture changed and the FDP lost its strategic position as king-maker.
3.   After German unification a fifth player, the post-communist PDS, which still holds a prominent position in the East and is totally irrelevant in the West, managed to get into parliament. This made forming a government potentially much more complicated because no other party was able or willing to form a coalition in which the PDS was the only partner or one among other partners. From 1990 until 1998 the sheer existence of the PDS made an alternative to the conservative–liberal coalition of CDU/CSU and FDP impossible. With its defeat in the 2002 federal elections, the PDS has probably lost its influence at the federal level for good, resulting in a clear-cut situation: on the one hand the red–green government, on the other the joint opposition and potential coalition of CDU/CSU and FDP.

This discussion, however, would be incomplete and misleading if it did not take into account the situation at Länder level, where various coalitions and potential coalitions and a fundamentally different situation in East Germany present a much more colorful picture.

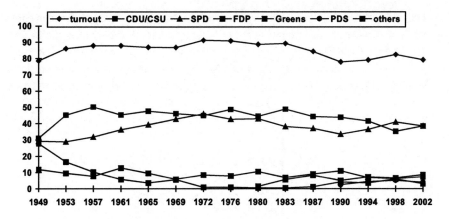

Figure 3 Federal Elections 1949–2002 (%)

It should be mentioned that there has never been such a thing the absolute dominance of one party, even during the two periods – from 1949 until 1966, and between
1982 and 1998 – when the CDU/CSU governed in coalition with the FDP. In the
Länder, governments are quite often voted for which are of a different composition,
with the main opposition party in the federal parliament as governing party in some
of the federal states and enjoying a decisive influence on federal legislation via
the Bundesrat. The German voter tends to use state elections to check the federal
government of the day.

Coalitions and Coalition Governments

Germany has witnessed a remarkable continuity of governments and coalitions. All
governments at the federal level have been coalition governments, even in the years
after 1957 when the CDU/CSU commanded an absolute majority in the Bundestag.
Governments and chancellors in the Federal Republic tend to stay in power for a
comparatively long time. The first chancellor, Konrad Adenauer, remained in office
for thirteen years, Helmut Schmidt governed for eight years, and in 1998, when he
was voted out of office, Helmut Kohl had been in office for sixteen years.

Changes of coalition have been far from routine events. Instead they are turned
into decisions about a 'new politics' and 'fundamental political' change, as the
term 'Wende' (turn), used in 1982 after the Kohl government was voted into office,
implies. Yet despite the domination of Chancellor Helmut Kohl and later Gerhard
Schröder over their parties and the governing coalitions, changes in the party system
and voting behavior are evident, with uncertain effects on coalition formation.

Forming a coalition becomes more and more difficult because of shifting party
loyalties within the electorate, the growing volatility of voters, and a tendency

Table 2 Federal elections 1949–2002 (%)

	1949	1953	1957	1961	1965	1969	1972	1976	1980	1983	1987	1990	1994	1998	2002
Turnout	78.5	86.0	87.8	87.7	86.8	86.7	91.1	90.7	88.6	89.1	84.3	77.8	79.0	82.3	79.1
CDU/CSU	31.0	45.2	50.2	45.3	47.6	46.1	44.9	48.6	44.5	48.8	44.3	43.8	41.5	35.2	38.5
SPD	29.2	28.8	31.8	36.2	39.3	42.7	45.8	42.6	42.9	38.2	37.0	33.5	36.4	40.9	38.5
FDP	11.9	9.5	7.7	12.8	9.5	5.8	8.4	7.9	10.6	6.9	9.1	11.0	6.9	6.2	7.4
Greens									1.5	5.6	8.3	5.0	7.3	6.7	8.6
PDS												2.4	4.4	5.1	4.0
Others	27.8	16.5	10.3	5.7	3.5	5.5	0.9	0.9	0.5	0.5	1.2	4.2	3.5	5.9	3.0

Table 3 Governments, Coalitions, and Federal Chancellors 1949–2002

Term of government	Chancellor	Coalition	Changes during term of office
1st Legislature, 1949–53	Konrad Adenauer	CDU/CSU–FDP–DP	None
2nd Legislature, 1953–8	Konrad Adenauer	CDU/CSU–FDP–DP–GB/BHE	GB/BHE quits coalition 1955; FDP splits, ministers form FVP and stay in government; the party leaves coalition 1956
3rd Legislature, 1957–61	Konrad Adenauer	CDU/CSU–DP	Most of the MPs of DP join CDU in 1960
4th Legislature, 1961–3	Konrad Adenauer	CDU/CSU–FDP	Adenauer resigns in Oct. 1963
4th Legislature, 1963–5	Ludwig Erhard	CDU/CSU–FDP	None
5th Legislature, 1965–6	Ludwig Erhard	CDU/CSU–FDP	FDP leaves government in Oct. 1966; minority government until Dec. 1966
6th Legislature, 1966–9	Kurt Georg Kiesinger	CDU/CSU–SPD	'Grand coalition'
6th Legislature, 1969–72	Willy Brandt	SPD–FDP	After defections from coalition and a failed 'constructive vote of no confidence,' early elections in 1972
7th Legislature, 1972–4	Willy Brandt	SPD–FDP	Brandt resigns in May 1974
7th Legislature, 1974–6	Helmut Schmidt	SPD–FDP	None
8th Legislature, 1976–80	Helmut Schmidt	SPD–FDP	None
9th Legislature, 1980–2	Helmut Schmidt	SPD–FDP	After FDP defects, Schmidt coalition is deposed by a vote of no confidence
9th Legislature, 1982–3	Helmut Kohl	CDU/CSU–FDP	Voted into office by new coalition
10th Legislature, 1983–7	Helmut Kohl	CDU/CSU–FDP	Early federal elections

Term of government	Chancellor	Coalition	Changes during term of office
11th Legislature, 1987–90	Helmut Kohl	CDU/CSU–FDP	None
12th Legislature, 1990–4	Helmut Kohl	CDU/CSU–FDP	First all-German elections
13th Legislature, 1994–8	Helmut Kohl	CDU/CSU–FDP	None
14th Legislature, 1998–2002	Gerhard Schröder	SPD/Greens–Alliance90	Voted into office by 1998 general elections
15th Legislature, 2002–	Gerhard Schröder	SPD/Greens–Alliance90	Voted into office by 2002 general elections

Notes: CDU Christlich-Demokratische Union Deutschlands
CSU Christlich Soziale Union (only in Bavaria)
DP Deutsche Partei
FDP Freie Demokratische Partei
FVP Freie Volkspartei
GB/BHE Gesamtdeutscher Block/Bund Heimatvertriebener und Entrechteter
Grüne/Bündnis90
SPD Sozialdemokratische Partei Deutschlands

toward protest voting. All political parties, whether governing or in opposition, are tempted to resort to a highly problematic political 'short-termism.' This works against coalition policies based on a political agenda and common political goal for a certain period of time, normally one legislature. Coalition parties are tempted to make their mark at the expense of the others in order to please their voters.

The Constitutional and Political Role of the German Chancellor

In most modern democracies the head of government has a prominent position. In the German system the chancellor's position is particularly strong. This is why the German system of government is often referred to as a 'chancellor's democracy.'

Taking England as a historical model, one must observe that since Walter Bagehot's *The English Constitution* of 1867 a shift has taken place from parliamentary democracy and cabinet government to prime-ministerial government, where the head of government is endowed, either by convention or, as in Germany, by the constitution, with wide-ranging rights and powers. The German chancellorship is a specific variant of prime-ministerial government.

The term 'chancellor's democracy,' rightly emphasizes the prominent role the head of government can play. But it also tends to underestimate several other variables, such as the composition of the party system, the representation of parties in parliament, coalitions, and, last but not least, the different personalities and leadership style of the federal chancellors. In more than fifty years the Federal Republic has had only seven chancellors, of whom two, Konrad Adenauer and Helmut Kohl, have governed for more than ten years. The powerful position of the chancellor is established by a series of articles in the Basic Law.

First, there is the right of the chancellor to determine policy guidelines (*Richtlinienkompetenz*): 'The Federal Chancellor shall determine and be responsible for the general guidelines of policy. Within these limits each Federal Minister shall conduct the affairs of his department independently and on his own responsibility' (Article 65). Because most of the chancellors have remained in power for several years, and have had great authority in the cabinet, the relationship between the right to determine policy guidelines and the personal responsibility of ministers has changed. Strong chancellors tend to define the right to determine policy in broad terms and to interfere with the work of individual ministries. Helmut Kohl, in particular, has in recent times declared an increasing number of ministerial decisions to be 'a matter for the boss,' so that a *de facto* shift of competence from the ministers and the cabinet to the chancellor has occurred. Just as during the Thatcher era in Britain, tendencies that undermine parliamentary practices and replace them with quasi-presidential decisions have become marked.

Second, and above all, the chancellor's strong position, provided he has a parliamentary majority, resides in the 'constructive vote of no confidence' (Article

67), which is to be seen as a reaction against the 'negative majorities' of the Weimar Republic. This instrument has been used only twice in the history of the Federal Republic – in the unsuccessful attempt to bring down Willy Brandt in 1972 and in the successful overthrow of Helmut Schmidt in 1982; this is how Helmut Kohl became chancellor. It is almost impossible to remove a chancellor from one's own party merely because he is regarded as too weak and 'past his sell-by date,' as, for instance, Helmut Kohl was perceived to be in the early summer of 1989. An internal leadership battle would inevitably split the governing party and make it difficult for any challenger to forge a parliamentary majority. The chancellor's constitutional right to lay down the guidelines of government policies, to appoint cabinet ministers, to mediate in conflicts between ministers and departments, and, above all, to dismiss ministers puts the chancellor in a very strong position.

Given the prolonged tenure of most of the chancellors (Konrad Adenauer 1949–63; Helmut Schmidt 1974–82; Helmut Kohl 1982–98), their authority was great and grew over the years, whereas ministers stayed in office for far more than one term of parliament in rare instances. The longer a chancellor stays in office, the more he tends to intervene in the affairs of government departments, mostly to the disadvantage of the cabinet minister concerned. Those political problems that are highly controversial or receive close public attention are often declared matters to be resolved by the boss (*Chefsache*). This goes beyond the constitutional mandate to provide guidelines for government policies and could lead, as in the times of Konrad Adenauer and Helmut Kohl, to a quasi-presidential style of politics.

Third, most German chancellors have also been leaders of their parties: Konrad Adenauer, Willy Brandt, Helmut Kohl, and Gerhard Schröder until 2004. A chancellor is heavily dependent on the support first of his own party and second of his coalition partner. In order to achieve the first, a chancellor is always in a good position if he leads his party. The longer the chancellor is in office, the more he is tempted to transform the party into a political organization for the support of the government of the day and his or her own position as chancellor. The result of this exercise is mixed. While support for the chancellor and his government is necessary in order to secure power, it causes problems to the function of parties as societal organizations able to express and coordinate the ideas, interests and political views of large groups of citizens and potential voters. Therefore, party democracy and chancellor democracy in Germany are intertwined and bound together in a delicate relationship.

Fourth, German chancellors have command over a strong and influential policy unit, which helps them to 'determine ... the general guidelines of policy,' as the Basic Law puts it. In the early years of the Federal Republic, the first chancellor, Konrad Adenauer, immediately after being elected into office, invented an institution which is not mentioned in the Basic Law, but has become one of the most important instruments at the chancellor's disposal: the Federal Chancellor's Office (*Bundeskanzleramt*). It started as a small office with only a dozen or so civil servants and has expanded since then to an administration of about five hundred employees.

In the early 1970s, the Chancellor's Office was transformed into a central institution of governance.

The Federal Chancellor's Office also has the task of supervising the Federal Intelligence Service (*Bundesnachrichtendienst*), which deals with espionage and counterespionage, whereas the other intelligence units are attached to the ministrie of defense and the interior. The Chancellor's Office also hosts the Federal Security Council (*Bundessicherheitsrat*), a cabinet committee which discusses all security issues. The Chancellor's Office probably played the most decisive role in its entire history during German unification. The then head of the office, Wolfgang Schäuble, was the main architect of the two treaties that paved the way for the accession of the GDR to the Federal Republic on October 3, 1990. During this process the heads of cabinet departments were more or less sidelined and all strategic decisions were taken by the Chancellor himself – with the exception of the foreign dimension, where the liberal Foreign Minister, Hans Dietrich Genscher, played an important role.

The carefully drafted institutional structure and sheer size of the Chancellor's Office make it a powerful tool for the chancellor to pursue his political ideas. These ideas, however, are quite often born in an informal environment. 'Kitchen cabinets,' composed of informal advisers and spin doctors, play, as in nearly all modern governments, an important role, as do – due to the German system of coalition governments – informal meetings of representatives of the parliamentary parties and so-called 'coalition committees.' These committees were first established in 1961 at the beginning of the last term of the patriarch Konrad Adenauer, and they turned out to be a blow to Adenauer's leadership role.

Chancellor Democracy and Party Government – from Adenauer to Schröder

As already mentioned, the role of the German chancellor was markedly shaped by the style of government of the first head of government, Konrad Adenauer. He was the dominant political figure in the early years of the Federal Republic and held the post from 1949 until 1963. His extraordinary authority was due to specific political conditions. Even before the Federal Republic was founded in May 1949, he had served as president of the Parliamentary Council that drafted the Basic Law. It was he who had direct access to the representatives of the military governments of the three Western Allies and later to the Allied High Commissioners for Germany. He served as *de facto* foreign minister even before the Federal Republic was allowed to conduct its own foreign policy in 1952. Last but not least, he managed to become the leader of a new type of party, the inter-confessional Christian Democrats that ruled the Federal Republic for more than thirty years. When Adenauer left office in 1963 at the age of 87, the Federal Republic had been transformed into a Western democracy firmly embedded in the European Community and Western institutions.

The unhappy chancellorship of the previously successful economics minister and 'father of the economic miracle,' Ludwig Erhard, lasted only three years. His short term of office ended with the first economic crisis in post-war German history and led to a 'grand coalition' (1966–9) under Kurt-Georg Kiesinger (CDU) as chancellor and Willy Brandt (SPD) as his deputy and foreign minister. Kiesinger was not a strong political figure. As head of government of the grand coalition, his prime function was to be a moderator not a leader. Nevertheless, his chancellorship was marked by far-reaching reforms of the political, economic and social system – a response to the first economic crisis the Federal Republic underwent in the years 1965–6. The grand coalition was meant to be an exception to cope with political and economic problems. When, after the federal elections in 1969, a parliamentary majority of the SPD and the Liberals decided to form a coalition, the CDU/CSU lost power after twenty successive years in office.

Willy Brandt, the charismatic political leader of the Social Democrats, who had spent his early years in Norwegian and Swedish exile, took over the chancellorship in 1969. In his inauguration speech, he promised 'to open democracy further' (*mehr Demokratie wagen*), to strengthen civil society, and to overcome authoritarian traditions in German political life, a promise that resonated powerfully in German society, especially among young people. The new government created a reform agenda that was meant to liberalize the social and political system, which was still mired in problems stemming from the old authoritarian German idea of the state as main political actor and civil society as subordinate. Reforms of the welfare state, health service, and higher education, and the liberalizing of the penal code were just a few of the major reforms put forward by the coalition of Social Democrats and Liberals.

In his five short years as chancellor, Willy Brandt achieved a historic success with his policy of détente toward the East (*Ostpolitik*) and the GDR. Willy Brandt had to leave office after one of his closest aides was exposed as a spy for the GDR, but he remained chairman of the party and an influential player behind the scenes. His influence was further increased in line with his international reputation. In 1971 he was awarded the Nobel Peace Prize, and he was later known as a passionate advocate on behalf of the developing world.

His successor, Helmut Schmidt, had served as minister of defense and minister of finance in the Brandt government. Schmidt managed to lead the Federal Republic during a turbulent period, marked by a worldwide economic crisis, terrorism and strained East–West relations in the late 1970s. When East–West relations deteriorated after the Soviet invasion of Afghanistan in December 1979, Schmidt was one of the Western leaders who decided to lean on the Soviet Union to pull out of Afghanistan and reduce its huge nuclear arsenal and missile program. He was the one who invented the idea of the so-called 'twin-track decision' of NATO to deploy new mid-range atomic missiles and, at the same time, to offer new talks on disarmament. This policy was strongly opposed by many members and representatives of the SPD, including some prominent one. The same can be said of his attempts at creating an austerity policy in order to get the federal budget in shape and cut down on state subsidies.

When in 1982 the Liberals decided to change allegiance and form a government with the Christian Democrats in order to put the economy and the state budget back on an even keel, it was partly due to the weakness of the chancellor, who had lost the support of his own party. Helmut Schmidt was voted out of office by a constructive vote of no confidence in parliament, and Helmut Kohl was elected chancellor.

The lengthy chancellorship of Helmut Kohl and the equally extended spell in opposition of the SPD show that there is a close relationship between parties and government and that governing has important consequences for government and opposition parties alike. The CDU, which under the leadership of Helmut Kohl in the late 1970s had been transformed into a modern party with an effective party apparatus, has, step-by-step, been shaped into nothing more than a machine to support the government and the chancellor. When Helmut Kohl was voted out of office in 1998, the party fell into a deep crisis, and it was years before the party recovered. As a result of the offices of chancellor and party leader being combined, the CDU, as in the days of Adenauer, had degenerated into an 'organization to re-elect the chancellor' with comparatively little life of its own. More or less the same thing happened to the SPD after it came to power in 1998. Just like his predecessor, Gerhard Schröder, during his first years in office, tried to streamline his party into a support machine for his chancellorship. After his surprising re-election in 2002, he was forced to change his political agenda in 2003 in order to respond to the growing economic and social crisis in Germany. Under the title 'agenda 2010' he initiated a radical reform of the German welfare system, which flew in the face of social democratic traditions. As a result, he had to resign as party chairman in spring 2004 and to hand his job over to a talented apparatchik, Franz Müntefering, who represents the more traditional views and deep-rooted convictions of the SPD rank and file.

German chancellors have to be strong leaders and moderators in one person. As in most parliamentary democracies, the German chancellor is normally also leader of the main governing party. In contrast to British prime ministers like Margaret Thatcher and Tony Blair, who were strong leaders of their parties and able to mobilize party support, German chancellors have to take into account the views of their coalition partners in order to keep the government running. Strong party leadership has to be combined with the ability to make and to sell compromises with the coalition partner.

Institutional and Political Constraints

History has shown that, besides personality and leadership style, the success or failure of a chancellor is heavily dependent on other variables, notably the influence of parliamentary groups and representatives of parliament. The chancellor is subject to many constraints:

- With one exception (1957–61) no party has had an absolute majority in the Bundestag. Every chancellor needs coalition partners, but, if the parliamentary arithmetic permits, the partners can threaten to leave the coalition and side with the opposition.
- The chancellor and government majority have to contend with the Bundesrat, which may well have its own political complexion since different coalitions exist in the Länder. But even if the governing parties have a majority in the Bundesrat too, the decision of a state government is often dictated more by its own interests than by party loyalties.
- The complicated legislative procedure and the structure of public administration make necessary a permanent search for cooperation and harmony between the federal government and the Länder, and reduce considerably the ability of the former to shape political decision making.
- All government decisions are subject to control by parliament, but above all by the Constitutional Court, as shown in the case when the court ruled positively on whether German soldiers could serve in the Balkans.
- The Federal Republic has a powerful Central Bank (the *Bundesbank*), which by law pursues an independent monetary policy and thereby exerts a crucial influence on the economic and financial policy of the government.
- The scope for activity of all governments in the European Union is becoming ever narrower, as European laws and decisions by the Commission and the Council of Ministers are gaining increased importance.

The Basic Law created a representative democracy and parliamentary government. The strong position designed for the head of government, however, created the basis for what has been called a plebiscitary component of German democracy. In laying down the concept of the chancellor's competence to determine cabinet policies in Article 65 of the Basic Law, and fending off 'negative' coalitions with the 'constructive vote of no confidence' in Article 67 of the Basic Law, the drafters of the constitution created a specific variant of prime-ministerial government, in which, as an election slogan of the CDU/CSU put it in 1969, 'everything depends on the chancellor.' Polemically one could argue that general elections in Germany have been degraded into an American-style contest between more or less charismatic figures for the post of federal chancellor. This development contradicts the original intentions of the drafters of the constitution, who wanted a strong government in a parliamentary and strictly representative system, not a quasi-presidential system.

–7–

The German Party System

The modern German party system developed in the second half of the nineteenth century. Parties in Germany do not originate from parliament and parliamentary groups or factions but from social and political movements. While the first all-German constitutional convention of 1848 was dominated by gentlemen, lawyers, and representatives of the new middle classes – a social composition very similar to that of other European parliaments – the political scene after the failure of the liberal revolution of 1848 was dominated by attempts of the ancien régime to regain total control over the land. Social and political movements were born in response, and out of these movements came the Social Democrats, the Catholic Center Party (*Zentrum*), agrarian parties, and ultra-nationalist groups.

Germany came late to democracy – in the period after World War I – and by that time there was already a party system that had developed outside and sometimes in opposition to parliament. Parliamentary parties actually exercised less influence than those with a power base outside parliament: the Social Democrats, Liberals, Conservatives, and Catholic Center Party, founded in 1870 to challenge the Bismarckian attempt to establish Prussian political and cultural dominance in the German Empire at the cost of other regions and the Catholic minority. In the Weimar Republic, the Center Party, along with the Social Democrats, played a key role in challenging the democratic republic. Given the authoritarian tradition and the lack of democratic institutions, it was some decades before all relevant parties accepted the rule of law as the basic principle of state and society. It took time for the ideas and values of parliamentary democracy and political equality among citizens to take root.

The Weimar Republic – the first German republic of its kind – was characterized by a destructive dualism among parties. On the one side, there was the Center Party and the Social Democrats, along with some smaller progressive liberal parties that defended democracy and the republic against antidemocratic political groups and parties. On the other side, were the enemies of the newly founded democratic republic–representatives of the ancien régime, the conservative parties, and organizations that longed for the old German Empire and the Kaiser. On the extreme right, the Nazis challenged the legitimacy of the Weimar Republic, and on the extreme left, the Communists did. When the Weimar Republic ran into trouble during the international economic crisis of the late 1920s, the democratic parties were neither willing nor able to unite together in a concerted attempt to thwart the enemies of the republic. As a result, new antidemocratic mass movements grew in strength – the Communists and the Fascists.

A strong authoritarian tradition helps explain the weakness of the democratic parties. This history infected the new democracy such that while the state and its institutions claimed to represent the public good, the republic was widely perceived as politically impotent. There was a general mistrust of political parties, and the Nazis played upon this deep-rooted resentment. The National Socialists succeeded in winning over social and political groups at the center of society who were yearning for a party that emphasized national unity and pride – ideals that were largely disregarded by parties on the left. In March 1933 these reborn nationalists finally handed over the Weimar Republic to Hitler and his henchmen.

The Constitutional Role of Parties in the Basic Law

It was against this background that the founders of the West German democracy of 1949 established political parties as the main political actors. The constitution awarded them significant power, and parties were prominently mentioned as an integral part of the political organization of German democracy.

The Basic Law provides political parties with remarkable power. They are positively mentioned as institutions acting as intermediary political forces between state and society and as institutions expressing the political will of the people. Parties were constitutionally accepted and established as part and parcel of the political system. Article 21.1 of the Basic Law states: 'Political parties shall participate in the formation of the political will of the people. They may be freely established.'

This central role of political parties has been confirmed by the law concerning political parties and, more importantly, by the German Constitutional Court. The court interpreted the formula 'political parties shall participate in the formation of the political will of the people' as a mandate to overcome the discrepancy between the factual influence of parties in political life and their legal position as set out in the constitution, as had been the case with the Weimar constitution. In an early decision in 1952 the Constitutional Court described political parties as social and political organizations which were granted a special legal status as an 'integral part of the constitutional structure and the political life formed and regulated by the constitution.' The positive view vis-à-vis political parties has been influenced by constitutional lawyers like Gerhard Leibholz, who in the 1930s emigrated to Britain and later became the first president of the German Constitutional Court. The term 'party democracy' acquired a positive connotation as an expression of the fact that parties in modern societies are the principal political actors in state and society.

Given the German experience with antidemocratic movements and parties, the framers of the Basic Law put great emphasis on providing checks against any attempt by a political party to destroy democracy by legal or illegal means. Based on the concept of 'militant democracy,' the framers of the Basic Law took the decision to bind the exceptional political role of parties to certain conditions: 1. Parties have to accept the rules and procedures of democracy. 'Their internal organization must conform to democratic principles' (Article 21.1 Basic Law). 2. Parties can be outlawed if they fail to do so and if they fight against the democratic system. Article 21.2 states that parties which, 'by reason of their aims or the behavior of their adherents, seek to undermine or abolish the free democratic basic order or to endanger the existence of the Federal Republic of Germany shall be unconstitutional. The Federal Constitutional Court shall rule on the question of unconstitutionality.' And so it did. Twice, in 1952 and in 1956, it published, by request of the government, a verdict against the neo-Nazi *Sozialistische Reichspartei* and the Communist Party.

The Party System of the 'Old' Federal Republic

The party system of the old Federal Republic until 1989 was characterized by two elements: concentration and polarization. In the Weimar Republic, the German party system had been highly fragmented. Parties tended to address the interests of specific groups, such as farmers, or regional interests. They were more often disguised interest organizations than modern multi-issue organizations. This partly explains why they could not deflect the growing power of the Communists or Fascists, who pretended to support and defend the rights of ordinary people and appealed to those who did not feel represented by traditional parties. The only exceptions were the Social Democratic Party, with strong roots in the working classes and in the public sector, and the Catholic Center Party, prominent among Catholic workers (quite often of Polish origin) and the Catholic establishment. Given this historical experience, it becomes understandable that the idea of avoiding the old fragmentation led to the creation of parties that could unite several sectors of society.

Party concentration is mainly due to two factors. First, the Western Allies had the right to license new political parties. Any attempt to establish a new political party had to undergo a thorough process of scrutiny by the Allies. Second, the lessons learned in the final years of the Weimar Republic and the years after its defeat led to a remarkable reconstruction of the political Center. The Christian Democrats (CDU and CSU in Bavaria) established themselves as the dominant political party of the Center-right for more than thirty years. They managed to integrate conservative and national-liberal traditions as well as Protestants and Catholics, overcoming a cultural divide between these two denominations dating back to the Thirty Years War of the seventeenth century. That led to the end of the fragmentation of bourgeois politics that characterized the German Empire and the Weimar Republic.

Because of the Cold War and the division of post-war Germany, the Communist Party never gained a significant stronghold in the Federal Republic. The Social Democratic Party (SPD) became the only legitimate representative of the political left. The Free Democratic Party (FDP) overcame the final division within the liberal camp between the Prussia-oriented and openly nationalist 'National Liberals' and the progressive liberals who longed for a free-market economy.

The German political system was shaped by these three parties: Christian Democrats, Social Democrats, and Liberals. In the formation period of the Federal Republic the bourgeois parties formed an informal political bloc to keep the Social Democrats out of office at the federal level – on the Länder level coalition governments with the SPD were formed if necessary, without ideological reservations. It was only in the late 1950s, at a party congress in Bad Godesberg near Bonn, that the SPD managed to transform itself into a center-left political party – a move that could be compared with the creation of New Labour in Britain in the 1990s. That reform helped the Social Democrats to become a serious contender for political power, and exactly ten years later in 1969 they finally succeeded in taking over the federal government.

Astonishingly, no radical party of the right has ever made it into the Bundestag. In the years following the end of World War II, the Western Allies forbade the reorganization of the radical political right. After the founding of the Federal Republic – when the Allied powers to license political parties were terminated – some radical right-wing parties were founded but did not succeed in gaining a mass following. Nevertheless, in 1950 the federal government took the decision to go to the Constitutional Court in order to outlaw one of the more prominent parties on the extreme right, the *Sozialistische Reichspartei* (SRP), the Socialist Party of the German Empire, as an extremist, antidemocratic party in the tradition of the Nazi movement. In 1952 the court delivered its verdict. The court outlawed the party by upholding the view that the SRP was challenging the democratic order of the Federal Republic and similar in character to the Nazis. A corresponding decision was made in 1956 vis-à-vis the Communist Party, which the court considered part of an international political movement of a totalitarian character.

The decisive stabilizing factor in German post-war political history centers around the party system. The concentration of power has been centered on two major parties – the Christian Democrats and the Social Democrats, and to a lesser degree the smaller liberal party, the FPD. This has established a confrontation between the left and the right, with the liberals in the middle. While in the first German Bundestag of 1949 twelve parties managed to gain seats, from the mid-1950s to 1983 only these three parties were represented in the lower house of parliament. In some Länder, however, smaller parties succeeded in gaining more than 5 percent of the popular vote necessary to be represented in parliament. In the 1960s and 1970s the two major political parties, CDU/CSU and SPD, which presented themselves to the electorate as 'parties of the people' (*Volksparteien*) were supported in general elections by nearly 90 percent of the electorate. Both parties were quite successful in preventing the formation of new fringe parties on the right and the left due to their ability and willingness to integrate more radical groups into their ranks and thus the political mainstream, as long as they accepted the rules of the democratic game.

In the 1950s the CDU/CSU successfully stymied the rise of populist right-wing political movements, often formed by organizations of refugees from Czechoslovakia and those eastern parts of Germany now administered by Poland. With less positive results, the SPD tried to integrate the younger generation which revolted against the status quo in 1968 and the early 1970s. Some of the rebellious youngsters of 1968 made their way through the institutions, the press, and the universities and into politics. The red–green government of 1998 was basically composed of former 'angry 1968ers.' Others did not comply with democratic rules and ended up in fringe parties, political splinter groups and some even in 'armed struggle' and terrorism. The cultural and political revolt of young people in the late 1960s resulted in a fundamental cultural and political change, and a development that could be termed participatory revolution.

Political participation and direct involvement of citizens in political affairs were no longer met with suspicion or seen as a potential threat to the representative democratic institutions, as in the early years after World War II, but as a precondition for a sustainable democratic order and civil society. Parties and organized interest groups such as trade unions were often accused of being corrupted by 'the system,' of having become part and parcel of the power structure of the state, and of acting on behalf of their functionaries rather than their members and supporters. Instead of the traditional highly bureaucratized organizations, detached from 'real life' and the needs of the people, 'new social movements' should be formed to shake up the petrified political structures and act as guardians of those without power, those who are marginalized and/or unable to express their interests, those who have no voice in society.

Starting in the early 1980s, hundreds and thousands of 'citizens' initiatives,' self-help groups, cooperatives, NGOs, and other groupings of individuals mushroomed in West Germany. All these groups and organizations were considered to be as part of a new social movement, concerned with environmental issues, sustainable development, peace and nuclear disarmament, and new concepts of education, health, and culture, to mention only a few.

The traditional political parties reacted with a mixture of consternation and hostility. These new social and political groups and organizations were, quite rightly, perceived as a threat to the monopoly of the political parties (and traditional organized interests) as privileged political and social actors. As long as the groups were founded and organized on a local level, as single-issue groups, committed to tackling problems like urban or regional planning, opposing the erection of nuclear power-plants, or carrying out actions to preserve the local environment, this monopoly of the traditional institutions and organizations could be maintained. However, the more these new groups and citizens' initiatives started to build regional and national networks, the more they managed to acquire the minimal standard of institutionalization necessary to become influential actors in political and social conflicts, and the more they transformed themselves into multiple-issue organizations, the more they became a serious competitor in the established political institutional system.

These new groups and networks were successful in putting new political, social, cultural, and, above all, environmental issues on the political agenda. But they failed to gain a decisive political influence as long as they hesitated to accept the importance of political parties and parliamentary representation. In modern democracies only parties, if endowed by the voters with a mandate in parliament, have the ability and the power to set a new political agenda and to influence political decisions directly.

When, after years of fierce discussion, the step of forming a new party was finally taken, the new political formation, the Greens, shook up the traditional three-party system. Within three years of its foundation in 1980, members of the 'anti-party party' became members of the Bundestag. Greeted by the old parties like badly behaved children, the Greens established themselves as the only successful new political force in the history of political parties in the Federal Republic and were soon accepted as junior partners in Länder governments. It was not until 1998 that the Greens (since 1991 united with the East German Alliance 90) became a coalition partner in the federal government. When the Greens entered the political arena as a fourth political player in parliament, the Liberals lost their strategic position as 'king-makers.' With a short interruption between 1966 and 1969, when a so-called 'grand coalition' of the CDU/CSU and SPD governed the country, the FDP had served as the junior partner in all federal governments: until 1966 with the Christian Democrats, from 1969 until 1982 with the Social Democrats, and, after switching allegiance in 1982, again with the CDU/CSU until 1998.

Mention must also be made of extremist parties on the political right. After some failed attempts to regroup the extreme political right after the war and the ruling of the Constitutional Court in 1952 to outlaw the SRP, it took more than a decade before new groups on the right emerged. In 1964 the 'National Democratic Party' (NPD) was founded by right-wing extremists, neo-Nazis, and some fringe conservatives. In the 1960s it had some electoral successes at the Länder level and nearly overcame the 5 percent hurdle in the 1969 Bundestag elections.

In the late 1980s and early 1990s two parties on the extreme right were temporarily successful, the 'German People's Union' (DVU) and the so-called 'Republicans.' As with the NPD in the 1960s, they managed to get votes with populist and xenophobic slogans and by mobilizing public sentiments against those in power, be it in politics, social life or elsewhere, especially among marginalized social groups and/or regions or communities struck by economic and social problems – in short, among those who are or fear becoming the losers in the process of economic and social modernization.

A Brief Portrait of the Major German Parties

A commentator on the political system of the Federal Republic of Germany in the late 1940s would have been tempted to predict that the fragmentation and division of the party system that had characterized political life in the Weimar Republic would reemerge. Dozens of parties competed in local, regional, Länder and federal elections, and local and regional parties gained strong influence in some parts of Germany, especially Bavaria and Lower Saxony, where the old divide between right and left was as deep and uncompromising as in the inter-war period. Twelve political parties were represented in the first German Bundestag in 1949.

But ten years later the picture had fundamentally changed. Most of the smaller and regional parties had become politically irrelevant – many of their members and functionaries had either given up their political activity or joined other, more successful parties. Christian and Social Democrats competed to become the leading political force in West Germany, and the Liberals held a very comfortable position in the Center of the political spectrum because they were, due to the German electoral system, needed to form a majority in parliament.

Immediately after the war, conservatism in West Germany was stigmatized by the support that the Nazi movement had received from conservative and right-wing parties at the end of the Weimar Republic. Many conservative politicians had collaborated with or later joined the Nazi movement. When the Western Allies started implementing democratic structures in West Germany at the local level, they recruited reputable conservative politicians from the Weimar era, men and (fewer) women who had not become involved with the Nazis. As the political right in the Weimar Republic had been fragmented, the search for a strong conservative political party was very high on the agenda.

In the post-war years it seemed as if the old divisions in the conservative camp would reemerge. Conservative political groups were mushrooming. Because of the very limited freedom of movement, especially from one zone of occupation to another, cooperation and coordination among these groups and potential political leaders were nearly impossible. As a result, a patchwork of conservative and right-wing political groups emerged locally and gradually developed regional and national networks. This was true for all other political groups as well, excluding the Communists, who were effectively orchestrated by Moscow.

In 1945 attempts to form 'national' organizations by politicians residing in Berlin were met with reluctance and sometimes stiff resistance from regional leaders. Neither the party executive of the Christian Democrats, led by Jacob Kaiser, one of the founders of the CDU in Berlin, nor the Central Committee of the SPD under Otto Grotewohl (who later became Prime Minister of the GDR) was accepted as the national executive of these parties. Even the legitimate party leadership of the SPD, residing in exile in London, was sidelined. The leading political figures of post-war Germany were politicians who had not held prominent political positions at the national level in the Weimar Republic: Konrad Adenauer in Cologne and Kurt Schumacher in Hanover. Traditional German particularism, Nazi centralism, and the division of Germany into four zones of occupation created a sense of regional identity which became one of the hallmarks not only of the political parties but also of the West German state and society as a whole.

All German parties have strong regional identities, and it took some decades before the party headquarters became the center of party political life. The Christian Democrats exemplify this. In Bavaria the Christian Social Union (CSU) was founded as and has remained a regional party reflecting the identity of Bavarians as a separate German tribe as well as their more conservative views compared to the CDU in the rest of the Federal Republic. The CSU managed to exert a strong influence on the bigger CDU because of its strength and political success in this particular state.

Compared with the conservatives, the SPD always had a more centralist concept of politics and political organization, but even then local identities play an important role. The party organization of North-Rhine Westphalia, the former industrial heartland of West Germany, traditionally plays a vital role in the SPD as bearer of the old working class tradition, while in the Hanseatic cities of Hamburg and Bremen, both heavily influenced by trade and commerce and close cultural links with Britain, a more liberal creed of Social Democrats dominates.

The divisions created by German regionalism were most visible in the case of the Liberals. They formed local parties in an unorganized manner and with a variety of names, and it took three years before they joined the ranks of the Free Democratic Party (FDP) in 1948. Even then local and regional liberal groups survived until the mid-1950s, when the process of concentration within the post-war German party system stopped. The united Liberal Party was nevertheless marked by deep political, ideological, and regional divisions, mainly between so-called National Liberals (sometimes former hard-core Nazis), most prominent in small towns and rural areas, and a more progressive political wing which dominated in the big cities.

The Christian Democrats

The Christian Democratic Union (CDU) and the Bavarian Christian Social Union (CSU) are distinctly post-war creations. After a bumpy start the CDU/CSU became the dominant political force on the center-right of the political spectrum. This is particularly due to a sharp break with the tradition of German conservatism. The CDU, and to a lesser extend the CSU, are not conservative parties in the traditional German sense: backward looking, antirepublican, antidemocratic, or at least skeptical vis-à-vis a democratic polity and society. Both parties started more as a political alliance of different groups (*Sammlungsbewegung*), trying to unite as many political groups and individuals on the center-right, rather than as a party with a clear-cut political message and a coherent program.

Both parties were founded by groups of former Weimar center-right Conservatives, National Liberals and even Christian Socialists in order to unite all political forces that combined general Christian principles with politics. They were composed of heterogeneous groups of Protestants and Catholics united behind the principle that a new German democracy should be reconstructed along Christian and humanitarian lines, without an exclusive denominational orientation. There was a general feeling that the traditional differences between Catholics and Protestants must be bridged. An overarching Christian party was meant to become an integrating force in the new political system. Even though most of the political leaders of these two 'sister-parties' were Catholics (partly due to the dominance of Catholics in West Germany, as opposed to the traditional Protestant East), both parties crossed the boundaries that had divided the party system in the German Empire and the Weimar Republic, where the Catholic Center Party (*Zentrum*) and Protestant parties fought each other vigorously to the disadvantage of democracy.

The accession of the Nazis to power had widened the gap between Catholic and Protestant political groups, because many Protestants were early supporters of the Nazis (they had their biggest electoral successes in the early 1930s in conservative Protestant regions), while political Catholicism, at least until March 1933, withstood all attempts to fall in line with the Nazi movement. That split was only partially healed by the joint resistance of Protestant and Catholic individuals and political representatives under the Nazi regime. Nevertheless, the overcoming of the denominational divide, a political decision taken by the leaders of both camps, was not to be taken for granted after more than three hundred years of bitter division. The CDU/CSU helped to overcome the traditional association of the German middle classes with right-wing and extreme nationalist parties that undermined the first attempts to create a democratic system in the inter-war period.

The foundation of the CDU and CSU after World War II proved to be the most fundamental political innovation in the history of modern German parties. The CDU/CSU became a reservoir for different social and political groups with both Catholic and Protestant affiliations. As a party at the center of society, as a political force which pursued policies that led to an unprecedented economic and social recovery in the early years of the Federal Republic, and with its successful (though heavily contested) Western orientation, the CDU/CSU functioned like a sponge that could absorb smaller parties on the center-right and the single-issue parties founded after the war. Over a period of less than a decade, the CDU and the CSU managed to become the prototype of a 'catch-all party,' or, in German terms, a 'people's party' (*Volkspartei*), a political movement that was broadly based, programmatically vague, and appealed successfully to a wide spectrum of the electorate.

The CDU/CSU gained most in those parts of West Germany with a traditional Catholic milieu formerly leaning to the Center Party. The support of the Catholic episcopate proved to be a decisive factor in the early years. The CDU/CSU could also rely on strong support from big business and the owners of middle-sized firms, who represent the backbone of German industry. Until the mid-1970s, the party was only a semi-professional organization and relied heavily on the support of local elites, such as doctors, teachers, priests, craftsmen, and entrepreneurs. Only after being pushed out of power in the Bundestag elections of 1969 did both parties start to reinvent themselves as modern political organizations, equipped with a professional party apparatus and trained party officers. The party headquarters in Bonn and Munich became the political center of stream-lined election campaigns, and they managed to set the political agenda for party representatives and deputies at the federal, Länder, and local level.

Even though conservative parties in Germany never embraced the idea of developing sophisticated programs and political visions, in the mid-1980s the CDU/CSU quite successfully adopted the idea that a modern conservative party had to present itself to the voters as a political force able to combine both traditional values and modern ideas, tradition and progress, favoring free enterprise and, at the same time, securing social welfare and support for the needy.

The reform processes transformed the CDU and the CSU into modern parties on the Center-right of the political spectrum. Without any interruption the CSU has ruled Bavaria for more than forty years and until 1998 was the party in power at the federal level for nearly forty years.

The Social Democrats

Just as the political right underwent fundamental changes after World War II, the revival of the traditional left was also inevitable. Both major parties of the left, the Social Democrats and the Communists, were the first victims of Nazi barbarity and political persecution. Both had fought against the Nazis even after all the other parties, with the so-called Enabling Act of March 1933, had granted the Nazi government unlimited powers. It is against this background that both parties were perceived as the only legitimate political forces not compromised by collaboration with the Nazis. The SPD proclaimed its natural right and duty to rule the new democratic Germany, because all others had succumbed to the pressure of the Nazis. As to the credentials of the Communist Party, it was not to be forgotten that the Communists had been at the forefront of destroying the Weimar democracy and were, like the Nazi movement, also guilty of bringing down the first German democratic republic in 1933.

The Social Democratic Party and the Communist Party were refounded immediately after the end of the war. Ideas of forming a united party on the left, prominent among many former politicians and survivors of the concentration camps, failed due to a *de facto* veto by the Soviet administration in East Germany. Consideration was also given to creating a center-left party after the model of the British Labour Party. These ideas were met with stiff opposition from leading members of the old SPD, mainly Kurt Schumacher, who became the charismatic leader of the West German SPD. The leaders of the Social Democratic Party, who had survived Nazi terror in prisons and concentration camps and been forced into early political retirement in 1933, and others who had returned to Germany after years in exile wanted to reestablish the old Social Democracy that, after seventy years of existence, had been persecuted and destroyed by the Nazi regime in 1933.

The SPD reestablished its organization in a traditional manner, with a highly centralized party organization and numerous social organizations such as trade unions, cooperatives, cultural organizations, its own press etc., in order to reconstruct the social-democratic political and cultural milieu destroyed by the Nazis. Hopes of governing the new democratic order in West Germany were disappointed at the first elections to the federal parliament in 1949. After the early death of its leader Kurt Schumacher in 1952, the SPD lost track of the new political, economic, and social developments and lost support even among its former combatants, the working class and civil servants. The party opposed the concept of a 'social market economy' and favored a planned economy and the socialization of industry. It rejected rearmament and the accession to NATO on the ground that it would close the door to the East and future unification. The poor showing in federal elections (at the Länder level the SPD was more successful) generated internal pressure for a programmatic and political reform concept and the broadening of its political appeal beyond its working-class base.

In 1959, at a famous party congress in Bad Godesberg near Bonn, the SPD agreed upon a modern program and abandoned its traditional role as advocate of socialism. It renounced its preference for nationalization and state planning in favor of the principles of a social market economy and economic competition. Finally, in a speech to the Bundestag in 1960, the strong man of the party, Herbert Wehner, acknowledged the Western orientation of the Federal Republic. The SPD accepted the NATO membership of Germany and became a vocal supporter of European integration and the European Economic Community as cornerstones of West German political identity.

After some years these decisions paved the way toward ending the SPD's long spell of opposition and finally led to government in 1966, first as a junior partner of the CDU/CSU and then, from 1969, as the political party in power for twelve years at the federal level and in many Länder. With the new *Ostpolitik* of the 1970s under the chancellorship of Willy Brandt, the party took a decisive step toward normalizing the Federal Republic's relations with the (communist) East without giving up the Western orientation which the GDR had so fiercely resisted for two decades. This new policy toward the East and a far-reaching reform agenda appealed to the hearts and minds of the younger generation in those social and political groups that were longing for domestic reform, a modern participatory democracy, and a new political culture. The leader of the party and first Social Democratic chancellor, Willy Brandt, became the political hero of a whole generation. Even after his resignation in 1974, he remained the most visible representative of the new democratic Germany – one that had finally overcome the ghosts of the past.

The late 1960s and early 1970s were times of considerable social and political change and severe political crisis, generated by a wave of terrorist attacks and politic-ally motivated murders conducted by extreme left-wing groups and organizations. Willy Brandt's successor, Helmut Schmidt, had a reputation as a crisis manager who could handle the nation's problems, ranging from the oil-related economic crisis of 1973 to domestic terrorism. Even though the chancellor's crisis management was quite successful, he and the leadership of the SPD under Willy Brandt (who remained party chairman after his resignation as chancellor in 1974) failed to recognize that a fundamental cultural change was taking place which, if not taken into consideration, would estrange the younger generation from social democracy. This was most visible in relation to the question of atomic energy. The trade unions and working-class supporters of the SPD favored nuclear energy and development projects that might threaten the environment in order to achieve economic growth and social benefits. Many younger, middle-class members of the SPD, however, sympathized with the new social and political movements that highlighted the potential dangers of unlimited economic growth at the cost of the environment.

Another rift arose over defense policy in general and disarmament in particular. The Schmidt government was ready to accept the deployment on German soil of a new generation of NATO nuclear missiles. The great majority of the younger population and the left within the SPD fiercely opposed that idea. The party responded half-heartedly to these new developments and failed to address the concerns of many people, even many of those who had joined its ranks or sympathized with the party in the times of Willy Brandt. Growing disillusionment among its supporters weakened the party and led, when the FDP coalition partner switched allegiance in 1982, to an abrupt end of the social democratic era and sixteen years of opposition.

The Liberals

Liberal parties date their origins back to the eighteenth-century Enlightenment, the ideals of the American and French revolutions, and the nationalist and constitutionalist ideas that, in some European states, culminated in revolutionary events such as those of 1830 and 1848. In the aftermath of the French Revolution and Napoleonic rule, liberal political clubs and organizations were founded all over Germany, especially in the south and west, where French cultural and political influence had been most visible.

As Germany was no national state like France or the United Kingdom, nationalist ideas were highly influential in German liberal circles. The formation of a German nation state and a constitutional and democratic republic was the political vision of the Liberals. After the failed democratic revolution of 1848 and the unification of Germany under Prussian terms in 1871, the Liberals split and did not unite again until after the Second World War. Until then, German liberalism was always divided into two main streams and at least two party organizations: Progressives, who opposed the semi-democratic, authoritarian political system in Germany, and National Liberals, who made their peace with Bismarck and later heavily supported expansionist political concepts pursued under the reign of the German emperor Wilhelm II. During the Weimar Republic that split continued and added to the relative weakness of liberal ideas in Germany. Liberals in Germany were, unlike their brethren in Britain and France, not unanimously staunch supporters of parliamentary government and liberal democracy.

It was not until after World War II that serious attempts were made to overcome this historical divide and to create a united Liberal Party. But more than with the Center-right, this proved to be a difficult task. Licensed by the occupation forces before the Federal Republic was founded and after some struggles over political influence and its programmatic profile, it lasted until 1948, when the Free Democratic Party (*Freie Demokratische Partei*, FDP) was finally founded. At that time, nobody could have predicted that the Liberals would become the most successful German party relative to its electoral support. As the third party in what developed within a decade into a three-party system, the FDP was needed as a potential coalition partner by the two main contenders, CDU/CSU and SPD. With only one exception prior to 1998, the FDP was a junior partner in government most of the time.

It was the FDP which held the balance of power in the Bundestag and which, by switching its political allegiance, decided whether the Christian or the Social Democrats could govern. This proved to be an extremely comfortable position, and the political role the FDP played in the West German political system far outstripped its weight relative to the size of its electorate. The Liberals never won more than 12 percent of the vote in general elections. Even though the two tendencies of German liberalism were united within one party, the FDP had to cope with the legacies of the historical split. Unity was a relatively rare commodity in the party's post-war history and led to a number of severe controversies and the defections of prominent Liberal politicians to other parties. The nationalist wing held the upper hand until the late 1960s, when the party drifted to the center-left and lost more than a third of its electorate. Nevertheless, the FDP was the only small party in the center of the political spectrum that was able to avoid total absorption by the CDU/CSU in the 1950s and 1960s.

After more than fifteen years in power as a junior partner of the CDU/CSU, the FDP – under a new younger leadership in 1969 – took the chance of forming a coalition with the SPD. This was a decision many national Liberal Party officials and quite a few voters never accepted. It caused serious rifts within the party and led to a number of defections. Some Liberal deputies in the Bundestag left the party to join the CDU/CSU, which in 1972 cost the government its majority in parliament and led to early elections.

A second turning point occurred in 1982. The Liberals left the coalition with the Social Democrats only two years after elections, which led to the toppling of Chancellor Helmut Schmidt and the voting of Helmut Kohl into office by means of a constructive vote of no confidence. This led to bitter discussions within the party and the defection of many prominent representatives of the left wing. In the years to come, the FDP was little more than a liberal corrective to the conservatism of some factions within the CDU and especially the Bavarian CSU.

It was in the early 1980s that the FDP gradually lost its privileged position in the German party system. There was a new political actor on the scene – the Greens. Within a few years, they would serve the Social Democrats as junior partner in Länder governments and ultimately at the federal level. The FDP's role as king-maker was terminated for good.

The Greens

When it was founded in 1980, the Green Party started as the political arm of so-called 'new social movements.' These movements had heavily influenced the political process in Germany during the second half of the 1970s, after the decline of the leftist political groups which had spread after the youth revolt of 1968. In the 1970s environmental issues began drawing widespread publicity. Environmentalists started to organize local single-issue groups and step-by-step created a network of environmental initiatives and organizations. These initiatives and political groups had been founded at a time when more and more people were losing confidence in the ability of the traditional parties, often denounced as 'system parties.' They confronted new political, economic, and social issues head on and considered strategies for tackling these difficult problems.

These groups and initiatives, as successful as they were at the local and regional level, failed to influence political decisions at the federal level because they could not, as other interest groups could, rely on support in parliament and among legislators. That is why the environmental movement entered a new phase in the late 1970s. In the view of many supporters of the new social movements, the 'old' parties appeared oblivious to the pressing environmental concerns of the day and the question of creating a new party became more and more urgent.

The cultural shift in the 1970s changed the perception of politics among many young voters. They refused to be satisfied with the arguments that *realpolitik* did not allow for vision and that politics is, to paraphrase the German sociologist Max Weber, like drilling thick planks. They longed for an immediate, unconditional, and uncompromising change in political attitudes and quick solutions. Frustrated by the lack of progress as a non-parliamentarian movement with little or no influence on legislation and political decisions at the top, they established local and regional ecological electoral lists and parties to take part in elections and work from inside the system. The first of these lists appeared in 1977 in local elections in Schleswig-Holstein, and in 1979 an ecological party won representation in the state legislature of the city of Bremen. In the same year a consortium of environmental groups put up a list for the first European elections. Under the label 'Other Political Associations: The Greens' they were unexpectedly successful with 3.2 percent of the votes, a result which spawned attempts to found a new ecological party to run in the 1980 Bundestag elections.

Forming a new party was nevertheless a high-risk strategy because all previous attempts had more or less failed. After the initial period immediately following the war, no new party succeeded in winning parliamentary seats in the German lower house of parliament. Extraordinarily favorable circumstances helped the Green Party (*Die Grünen*) to come into being and to survive the litmus-test of party competition and electoral success.

The Greens came into being as a *de facto* single-issue party: saving the environment. Its further rise as a fourth political actor on the national political scene was due to the confrontation that arose in the early 1980s following the Soviet invasion of Afghanistan and the Reagan administration's launching of a new Cold War against the Soviet Union. NATO, under the influence of Chancellor Helmut Schmidt, developed its 'twin-track decision' to deploy new middle-range atomic missiles in Europe, mainly on West German soil, in order to force the Soviet Union into negotiations over nuclear disarmament. These plans, supported by the German government, not only estranged many young people from the SPD but also fueled a political mass movement not seen in West Germany since the fierce confrontation about rearmament in the early 1950s. The Greens, originally founded as a party for the protection of the environment, spearheaded the popular movement for nuclear disarmament, which brought millions to the streets.

This might explain why, after a poor showing in the 1980 federal elections (they gained only 1.5 percent of the popular vote), the Greens in the following years won representation in as many as six state legislatures and many local parliaments. In the 1983 federal elections, which were held after the SPD fell from power in late 1982, the Greens managed to gain 5.6 percent of the vote and entered the Bundestag, greeted by the traditional parties with a good deal of suspicion and even hostility. After long and fierce struggles between different party groups – the so-called realists (*Realos*) and fundamentalists (*Fundis*) – over whether to remain a protest movement with representation in parliament or a new type of parliamentary party, the realists finally got the upper hand. In 1983, in the state of Hesse, the Greens for the first time formed a coalition with the SPD and took over the Department for Environmental Affairs. Joschka Fischer was inaugurated as the first Green minister.

After the nuclear disaster at Chernobyl in the Soviet Union in May 1986 the 'green cause' seemed unbeatable. A party congress demanded the immediate dismantling of all nuclear power plants and the withdrawal of the Federal Republic from NATO – both goals with no realistic chance of being accomplished in a coalition with the SPD. Nevertheless, support for the Greens rose after Chernobyl and in the 1987 federal elections the Greens gained 8.3 percent of the popular vote. It seemed as if they had finally managed to establish themselves as a permanent member of the club of parliamentary parties.

Next came German reunification. The Greens survived a crushing defeat because they had not addressed the political issues of the day. Showing open distrust and negative feelings toward the prospect of German unification did not make them popular. Slogans like 'Germany never again,' and talk of a new *Großdeutschland* and a Fourth Reich were quite popular in Green circles but were alienating to many voters who might share the Greens' environmental stance. It was only as a result of the East German citizens' movement – Alliance 90 (*Bündnis 90*) – forming a loose pact with the western Greens, and later, in 1992, finally joining them under the new name *Bündnis 90/Die Grünen*, that the West German Greens survived as a political party.

The Establishment of a New Democratic Party System in East Germany (1989–90)

The revolution in the GDR and German unification led to considerable changes in the party system. First, the foundation of new democratic parties and the attempts of the old GDR bloc parties to secure their future in a democratic order transformed the political landscape. In the month following German unification in October 1990, the new rudimentary party system in East Germany had, once again, to be adapted to fit the demands of an all-embracing party system of the united Germany.

The new party system in the GDR developed in several phases. In contrast to most other communist countries in East and Central Europe, the GDR was officially a multi-party system. However, in practice the so-called 'bloc parties' were never anything more than subordinates of the Socialist Unity Party (SED). One would expect that, after the revolution, these bloc parties would cease to exist and new democratic parties would be created. Many observers considered citizens' groups like New Forum or Democracy Now as the organizations which would provide the basis for a new democratic party system in East Germany, but those groups were reluctant to convert into political parties.

It is surprising that the bloc parties continued to survive and, moreover, were able to fashion themselves – at least superficially – into parties in the Western mold. They ceased to see themselves as the mouthpieces of certain ideological concepts or as representatives of certain social groups. The parties suppressed their ideological orientation and cut themselves loose from their incriminating past by adapting as quickly and as quietly as possible to the pattern of Western style catch-all parties.

In the fall of 1989 the bloc parties cut the umbilical cord to the SED. New political organizations were founded by the citizens' movement, which, in a second phase, constituted themselves as parties in 1990. They changed their leadership and underwent a programmatic change, and, in particular, abandoned socialism as a political goal. A third phase, which bore the imprint of the campaign leading to elections to the People's Chamber on March 18, 1990, was dominated by the attempt to set up alliances and electoral unions in order to prevent the fragmentation of the new party system in its infancy.

In response to the direct influence and pressure exercised by the CDU and, in particular, Chancellor Helmut Kohl, the CDU, the DSU (which was closely associated with the Bavarian CSU), and the Democratic Renewal (*Demokratischer Aufbruch*, DA), which had originally been part of the citizens' movement, joined forces, in spite of their different views and internal conflicts, to form the Alliance for Germany. The liberal camp saw the founding of the League of Free Democrats (*Bund Freier Demokraten*) by the Liberal Democrats of the GDR, and the German Forum Party (*Deutsche Forumpartei*).

The unexpected victory of the Christian Democrats in the elections of March 18, 1990 gave added impetus to the unification process and to the restructuring of the party system after the model of the Federal Republic. This development determined the course of political debate in the summer of 1990 and came to an end in the fall of 1990 with party congresses that saw the merging of the CDU, SPD and FDP parties in the two German states. The post-communist Party of Democratic Socialism (*Partei des Demokratischen Sozialismus*, PDS), successor to the SED, tried to expand into the West, but to little or no effect. Only the Greens and the citizens' movements of the GDR insisted on their autonomy.

While the renewal of former bloc parties such as the CDU and the Liberal Democrats (LDPD) was guided by the classic ideas of Christian and liberal politics, the Democratic Farmers' Party *Demokratische Bamernpartei Deutschlands*,(DBD) and the National Democrats (NDPD) experienced considerable difficulties of reorientation, which ultimately sealed their fate as autonomous parties.

The East German CDU as a former bloc party, was met with reservations by the western CDU, but these were dropped when the results of the elections to the People's Chamber demonstrated that the electors had 'forgiven' the eastern CDU for its past close relationship with the SED. The decision to lend full support to the CDU in the east was based on a number of considerations: the CDU in the east disposed of what was still a considerable number of members, large assets, and above all a fully fledged party organization which was of great importance for the coming federal elections.

The CDU derived additional benefit from the fact that in the summer of 1990 it took over what was left of the DBD. Beyond that, the election results of the two other partners in the Alliance were sobering. The German Social Union (DSU), supported by the Bavarian CSU, had fallen well short of achieving its aim of becoming the dominant conservative force in the south of the GDR, and the DA had shrunk below the point of significance. The end of the Alliance meant that a struggle within the Christian-Democratic camp was inevitable. This lasted through the entire summer and ended, after the elections to the Bundestag on December 2, with the CSU clearly losing ground within the all-German party spectrum.

The successes of the CDU in the GDR did not mean, however, that it was able, after its merger with the western CDU on October 1, 1990, to exercise any real influence on the fortunes of the enlarged party. This was true despite the fact that its approximately 200,000 members (compared with the 680,000 members in the west) represented about a quarter of the total membership. This is equally true of the Liberals, and even more so of the Social Democrats. Only very few politicians from the east managed in the years to come to obtain a prominent role – the head of the CDU, Angela Merkel, and the president of the Bundestag, the SPD politician Wolfgang Thierse, are among them.

The Liberals underwent a similar development to that of the CDU. They supported the quickest possible unification of Germany within a European peace order, the rule of law, and a free market economy. The party merged with the NDPD and, at a party conference in August 1990 joined, the western FDP.

Mention must finally be made of the SED's successor party, the Party of Democratic Socialism (PDS), which attempted to throw off the shadow of the past and to present itself as a modern socialist party. Within five months, between October 1989 and February 1990, the party lost nearly two out of three of its 2.3 million party members. Many of them were reform-minded younger people.

Initially the various attempts to found new parties free of guilty associations from the past appeared more important than the reform of the old bloc parties. These attempts were closely associated with the idea that a new political system could be constructed in the GDR, which could then, as part of a gradual process, be unified with the Federal Republic. But even in the period leading up to the March elections (the date of which had been brought forward under the ever increasing pressure of public opinion) it became clear that these new parties were only to be transitional phenomena.

In the early fall of 1989 a new Social Democratic Party was founded in the GDR outside the bounds of legality. At that time it called itself the Social Democracy Party (SDP), in order to demonstrate its independence from the western SPD. On January 13, 1990, at a conference in Berlin, the party renamed itself the SPD and thereby underlined its claim to be the successor of the old Social Democratic Party which had been compelled in 1946 to become part of the SED. More quickly than any of the other parties, the SPD of the GDR developed into part of an all-German party. As early as February Willy Brandt had been elected as its honorary chairman. In its program the SPD clearly recognized its duty to its origins. Its founders had been part of the human rights, peace, and ecology movement in the GDR. From the outset it consciously placed itself in the long, tried-and-tested tradition of German and international social democracy, and drew its self-confidence from the rich traditions and heritage of the labor movement, of humanism, and of Christian ethics, and its rootedness in the opposition movement against the SED regime. More clearly than in the case of the western SPD, it was able to see itself as a 'broad democratic people's party,' which had a strong ethical base and was open in particular to its citizens' movements.

After the elections to the People's Chamber, the SPD faced a serious crisis. It was confronted by the problem of how, linked in a grand coalition with the CDU,

DSU and the Liberals, it could develop its own distinctive profile. Its claims to be the party of the workers and the 'little people' had been discounted by the voters – the workers had largely voted for the CDU. Unlike the former bloc parties, the SPD did not have a functioning party apparatus at its disposal. It was not present in many communities and districts. Because of the GDR's desperate situation, which made the need for a broad government alliance imperative, it was not able to keep its electoral promise that under no circumstances would it enter a coalition with the right-wing conservatism of the DSU. Joining the government caused considerable internal tensions between the approximately 30,000 rank-and-file members and the party leadership, which, for reasons of state, joined in forming a grand coalition.

During the difficult phase of transformation in the GDR, the SPD was unable to develop its own distinctive profile. In the months leading up to unification it too became a prey to West German party tactics. The electoral program of the western SPD's candidate for the chancellorship, Oskar Lafontaine, had as its central focus the expected negative financial and social effects of unification. The western SPD condemned the federal government's policy of taking unification to mean only the unification of the two states, while for Social Democrats this term also implied the equalization of living standards. As subsequent developments in the former GDR showed, this was not unjustified criticism. However, it took no account at all of the mood in the GDR, where these arguments were understood as criticism of the people's wish to see Germany rapidly unified.

The merger of the eastern and western SPD had no decisive impact on internal party structures. While it is true that the last chairman of the SPD in the GDR, Wolfgang Thierse, was elected a deputy chairman, the unification of the two parties was otherwise more in the nature of a friendly take-over. Given the disparity in the membership figures (approximately 800,000 in the west and only about 25,000 in the east), it would have been difficult, of course, to secure greater representation for members from East Germany.

The German Social Union (DSU), formed on January 20, 1990 from a dozen small Christian and conservative groups and parties, presented itself as the eastern counterpart to the Bavarian CSU. Initially, it was highly critical in particular of the CDU as an old bloc party and could be persuaded only with great difficulty to join the 'Alliance for Germany.'

After its poor showing in the March elections, the DSU took on right-wing, populist traits. The western CDU had largely broken off contacts with the DSU and concentrated on supporting the CDU in the east. There were moves in the DSU to establish a permanent presence in all regions of the GDR. But this ruled out a merger with the CSU, since it would have meant that the CSU had ceased to limit its political activities to a certain region and had therefore brought to an end its parliamentary alliance with the CDU in the Bundestag. The example of the DSU demonstrates particularly clearly that the unification of Germany had an impact on the party system in the whole of Germany and not just on the territory of the former GDR.

In the summer of 1990, during the run-up to the Bundestag elections, a bitter dispute raged on the subject of electoral law, the real cause of which was the problem of the future structure of the party system. The CSU had derived its importance in the old Federal Republic from the fact that it also represented an important conservative bloc within the parliamentary alliance of CDU and CSU. Its influence would have been considerably reduced by the expansion of the national constituency. For that reason it was interested in finding a counterpart in the eastern regions of Germany. Since no firm party alignment existed, the western CDU also had a strong interest initially in not allowing potential voters in the GDR to drift to the right.

The DSU appeared to present an attractive proposition to these groups of voters. But, following its bad showing in the March elections and the halving of its share of the vote at subsequent local elections, it was clear that an autonomous conservative party to the right of the CDU had no prospect of success. So in the summer the DSU finally became a bargaining chip for the CSU in its struggle to maintain its influence in federal politics.

In January 1990 attempts were made to unite all opposition groups within one political alliance which would appeal to the voters in the forthcoming elections. These plans failed because the Social Democrats did not join. After this failure 'New Forum,' the 'Initiative for Peace and Human Rights,' and 'Democracy Now' joined forces in February to form 'Alliance 90' (*Bündnis 90*). The alliance saw itself, and still sees itself, because of the experience of dictatorship, as a coalition of groups are intent on defending the individual and social rights of all citizens. All three groups aimed at the protection of human and civil rights, achieving a society based on solidarity, the maintenance of a state built on the rule of law, and the necessary democratization of state and society. Also common to them all was the idea that it should be possible to represent the interests of citizens both within and outside of parliament without having to set up as parties.

Disputes repeatedly broke out between New Forum and the other groups. At the heart of these controversies were both the problem of alignment within the traditional right–left spectrum and organizational questions. In line with the tradition established at its foundation, New Forum saw itself as a political group that could not be assigned to the left-wing camp. It had a variety of links to conservative ideas and values and rejected any form of organization which might resemble a party. Some of the leading members later joined the ranks of the CDU.

The German Party System after Unification

At first glance, German unification had no decisive impact on the German political system at the federal level. As in the years before 1989, two political blocs competed to form the government, the Christian Democrats and Liberals on the Center-right and the Social Democrats and Greens on the Center-left. Due to the complicated

German electoral system and special regulations for the first all-German elections, the post-communist East German PDS was elected to the Bundestag in fall 1990 and twice again in 1994 and 1998. In the 2002 general elections the party failed, as before, to pass the 5 percent threshold and also failed to gain direct seats in three constituencies, which was necessary to be represented in parliament.

Even though the PDS did not, until 2002, play an important role in national politics, its pure existence has changed the German party system. One could speak of a divided party system. In the first decade after unification the two smaller parties, the Liberals and Greens, played no role in East Germany, mainly due to their programmatic ideas, that attracted predominantly middle-class voters. East Germany, however, was a 'classless' society. On the other hand, the post-communist PDS was not able to attract West German voters, with a few local exceptions in smaller university towns. Even though the PDS remained a regional party, based in the East of Germany, it could, at the national level, present itself, rightly or wrongly, as 'the voice of the East Germans.'

Below the federal political level, in the Länder, regions and local politics German unification led to a divided party system: the four 'traditional' parties of CDU/CSU, SPD, FDP and the Greens in the west and a three-party system, composed of CDU, SPD, and PDS, in the east. For more than ten years, in most of the eastern Länder parliaments, the Christian Democrats, Social Democrats and PDS were the only political parties. Governments could only be formed with or against the PDS. The CDU was not prepared to cooperate with the ex-communists at the Länder level. This does not mean that they were as reluctant to do so at the local level, in the counties, cities, and municipalities. The unwillingness of the CDU to consider forming a coalition with the PDS in a Länder parliament provided for a comfortable strategic position for the PDS. It supported an SPD minority government in Saxony-Anhalt from 1994 until 2002, and it formed the first 'red–red coalition' in Mecklenburg-Western Pomerania in 1998 and in Berlin in 2001.

The PDS remains a special kind of party in the east. Even though electoral support for the PDS in the east is weakening and its charismatic leaders have left Center stage, it still plays a decisive role in the east of Germany. This is mainly due to its societal foundations. The PDS is the only party in the east with a broad membership and electoral support from all strands of life. Nevertheless, it is currently confronting the fact that many of its supporters are aging and that a fond nostalgia for the GDR is fading away.

The most likely scenario for the future development of the German party system is the consolidation by the traditional western parties of their electoral support in the east. Nevertheless, for some years to come the PDS will remain a regional party of some influence. It is highly unlikely, however, that the party could manage to become a national player in the future.

The political and party system of the old Federal Republic has proved able to cope with the unprecedented challenges of political revolution in East Germany and German unification. All indicators point to a continuation of the party system. However, there is still a political division between east and west. For some years, the balance between governance and representation was disrupted because of the relative success of the PDS in the east. Since their defeat in the 2002 elections, the post-communists have not played a role at the federal level. It seems as if the division of the united Germany into two regional systems (the traditional four-party system of CDU/CSU, SPD, FDP, and the Greens in the west, and a five-party system in the east, with the PDS as the only party with a strong societal basis and the Liberals and Greens on the margins) is finally coming to an end.

However, the German party system is in a state of flux. Since the concentration process of the 1950s, the only successful extension to the party system in the Federal Republic has been the founding of the Greens in the 1980s. The changes after unification were numerous, mostly in the form of failed attempts by right-wing populist parties. Although general support for political parties is in decline, the tendency for the party system is toward stability and consolidation. This is in stark contrast to other European democracies, such as Italy or France, where the traditional party system that evolved after the Second World War has crumbled in the 1990s, and populist parties have gained considerable political support.

–8–

The Power Structure of the German Democratic Republic

The GDR was always an 'occupation regime' (Samuel Huntington). In the aftermath of the Second World War, the political system established in East Germany reflected the will of the Soviet Union to build a cordon sanitaire of socialist states in Eastern Europe, including the eastern part of Germany. From the early days until its end in 1990, the German Democratic Republic was directly linked to the Soviet Union both politically and militarily.

Dictatorship of the Proletariat or Socialist Democracy – The Political System of the GDR

From its earliest days, the GDR was labeled a 'dictatorship of the proletariat' and a 'socialist democracy,' determined to fulfill its historic task of establishing a socialist order on behalf of the working class. The hierarchical power structure – based on the ideas of Lenin as expressed in his 1902 writing 'What is to be done?' – constituted a separation of the political superstructure from society. The communist Socialist Unity Party (SED) was concerned with directing and controlling all sectors and all levels of society. Its omnipotence was not restricted simply to state organization but encompassed the economy, education, culture, and so on. The organizational and leadership guiding principle was 'democratic centralism,' which meant that every organization and every institution had to accept the leading role of the SED. Democratic centralism preserved the concentration and unity of power in the hands of the SED by transposing its principles from the party to the state, the 'allied parties,' and to all other organizations and institutions, whether they be factories, the public administration, schools, or universities.

The power structure of the GDR was, from the point of view of Marxism-Leninism, made up of the following:

1. The Communist Party, known as the Socialist Unity Party (SED) in the GDR, was the 'politico-organizational center of society.' The SED defined itself as the 'battle-proven vanguard' and leading force of socialist society and the state.
2. The state was interpreted as the chief instrument of the working class led by the Communist Party in the formation of a developed socialist society. As a form of

123

'dictatorship of the proletariat,' it also embodied the specific thinking of the SED about what it termed 'socialist democracy.'

3. The law had some regulatory functions but was in general, and quite often, subjugated to the political will and instructions of the communist SED.

4. The fact that the GDR defined itself a 'multi party system' did not mean, however, that the so-called 'allied parties' had any real input into political matters. They recognized and accepted the leadership of the SED without reservation and served as willing political instruments of the SED, which constantly tried to extend its grip on power beyond the boundaries of its own organization.

5. There were only associations that had been approved and controlled by the Communists. These so-called 'mass organizations' accepted the leading role of the SED in all political, social, and cultural matters. Freedom of association was mentioned in the GDR constitution (Article 29), but in practice the SED maintained a monopoly on it, the only *de facto* exception being the churches. The Protestant Church, in particular, was the closest thing the GDR had to an independent association.

6. The National Front included all parties and mass organizations and, in particular, organized the 'elections' for the rubber-stamp People's Chamber (*Volkskammer*) and the representative assemblies at the regional and local level.

The GDR constitution described the *Volkskammer* as the supreme representation of the people. The official view of this parliament was the direct opposite of its real function within the framework of democratic centralism. It was described as the supreme organ of government, deciding on all fundamental aspects of government policy. Looked upon from the outside, the *Volkskammer*, like all other representative bodies within the political system of the GDR, was nothing more than a voting machinery for sanctioning decisions which had been taken beforehand by the SED leadership. All its decisions were passed unanimously (with the single exception of the abortion law which was opposed by some CDU members). The significance of the People's Chamber may be judged by the extraordinary infrequency of its sessions – normally twice a year for a day or two at the most. The chamber operated more as an executive instrument of the party and government than a deliberating and decision-making institution.

As is standard, the GDR had a government – the Council of Ministers (*Ministerrat*) – but this body had no actual power. In reality, decisions were made by the Politburo and the Central Secretariat of the SED and had to be executed by the government. After the death of the first president, Wilhelm Pieck, a collective body, the State Council (*Staatsrat*), was inaugurated as head of state. It represented the GDR under international law and was formally vested with the right to ratify international treaties. A special committee of the council, the National Council for Defense (*Nationaler Verteidigungsrat*), chaired by the president of the council, was designated as the highest legal body in cases of emergency and war. The presidency of this council was held by Walter Ulbricht and later by his successor, Erich Honecker. In late 1989 Egon Krenz, the 'young man' of Erich Honecker, took over the post, only to be ousted within weeks by the revolutionary events. Real power, however, rested with the Politburo of the communist SED. Originally a powerful body used by the General Secretary of the SED, Walter Ulbricht, to consolidate his power, the State Council under Erich Honecker lost many of its supervisory functions to party bodies or to the Council of Ministers, but empowered the General Secretary of the ruling SED with the position of head of state.

Mention must also be made of the two most powerful institutions besides the ruling party: the armed forces and state security services. After the accession in January 1956 of the GDR to the Warsaw Treaty Organization (or Warsaw Pact as it was generally referred to), the National People's Army (NVA) was instituted. The East German leadership had actually been commanding the military, officially labeled as police forces, since as far back as 1946. As in other communist countries, the East German leadership had, from its inception, established a political police whose purpose was to protect the regime against all attempts to challenge its hold on power. Defending the GDR against all 'enemies,' 'slander hostile to the state' (*staatsfeindliche Hetze*), and 'subversive activities' of 'Western agencies and their zealots' inside the GDR was the self-proclaimed aim of the Ministry of State Security (MFS), or *Stasi* in GDR vernacular. The domestic role of the security services was to control the expression of politically untoward views and to check the growth of autonomous social and political forces in East Germany. With thousands of full-time staff members and officers and tens of thousands of informers (so called IMs), the *Stasi* held a firm grip on East German society. The Minister for State Security, Erich Mielke, a dubious former KPD security agent, was the most hated political official in East Germany.

Despite a certain uniformity of the political systems in all communist regimes, the power structure of the GDR differed from those in other socialist countries. Formally the GDR was a multiparty system. Besides the SED, some so-called 'allied parties' existed, which defined themselves as being in alliance with the Communists and therefore accepted their leading role in government and society unreservedly. Between them and the SED there was no struggle for political majorities or voters. These parties were represented in the national parliament and regional assemblies. The size of the respective factions was decided upon in advance of the elections in unity lists of the 'National Front.'

Founded in 1949, the National Front was – according to its constitutional status – an all-embracing form of 'alliance-policy' in 1968. Article 3 of the 1968/74 constitution reads: 'The alliance of all the forces of the people finds its organizational expression in the National Front of the German Democratic Republic. In the National Front ... the parties and the mass organizations unite all the forces of the people in working jointly toward the development of socialist society. In this way they bring all citizens to live together in a socialist community according to the principle that each bears responsibility for the whole.' The National Front was an alliance of approximately thirty parties, organizations, and federations, including among others the Socialist Unity Party of Germany (SED), the Democratic Farmers' Party of Germany (DBD), the Christian Democratic Union of Germany (CDU), the Liberal Democratic Party of Germany (LDPD), the National Democratic Party of Germany (NDPD), the Confederation of Free German Trade Unions (FDGB), the Free German Youth (FDJ), the Democratic Women's League of Germany (DFD), the German–Soviet Friendship Society (DSF), the German Red Cross of the GDR, and the League of Culture of the GDR (*Kulturbund*). Those parties and organizations which were represented in the *Volkskammer* and regional assemblies were united in the so-called 'Democratic Bloc,' a sub-organization of the National Front. The following parties and organizations were members of the Democratic Bloc:

	Number of members	
SED	2,304,121	
DBD	106,000	
CDU	125,000	
LDPD	83,000	
NDPD	91,000	
FDGB	9.5	million
FDJ	2.3	million
DFD	1.4	million
Kulturbund	244,000	

After the 1986 elections, the 'Federation of Mutual Peasants' Assistance' (VdgB), with 560,000 members, also joined the Democratic Bloc.

As already mentioned, real power rested with the SED, the most important institution within the GDR's political system. The constitution made no detailed mention of the SED as far as its objectives, its organizational structure, or its predominance within the political system were concerned. The party defined itself as the vanguard of the working class and all working people, the 'highest form of socio-political organization,' and as the force of all working-class organizations, the state, and social organizations. Using the mechanisms of democratic centralism, the SED was able to command and control the entire political system and society as a whole. Nearly 60 percent of its over 2.3 million members were workers, nearly 5 percent collective farmers and approximately 22 percent members of the intelligentsia.

Like most communist parties, the SED was structured according to a 'territorial-industrial' principle. Its 'basic units' (*Grundorganisationen*) were primarily organized as groups of party members in public administration, schools, universities, cultural and scientific institutions, and so on. These basic units represented the lowest rung in the party hierarchy. Each subordinate party organization was subject to supervision and control by the superior one (district, regional, central level) – according to the principle of democratic centralism.

It is useful to understand what the various parties of the National Front stood for. The Christian Democratic Union of Germany (CDU) was intended to combine Christian faith and active commitment to the socialist society. For years it concentrated on cultivating close relationships with Christian peace organizations. It is significant to note, however, that the CDU did not play an important role in the improvement of relations between the churches and government in the 1980s because church leaders, quite rightly, did not consider the CDU an organization worthy of negotiating with. Only the SED could provide better conditions for the churches and their members. The Liberal Democratic Party of Germany (LDPD) mainly addressed skilled workers in cooperatives and small businesses, white-collar workers, and members of the intelligentsia. As with other parties, it accepted the leading role of the SED and democratic centralism as the principle for the organization of the party, as well as for the structures of society as a whole.

The National Democratic Party of Germany (NDPD), founded in April 1948, aimed mainly at integrating former members of the NSDAP (Nazi Party) and officers of the German *Wehrmacht* in the new political and social structure. It was also intended to reduce the membership of the CDU and LDPD, which at that time had not yet accepted the leading role of the SED. The Democratic Farmers' Party (DBD), also founded in 1948 by former Communists, was designed as a political home for small farmers and agricultural workers who resented the Communists. That is why, over the years, both the NDPD and the DBD became relics of the political struggles that marked the early years of the GDR.

None of these parties were sovereign political entities in the sense of a liberal-democratic party system. Instead, they were compliant instruments of the SED. Besides political parties, mass organizations like the Confederation of Free German Trade Unions (FDGB), the Free German Youth (FDJ), the Democratic Women's League of Germany (DFD), and the League of Culture of the GDR (*Kulturbund*) helped disseminate the politics of the SED. All these organizations were represented in parliament, and many of the members of the parliamentary groups of the mass organizations were also members of the SED.

Soviet-style socialist societies did not have assemblies of free deputies elected in accordance with the will of their voters and various interest groups. Instead, they had uniform, hierarchical political systems. Party membership had more in common with the traditional German Estates system, in which membership was based principally upon social status, rather than on socialist ideals of egalitarianism. Party cadres and the intelligentsia held the sole right of *de facto* owning the means of production to direct state and society and the patriarchal authority that was bound up with it. Party membership conferred, via the mechanisms of cadre policy, the right to join the higher ranks of state administration, mass organizations, scientific and cultural institutions, and, last but not least, parliaments and people's assemblies.

The representation of various social groups, parties and mass organizations in parliament did not restrict the SED's claim on political leadership. As the bearer of political power, the SED was not prepared to share it with others. All discussion of the sharing of power within the political and social system of the GDR, even an elevation of the 'multiparty' system to more pluralism, was strictly rejected by the SED. Until its very end, the SED was neither willing nor able to understand that the post-Stalinist political structures and procedures no longer maintained the pretense of democracy. Informal social groups and civil rights groups were mushrooming in all sectors of society. The quest for independent representation at all levels of the political system was growing.

In 1989 the so-called political and moral unity of the people and party broke down when citizens took to the streets, demonstrated for democratic liberties, and brought down a regime that – for more than forty years – had managed to maintain absolute power over them.

The Point of Departure: Creating a Socialist System in East Germany

The GDR was an unintended polity. Neither in the post-war plans of the governments of the war coalition nor in the thinking of German politicians during and immediately after World War II was the permanent partition of Germany into two states – one tied to the Soviet Union, the other allied to the Western powers – considered as an option. There was no common positive agreement over what to do with Germany after the period of occupation either.

It took only two years to transform the 'Soviet zone of occupation' into a Soviet-type political system. At that time it was not yet clear whether it would become a separate German state or whether it would remain under direct Soviet rule for years to come. When the two German states were founded in 1949, both were part and parcel of the strategies of the two main powers and opponents in the Cold War.

To many a political activist in 1945, a new democratic beginning for Germany under the auspices of the four Allies seemed to be a realistic possibility. In accordance with Allied agreements and in stark contrast to the more reluctant policy of the Western Allies, the Soviet Military Administration (SMAD) permitted the formation of political parties and trade unions in the Soviet zone of occupation on June 10, 1945 – only a few weeks after the end of the war. The structure and program of the new parties and organizations stressed the heritage of the democratic parties in the Weimar Republic and were all-German in scope.

Despite the efforts of many former members of the Social Democratic and Communist Party to overcome the division of the workers' movement, the Soviet Union in 1945 insisted on restoring the Communist Party under the leadership of old-style Soviet devoted cadres under Walter Ulbricht and Wilhelm Pieck. When the Communist Party of Germany (KPD) in June 1945 delivered its first political proclamation (it was written in Moscow), it did not even mention socialism or communism. Instead, it stated that Germany should become an 'antifascist democracy' with all civil rights and freedoms provided for the German people.

The KPD and the Social Democratic Party (SPD) were reestablished, with the Christian Democratic Party (CDU) and Liberal Democratic Party (LDPD) following a few weeks later. Within five months, the Soviet Union and its political Allies within the KPD changed their political strategy and started a campaign for the unification of the SPD and KPD, a campaign strongly opposed by leading SPD executives in the Western zones and only reluctantly accepted by leading SPD members in the Soviet zone.

In the immediate post-war period there were other developments in the Soviet zone – however short-lived – that gave the impression of democratic evolution rather than revolutionary change. For example, the first economic measures taken by the new administration – land reform, educational reform, and the expropriation of large enterprises – were fully endorsed by the general population. But this consensus started to splinter as the SED began to take over and suppress political opponents. The space originally left open by the admission of bourgeois parties into the political scene was being closed up. In 1948 the SED began to endorse openly the fundamental principles of the Stalinist program. The SED proclaimed itself a party of a new type, thus accepting the narrowing down of Leninist ideology in favor of a concept whereby the role of the proletariat is reduced to the fulfillment of the tasks set by the party leadership. The SED leadership, backed by the occupation power, had full authority to suppress deviating views by the use of physical coercion. The SED, as a Stalinist vanguard party, and the Soviet Military Administration (SMAD), as its *de facto* patron and a body of the occupation power, had a powerful and relentless grip on East German society.

The SED followed the Soviet Stalinist model; it abandoned the original concept of national peculiarities in building a socialist society in the east of Germany, and adopted Soviet planning and management methods, as well as central state planning, as the means for the reconstruction of the economy.

In taking the Stalinist path, the SED no longer relied on broad consensus or active support, nor even on the revolutionary potential of the proletariat. It distanced itself even from the legacy of the German workers' movement, as popularized by Karl Liebknecht and Rosa Luxemburg, in that it shunned the movement's democratic traditions. The proud legacy of the workers' movement had survived the Weimar Republic and fascism only to disintegrate under the SED. The SED assisted the Soviet Union in transforming the Soviet zone into the so-called 'People's Democracy,' as outlined by the Stalinist principles of alliance politics. The 'bourgeois' parties, such as the CDU and LDPD, were made to submit to the SED and forced to accept the principles of 'democratic centralism' as the structural basis of the new political order.

The Foundation of the German Democratic Republic

When the German Democratic Republic was founded on October 7, 1949, the political system in East Germany already bore all the signs of a Marxist-Leninist polity. Absolute political power rested with the Communist Party, the SED; democratic opposition was suppressed by all means, including state terror; and the economic and social basis of a liberal market economy was destroyed by state ownership of the means of production and central planning.

In May 1949 the 'German People's Congress' – in actuality an instrument of the SED – accepted a draft version of the SED-devised GDR constitution. The People's Congress elected a representative body called the 'German People's Council,' which became the provisional People's Chamber (*Volkskammer*) on October 7, 1949, the day the GDR was founded. The first elections in the history of the GDR took place on October 15, 1950. According to official reports, the turnout was 98.44 percent and 99.7 percent of the voters accepted the proposals of the 'unity list' presented by all parties and the National Front. Not until the first (and last) free elections of the GDR on March 18, 1990 did the citizens of East Germany have a genuine choice between competing candidates and parties.

By the time of the notorious Second Party Conference of the SED in 1952, the official tone had changed radically. Walter Ulbricht's report spoke of the division of the world into two camps, 'the camp of peace, democracy and socialism and the camp of imperialism.' No more mention was made of the national peculiarities of a socialist development in the GDR. Instead, the leading role of the Soviet Union as 'headed by the great Stalin, the leader of the people,' was accepted without any reservations. But unlike the Soviet Communist Party (CPSU), the SED was unable to claim that it had come to power as a result of a people's revolution and to rely on that mandate.

The Second Party Conference formally instituted the policy of transforming GDR society according to the Soviet model, with the 'planned building of socialism.' This transformation had commenced earlier as a revolution from above. The increasingly close adherence to the Soviet model led to the total abandonment of the notion of a German-specific path to socialism, as professed by the KPD/SED in the period immediately following the war. The adoption of Soviet planning and management methods, as well as the reconstruction of the economy to give precedence to heavy industry, clearly reflected the relationship between the Soviet Union and East Germany.

Broad sections of the population, including the working class, rightly understood the adherence to the Soviet model as a final act of subordination to the will of the occupying power. The working class was hit hard by the abandonment of democratic principles. Independent working-class organizations began to disappear. Organizational endeavors on the part of the working class were now channeled exclusively to a party (and to a trade union entirely dependent on it) whose views were tightly controlled by its inner circle. The party leadership, backed by the occupation power, now had full authority to suppress deviating views by the use of physical coercion. The workers' uprising of June 17, 1953 created such a challenge that the Soviet Union had to stage a military intervention in order to protect the 'achievements' of socialism in one of the countries within its hegemonic sphere.

The uprising of June 1953 was nevertheless significant. It marks the beginning of the SED's policy of reforming political and social structures. Especially after the Twentieth CPSU Congress of 1956, the SED very gradually began to replace its coercive methods with a strategy of social, political, and economic reform.

Overcoming Stalinism

The year 1955 was a crucial one in GDR history. Several watershed moments signaled a turning point in post-war German history: the signing of the Warsaw Treaty in May, the formal recognition of Soviet Union sovereignty (dissolution of the High Commission of the USSR in Germany, rescinding orders and decrees issued by the Soviet Military Administration (SMAD) and the Soviet Control Commission), the first appearance of the GDR at an international forum (as a delegation of observers at the conference of the foreign ministers of the four victorious powers in Geneva), and the corresponding developments in the Federal Republic (the Treaty on Germany, admission to NATO). The SED proceeded from the premise that the GDR was developing as a firm component of the world socialist system and was reinforcing the increasingly close alliance with the Soviet Union and the other socialist states.

Against the background of secured state prospects, the question of administrative structures, the improvement of planning and management methods, and the party's political, economic, and social objectives acquired a new significance. Reform attempts, started in 1955/6, were immediately stopped after the Soviet intervention in the Hungarian uprising in the fall of 1956. The events in Hungary and the social unrest in Poland were blamed on 'revisionist deviations' within the party leadership and among party intellectuals. This unrest triggered fears in the SED about its grip on power. The SED reacted by halting all reform attempts and expressing its determination to smash all efforts to put its power into question. But the fears of the leadership that the events in Hungary, and more particularly the Polish social unrest, could lead to new actions by the East German working class proved to be unfounded. Too vivid were the painful memories of June 17, 1953.

In 1956 the Twentieth CPSU Congress sent shockwaves throughout the communist states because of its condemnation of Stalin's crimes and his 'personality cult,' denounced by the Soviet party leader, Nikita Khrushchev, as contradicting the principles of socialism and 'collective leadership.' For the strongman of the GDR and devout follower of Stalin, Walter Ulbricht, this was a matter of serious concern. Referencing Hungary and Poland, the SED attempted to silence discussion, which it believed had gone beyond admissible limits. The leadership of the SED, which half-heartedly endorsed the Soviet line of denouncing Stalinist methods, strongly opposed all attempts to draw political conclusions from this fundamental change in the Soviet Union as 'revisionist' and against the interests of the working class. 'Revisionism' and 'revisionist deviations' were blamed mainly on leading party intellectuals who tried to use the historic chance for far-reaching reforms. The GDR missed a second opportunity, after the fundamental crisis of 1953, of reforming the outmoded political and economic system from within.

Technocratic Reforms in the 1960s

A series of crises led to the drastic step of erecting the Berlin Wall on August 13, 1961. Unrest was rife among the people as coercion became stronger and economic conditions worsened. Growing numbers of people were seeking refuge in the West, with hopes of better prospects for the future. Before the building of the Berlin Wall, hundreds of thousands of people, quite often the young and well educated, turned their backs on a repressive system and sought one that allowed individual freedom and privacy. Amazingly enough, the Wall provided the basis for the only consistent far-reaching reform attempt in GDR history, the 'New Economic System' (NÖS) of 1963.

The reforms of the 1960s can be understood as an attempt to overcome the negative consequences of an extremely centralized planning system, which could not serve a more advanced economy than that of the Soviet Union in the 1930s and 1940s, when it had originally been introduced. It was not without success in the years immediately after the war, when rebuilding the economy, the infrastructure, destroyed cities, and industries was high on the agenda, but now extensive growth had been replaced by intensive growth and what had been achieved was to be consolidated.

Under the impact of the shock produced by the events of June 1953, the de-Stalinization of 1956, the crises of the systems in Hungary and Poland, and opposition among the new communist intelligentsia in 1956–7, the SED was forced to admit that it was no longer in a position to function as a united center of action and to guide society centrally in all its details. Economic, scientific-technical and social developments, as well as the spreading differentiation and diversification of social processes and structures, compelled it to reconsider its own role.

Following a phase of experimentation lasting roughly from 1954 until 1963, the SED drew up the New Economic System, adopting ideas which it had condemned as revisionist only a short time previously. The SED had to concede that the GDR, like all other economically advanced countries, was confronting a new situation: it had to be capable of standing up to the challenges of the second industrial or scientific and technical revolution if it did not want to forfeit its future. At the end of the 1950s, the SED had learned the lesson that these challenges could not be solved using the established organizational concepts of excessive bureaucracy and centralization. But since it was neither willing nor able to overcome the other impeding factors (i.e. the system-dependent restrictions on organized individual or group interests), its attempts at reform remained of a purely technocratic nature. The experiment had to be modified after Nikita Khrushchev's fall in 1964 and was subsequently abandoned in 1968 when the next crisis erupted. The space for experimentation tolerated by the Soviets had become narrower and narrower. Under different conditions, NÖS might have become a model for technocratic reform of the socialist systems.

In the mid-1960s Walter Ulbricht's government also developed autonomous policy ideas in a variety of areas, independent of Soviet positions and no longer based on the utopian premise that communism was just around the corner. The idea of a 'socialist human community,' a conflict-free socialist society, took the place of utopian expectations. On closer inspection, the attempt to replace utopian, ideologically defined goals – which could be reached only by force – with new goals reachable during the lifetime of the living was a means to deny the existence of the real conflicts and contradictions of society. The SED was certain that it could build up a 'developed socialist system' with the help of scientific methods derived from cybernetics and systems theory. The building of socialism appeared to be the task of technocrats and specialists, and not of ideologues or Lenin's 'professional revolutionaries.' There were parallels to this line in Western theories of modernization, which were highly influential in the 1960s and 1970s.

Aside from the technocratic reflections, however, few voices in the GDR of the 1960s – unlike in Poland, Hungary, and Czechoslovakia – demanded political change. One of the few, and the most vehement, was Professor Robert Havemann in a series of lectures at Humboldt University in East Berlin. The violent suppression of the 'Prague Spring' of 1968 and the termination of Khrushchev's reforms in the Soviet Union (1968/9) put an end to all experimentation and condemned socialism in the GDR to another two decades of the old, centralist political control. For the GDR, Ulbricht's fall and replacement by Erich Honecker in 1971 was the end of the experiment, even though it opened the door to realistic cooperation of the SED with the West. It also created the preconditions for basic changes in the economic and social policy of the SED.

The late 1960s were characterized not only by an economic and social crisis, but also by serious problems in international relations. After giving up its inflexible and obstructive policies toward the GDR and other socialist countries, the Federal Republic came to share the general interest of the Western states and the Soviet Union in détente and became a leading force in designing a new *Ostpolitik*. The GDR under Walter Ulbricht feared that improved East–West relations would undermine its claim for full recognition as a state. It continued to resist obstinately even when the Soviet Union signaled that its policies toward the West were aimed at building a system of security and cooperation in Europe, which could not be achieved without changing the Soviet Union's position toward Germany, and especially Berlin, and improving German–German relations. The need for a change in leadership and policies was obvious.

The Honecker Era

When Erich Honecker became the first secretary of the SED in 1971, the economic, political and social system of the GDR was facing crisis. The aims and goals of the country's economic reforms (New Economic System) had not been achieved. Yet in 1963 the GDR had served as a peacemaker in the negotiations over economic reforms within the Council for Mutual Economic Aid (CMEA) or COMECON. The overthrow of Nikita Khrushchev in 1964 ended a period of reform in the Soviet Union that had begun in the late 1950s. The GDR tried until 1968 to develop its own model for reforming the economy and building up an advanced socialist society. After the invasion of Czechoslovakia by Warsaw-Pact troops, there was no longer a real chance of reform because the impact of a reform strategy could not be limited to the economic sector. The Czech example had shown the leaders of the ruling communist parties that reform of economic systems alone was a goal that could not be achieved, and that a reform strategy had to take into account the fact that different sectors of society needed to be united if reforms were to be implemented. They were not prepared to take that risk.

On the other hand, there was a strong need to reform and modernize society as a whole. The economic system suffered from over-centralized planning and regulation, inadequate development of market conditions, and a lack of devolved responsibility. The euphoric expectations regarding the effects of the scientific-technical revolution had proved to be an illusion. New 'home-made' social conflicts, which were not the result of the 'capitalist heritage,' had not been foreseen. The ideological idea that producing material goods is more valuable than developing the secondary and tertiary sector caused growing economic and social problems, in particular an inadequate investment in the infrastructure, especially housing.

The years following the Eighth Party Congress in 1971 marked a period of considerable socio-economic achievement in the GDR. The concepts 'crisis' and 'pre-crisis situation' seemed to be applicable only to the capitalist world, although symptoms of a deep crisis of 'real socialism,' especially in the case of Poland, could not be overlooked. The party congress suggested ways to solve the economic and social problems. One that had been for a long time considered utterly out of place in a socialist society was social policy. The congress initiated an explicit liberalization of cultural policy and involved the emerging political and social organizations (mainly the trade unions) in major decision-making processes. This remarkable change of course was dictated by the realization that there was no monolithic identity of interests between the individual, social groups, and the whole of society.

A policy of unity between the economic and social spheres of society became the basic driving force behind the SED. This policy change implied a far-reaching revision of the concepts which had marked the SED's strategy since the New Economic System of the early 1960s. There was not only a change in the political strategy and tactics; the theoretical assessment of the socio-economic situation had also fundamentally changed. The ruling party had to acknowledge that, even in an advanced socialist society, social problems remained and had to be solved if the political and social themselves were not to be put in jeopardy.

Social policy was meant to heal the adverse social consequences of economic policy and ensure, in the form of social planning, that they did not even emerge. Social policy embraced a range of concerns, including demographics, development, industrial labor organization, housing, urban and regional planning, health care, social security, leisure and recreation, relations in the workplace and in 'socialist combines,' and the supply of consumer goods and services available to the public. The 'unity of economic and social policy' implied a revision of the former policies of the SED. It included the admission that even a socialist economy could create social injustice that had to be healed by a paternalistic socialist welfare state. The SED succeeded in the early 1970s in setting new accents on its economic and social policy, and respect among the people for the new paternalism increased. Unfortunately, the worldwide energy crisis of the 1970s knocked the bottom out from under these ambitious reform plans.

The accession to power of the new leadership under Erich Honecker also led to changes in cultural policy, which, for a short period of time, led to liberalization, less control of the arts, and a more open-minded attitude of the SED, especially toward modern literature, theater and film. Many artists took the chance to free themselves from the ideological straitjacket of 'party mindedness' (*Parteilichkeit*) and 'socialist realism.' This more liberal approach of the party abruptly ended when some artists, such as the song-writer Wolf Biermann, called not only for more openness in cultural matters but also for political change. Biermann was eventually expelled to West Germany. Many of his colleagues protested this political move of the SED in an unprecedented public letter to the SED leadership.

The Biermann affair of 1976 was the first but not the last open confrontation between the ruling party and leading intellectuals, many of them devoted members of the SED. A few years later a new confrontation took place, when eight prominent writers were expelled from the official writers' union, which meant that they were banned from publishing in the GDR. This led to an exodus of some of the most prominent and internationally acknowledged writers in East Germany. The emigration of respected intellectuals to the West was a severe blow to the GDR's claim to be the political home for all progressive political and cultural movements, in contrast to West Germany which was said to suffer under the devastating influence of American popular culture and decadence. The Biermann crisis and the controversy with prominent writers led to a political crisis and demonstrated the unwillingness of the SED to open up the system to new ideas and unconventional views. Such an attempt made in the 1980s was by the new Soviet leadership under Mikhail Gorbachev which was strongly rejected by Erich Honecker and his comrades.

The final crisis of the GDR, however, was not triggered by disputes over cultural policies, nor even by the eruption of popular protest in the fall of 1989. There had been widespread unease with economic, social and political stagnation in the years before 1989. In addition, citizens of the GDR saw other socialist countries evolving. First and foremost, the Soviet Union, under the policies of glasnost and perestroika, was undertaking an unprecedented course in reform.

Considerable imbalances and the slowing down of growth rates characterized the economic situation of the GDR in the second half of the 1980s. At a meeting of the Central Committee of the SED in November 1984 Erich Honecker used the term 'turnaround' (*Wende*) to characterize the situation at that time. The party leadership was aware of the fact that new measures had to be taken to overcome stagnation. In the midst of the unfolding crisis in the socialist countries of Central and Eastern Europe – especially in 1980s Poland – the GDR was considered by many observers to be an island of relative peace and stability.

Although it was becoming increasingly clear that the political leadership could no longer read the signs of the times, observers outside the GDR did not have sufficient historical and sociological awareness to foresee what was to come in 1989. Everything appeared to be part of socialist normality. The fortieth anniversary celebrations of the GDR were designed to emphasize that it was a stable socialist republic and an esteemed member of the international community. Ironically, the bombastic self-congratulation of the Honecker leadership operated as a catalyst for a popular uprising. The fortieth anniversary festivities degenerated into an embarrassing funeral oration for a political and social system which had proved unable either to adapt or to reform, and for a ruling phalanx so removed from reality that it took its own proclamations of success at face value.

Only a few years earlier, it had been a very different picture. At the beginning of the 1980s the Cold War was at its height and the leadership of the GDR was praised for its relatively independent line from Brezhnev's Soviet Union. In fall 1987 Honecker was received in Bonn with full honors as the representative of the second German state. However, shortly thereafter regression – at first barely discernible to Western observers – set in, which was to lead within two years to the collapse of real socialism. Faced with the dramatic events unfolding in the Soviet Union, Hungary and Poland in the late 1980s, the SED became more and more concerned about the stability of the GDR's political and social system. Their concerns were not unfounded. There was a popular desire to reform the bureaucratic structure of society as a whole and to combine that reform with an increase in 'socialist democracy' and the rule of law.

By the end of the 1980s modernization of socialist systems had become a complex process that operated on different levels and in different sectors of society. But above all, it was no longer imaginable without democratization (though not necessarily in the sense of Western democratic theory). Modernization had become a goal that could not be achieved without rebuilding the whole economic, political and administrative structure, and the forms and methods of control. Last but by no means least, modernization required a different mentality and a new, more open framework for economic, political, social and cultural activities, with more participation and fewer bureaucratic restrictions.

The advent of perestroika in the Soviet Union arguably presented the GDR with its last opportunity to initiate a process of transformation. It was an opportunity lost. The SED and its notion of party-centralized planning and rule failed to grasp the complexity of the new problems. It failed to realize that since the 1960s social, cultural and political changes had occurred in the GDR that affected every political sphere. Neither the normative regulations in place nor the existing institutional system and state doctrine could cope with the new difficulties faced. 'Real socialism,' as the derivative of Stalinist rule, had proved to be a political and socio-economic system unequal to the demands of a modern society. It had failed once and for all, and the 'GDR model' collapsed in its wake.

The SED regime proved helpless and lacking in comprehension in the face of these developments. Over many years the political leadership had tried to limit the influence of Western 'imperialist' culture. It did not go as far as the North Korean regime, which allows only for fixed radio and television sets that only deliver party and state propaganda. Given that there were no language barriers, most GDR citizens were well informed via West German radio and television, which reported extensively on the situation in the GDR itself and, even more importantly, on the reform attempts and new social and political movements in other communist countries. The impact of the Western media on cultural and value changes in East Germany cannot be overstated.

Especially among younger people, cultural-political developments in the West were closely watched and influenced cultural orientations, values, and attitudes. Issues such as environmentalism, pacifism, and the quest for individual autonomy became as prominent among the youth of East Germany (and other communist countries) as in the West. Yet these developments by themselves would never have led to the overthrow of the SED regime, had the ailing party leadership not missed the import of these developments and the Soviet Union not failed to intervene by force, as it had always done previously.

The Collapse of the Old Regime

A session of the Central Committee of the SED in December 1988 was the scene of an unprecedented statement by the General Secretary of the Party, Erich Honecker. He said that there was 'no model which held for all the socialist countries.'

Instead, he referred to socialism 'in the colors of the GDR.' These statements were reminiscent of a famous essay from the early days of the SED in 1946, in which reference was made to a 'particular German road to socialism.' On closer inspection, however, it becomes clear that talk of circumstances specific to the GDR served only to distance the party from the reforms and strategy of Soviet Communists under Mikhail Gorbachev, which, in the eyes of the Honecker leadership, were expected to result in anarchy. The speech was quite rightly perceived by large sections of the party and GDR society generally as a rejection of any reform. The party leadership under Honecker was to remain loyal to this policy until the very end.

At first glance it seemed as if Honecker did not lack valid arguments in his favor. Was not the GDR the most industrially developed country in Eastern Europe? Did it not register the highest standard of living among the Eastern economies of COMECON? Had not the policies of glasnost and perestroika in the Soviet Union already resulted in major economic and social problems? This notwithstanding, the leadership did not acknowledge the severe economic crisis the GDR was facing and, first and foremost, failed to cope with one key aspect: for the first time since the early 1960s and the suppression of the 'Prague Spring' in 1968, the policies of glasnost and perestroika in the Soviet Union had cultivated the vague hope of a reform of Soviet-style socialism. A large number of intellectuals and even SED party members now expected the party to embrace these initiatives.

Glasnost and perestroika were greeted by the wider public and by members of the ruling party with great enthusiasm because one of the key contradictions between the people and the leadership in the GDR lay precisely in the lack of openness und the unwillingness to fundamentally reform the system. Honecker and the rest of the aging leadership wholly underestimated the ideological sea-change which the Soviet reforms had introduced.

Nonetheless, the uneasiness with the general situation was much more widespread than many in the GDR were prepared to concede. Social conflicts in the GDR were evident even in the leading party, with its more than two million members (nearly one fifth of the adult population). The party included both those who exercised absolute power – including the ever-present security apparatus of the *Stasi* – and many of those who were put under surveillance by the *Stasi*. The party was mammoth, comprising judges and prosecutors who pronounced hard-line political sentences and defense lawyers who in the same trials called for acquittal, those who banned films or books and those who made films or wrote books. The party was everywhere and all conflicts in GDR society were in a way also reflected within the rank and file of the party. This meant that the party, despite its self-perception as a cadre organization of committed revolutionaries in the style of Lenin and the early Bolsheviks, was a mass party with hundreds of thousands of opportunists and fellow travelers.

Moreover, there was no critical social science and very few clandestine publications (as in other socialist countries) that could provide a realistic picture of society. The published results of academic work in the social sciences were more or less reproducing the official image of the state of the GDR purveyed by the press and the party ideologues. The only source of independent news and information was Western radio and television, where the developments in Soviet Russia were intensively covered. This was one of the reasons why glasnost had become a utopia in the GDR: the people were as conscious as most party members of the fact that their reality was far removed from its ideologically prefabricated portrayal in the press, radio, and television of the GDR, which were in turn subordinate to repressive regulations, 'language rules,' and weekly briefings (*Argumentationen*) by the SED in order to ensure media uniformity. The above helps explain a joke often heard in the fall of 1989: a man goes to the police and applies, like tens of thousands at the time, for an exit visa. He is asked where he would like to go and replies: 'To the GDR.' When informed that he is already there, he says: 'No, I mean the GDR I read about in the papers.' This distortion of reality was not without its repercussions. Propaganda became a law unto itself and formed the worldview of those who used it.

Some leading political figures only grasped that they themselves had been viewing reality through ideological lenses when it was already too late. At the tenth session of the Central Committee of the SED (November 8–11, 1989), which decided to open the Wall, Egon Krenz, Erich Honecker's successor, conceded that the problems and questions under discussion had not come about overnight or in the previous summer, when people had left the GDR in their thousands. The SED had started from false economic premises, misinterpreted the international situation, and indulged in utopian thinking. The more the changes in the Soviet Union, Poland and Hungary progressed, the greater became the uncertainty in the geriatric leadership of the SED. It cocooned itself in a web of self-delusion and saw every attempt at change as an attack by the class enemy on what socialism had achieved. The mass exodus of predominantly young people was – as on August 13, 1961 when the Berlin Wall was built – attributed to the negative influence, propaganda campaigns, and wartime reporting techniques of the Western media, which, as the *Neues Deutschland*, the SED's 'central organ' put it on August 25, 1989, at the very height of the refugee crisis, gave the 'stage directions to encourage citizens to leave the GDR.' On October 2, 1989 the same paper stated that no tears should be shed for those who had left the GDR. This sentence, which provoked outrage in the GDR, was apparently penned by Erich Honecker himself and forwarded to the party newspaper through the Agitation and Propaganda Section of the Central Committee of the SED.

The fortieth anniversary of the founding of the GDR on October 7, 1989 was intended by the SED to be an occasion when the historic achievements of the GDR could be displayed to the eyes of the world. In an address which carried the grandiloquent title 'Through the people and for the people great things were achieved,' published in *Neues Deutschland* on October 9, 1989, Erich Honecker painted an idyllic picture of the GDR. The German Democratic Republic was crossing the threshold into the third millennium, secure in the knowledge that the future belonged to socialism even if 'influential forces in the FRG' were awaiting the chance to 'overturn the results of World War II and post-war history by a coup.' Instead of addressing the real problems facing the GDR, Honecker referred to a 'policy of continuity and renewal' which would ensure that in the future socialism would glow in the 'colors of the GDR.' In the illusory world of a political leadership which saw its life's work threatened by external forces, the party and the people remained united for the common cause.

At the same time, people were demonstrating on the streets and calling for a different kind of republic. Their talisman was Mikhail Gorbachev, who had been invited to the celebration by the SED leadership and had politely digested the proceedings. Tens of thousands of young people shouted both the official slogans, such as, 'the GDR is our Fatherland,' and 'Gorby, Gorby!' Only a few hundred meters away there were thousands of illegal demonstrators also calling 'Gorby, Gorby!' and demanding democratic rights and civil liberties. The failure of the leadership to introduce reforms of the political and economic system before it was too late pushed the GDR to the precipice of civil war and proved to be the final nail in its coffin. Only fortuitous circumstances prevented the peaceful revolution of October 9, 1989 in Leipzig from being put down like the demonstrations in Tiananmen Square in the spring of 1989, which cost hundreds of young lives.

When Honecker was toppled, only eleven days after the fortieth anniversary celebrations of the GDR many long-time observers were reminded of the spring of 1971, when Honecker's predecessor, Walter Ulbricht, suffered the same fate. Since the foundation of the GDR, power had been vested in two party chairmen. During the same period, the Federal Republic of Germany had had six chancellors: Konrad Adenauer, Ludwig Erhard, Kurt-Georg Kiesinger, Willy Brandt, Helmut Schmidt and Helmut Kohl. It was evident that the new leader of the SED, Egon Krenz, would be a transitional figure. Still, no one predicted that within two months Krenz would be on his way out as the last general secretary of an omnipotent state party

The downfall of the SED again testifies to the inability of the political system to reform itself from within. On October 11, 1989 the Politburo of the SED issued a statement, drafted under almost conspiratorial circumstances, on the situation in the GDR. The statement had been preceded by a dramatic turn of events. In September thousands of GDR citizens had tried to leave the GDR by traveling through Hungary, Czechoslovakia, and Poland. Hundreds camped out in the worst conditions imaginable on the grounds of the West German embassy in Prague. On September 25 the Czechoslovak party leadership had informed the SED leadership that it was no longer prepared to bear the consequences of an exodus now reaching panic proportions. It was afraid that the exodus from the GDR might jeopardize the internal political situation in Czechoslovakia. The question was whether the frontier between Czechoslovakia and the GDR was to be closed. This would have had unforeseeable consequences. The SED general secretary proposed an 'exceptional measure' to allow the people camped in embassy grounds to travel across GDR territory and settle in the Federal Republic. On October 4, violent demonstrations took place in Dresden, when people desperate to leave the GDR tried to storm the central railway station and climb aboard trains passing through en route for the Federal Republic. For the first time – and much too late – there were signs that the SED leadership was appreciating the true situation.

The people were offered a constructive and open dialogue. Regret was expressed at the exodus from the GDR. The leadership emphasized the need for solidarity, proposed a 'democratic community,' and called for 'active cooperation.' At the same time, however, accusations were made of far-reaching provocation by 'imperialist forces' that were trying to use the situation for their own means. The issue of removing travel restrictions had become a key indicator of the willingness of the SED leadership to change course and initiate *in extremis* a far-reaching reform of the system. Even if the party had exhibited this willingness by October, it would have been too late. The people and broad sections of the SED membership were no longer prepared to give credence to the desire of the SED leadership to reform under Honecker. His removal was already seen as overdue.

Preparations for Honecker's removal from office had been under way since late summer 1989 in a tight circle of certain Politburo members. The fortieth anniversary of the foundation of the GDR acted as a catalyst. Some top officials and members of the Politburo were planning a palace coup, but this could not take place without the agreement or at least the toleration of the Ministry for State Security and the Soviet leadership. The conspirators obviously did secure the support of Soviet advisors in the ministry and other organs of state security. At the session of the Politburo on October 17, 1989, Erich Honecker was removed from office.

The fall of Honecker and other leading members of the Politburo and the election of Egon Krenz as the general secretary of the SED left the impression that the SED leadership was content with cosmetic change only. The protestations of Egon Krenz and the Politburo that they wished to introduce new politics were not believed. To the majority of GDR citizens, Krenz was the loyal protégé of Honecker and the man responsible for the ballot rigging in the communal elections in the spring of 1989, and for brutal police interventions in October 1989. In the eyes of the new party leadership, the ousting of Honecker marked a turning point (*Wende*) that would enable the SED to regain the political and ideological offensive. Conflicting signals were given in this politically heated situation: promises of a new beginning and at the same time talk of political and ideological offensives and the old accretion of power to the general secretary of the party. The fact that Honecker's removal was announced not as a dismissal but as a retirement for health reasons left the credibility of the SED in doubt.

On the day of his election Krenz met a leading church figure, the first such communication after a long silence. He pursued open discussion with workers about the political situation. The State Council declared an amnesty for anyone convicted of 'crossing the border illegally,' and political prisoners were also to be released. The SED proposed an action program which contained what in earlier days would have been seen as far-reaching political concessions. Now they were recognized as the half-hearted efforts of a party desperately clinging to power. They included freedom of travel, extensive changes to penal law, reform of the political system and means of economic management, the education system, and the media, and, most significantly, a widening of the public realm.

The people of the GDR refused to believe that the SED leadership was able and willing to reform the political system and to overcome post-Stalinist socialism. The rebellion of the SED grass roots in the wake of new revelations of corruption, abuse of office and illegal deals, including officially tolerated arms trafficking, not only signaled the end of the Krenz 'era' after only forty-eight days. It also sealed the end of the SED.

The End of the State Party SED

On December 3, 1989 the entire Politburo of the SED resigned in an act unprecedented in over seventy years of Communist Party history. The resignation was sparked by a revolt at the party grass-roots level, which had been caught up in the popular mood for change and no longer trusted its new leadership to initiate root and branch reform. The fall of the Central Committee and the SED Politburo and the involuntary resignation of Egon Krenz as chairman of the State Council and the National Defense Council on December 6 illustrated the complete collapse of a political strategy devoted solely to damage limitation. Yesterday's revolutionaries either would not or could not grasp that a revolution was under way and that they were its 'counterrevolutionaries.' Despite the remarkable capacity of the 'renewed' SED leadership to adapt to changed circumstances, it was unable to regain the initiative. For weeks the leadership was left with no choice but to follow in the wake of the opposition movement.

The fall of Honecker could not prevent the collapse of the old order. The mass exodus of predominantly young people continued. Opposition groups made further gains. The belief that only radical and far-reaching reform could halt the disintegration reached into the deepest ranks of the SED. Individual groups within the SED had long attempted to stimulate a thoroughgoing reform process. After Mikhail Gorbachev's accession to power in the Soviet Union, pressure mounted on the party hierarchy to initiate wide-ranging reform along Soviet lines. For a number of reasons debate never went beyond the stage of informal discussions in small circles. Reformers made their views public for the first time in October and November 1989 and secured in the following weeks and months significant influence over the restructuring process of the political system.

At the same time, grass-roots discontent within the party and in the wider population mounted. It secured the replacement of the party leadership of Krenz, who had taken office in October. Discontent also forced the convening of an extraordinary party congress of the SED on December 8 and 16/17 – against the wishes of the leadership. This congress intended to transform the SED into a modern socialist party that would have to make a radical break with 'Stalinist structures.' Its new name, SED-PDS (Party of Democratic Socialism) combined two barely reconcilable political camps: Marxist-Leninists clinging to power and those promising an open debate and democratic deliberation.

Despite its radical self-criticism, the SED-PDS was scarcely able to lend credibility to its political transformation. Its influence on the running of the state was secured, albeit at a price. The SED-PDS forfeited much credibility even with its new, reform-minded leadership because, despite its efforts, it remained unable to shed old-style thinking and old apparatus structures and faced the accelerating changes in the political climate practically bereft of power. Saving the SED as the leading party in the GDR proved untenable. Despite the popularity of Hans Modrow, the new prime minister, the government failed to secure public confidence. The SED-PDS failed to lend credibility to the political transformation it had undergone.

The party remained largely powerless in the face of a rapidly changing political climate. Even after it had been renamed again as the Party of Democratic Socialism (PDS) in February 1990, the party could not escape its history. The series of scandals and comprehensive evidence of the complicity of leading members of the PDS in the old system could not, however, destroy the standing of the party in the eyes of long-standing members, as is demonstrated by the remarkable success achieved in the elections of 1990. This was in large measure due to the PDS's success in attracting not only old-guard communist support but also many of those who most feared the social costs of unification with the Federal Republic – first and foremost state servants, members of the security apparatus, and also a large number of intellectuals who had not yet abandoned the socialist ideal.

Structural Defects of the Communist System

The implosion of a political and social system which had hitherto been considered invincible demonstrated that the collapse of the GDR resulted not only from specific or accumulated errors but also from structural defects within the system. The system was based on the belief that a modern, industrial society could be planned and regulated from the center and that the Marxist-Leninist party exercised a monopoly on the scientific understanding of the laws of society. This belief contained the more fundamental reason for the emergence of authoritarian political and social structures that were neither flexible nor responsive to change. These structures could make only a belated and half-hearted response (if any) to the need for change and modernization.

This system has been termed structural Stalinism. It represented a political concept that can be characterized as the following: the SED conceived the political system as a homogeneous entity molded, directed, and controlled by the party. Within this nexus the independence of specific spheres of policy or a division of powers was not tolerated. Only a centralized policy based on standardized principles could in its view accomplish the social objectives of the party: the building of socialism and communism. Everything was subordinate to this goal. Only within this uniform complex of party, state, and society could a division of tasks between specific institutions and organizations be envisaged. Executive, legislature, judiciary, and all the state institutions and 'social organizations' could not question the leading role of the party. This Marxist-Leninist party defined itself as the 'political and organizational center of society.' The state was its 'principal instrument' in the formation of a socialist society. The mass organizations (the unions, youth, and women's leagues) and the fraternal parties were of their own free will to subordinate their interests to the leading role of the SED. Any suggestion of the independence of individual spheres of the political system or even of a division of powers would be regarded as a general attack on the basic premises of the state and the social order. All components of the political system were to pursue the same aims and function according to the same principles. This implied above all the recognition of 'democratic centralism' as the regulatory principle of the whole social order. Both the structure and the function of the political system of Soviet-type socialism clearly demonstrate that 'democratic centralism' as a regulatory principle assisted in securing the hegemony of the Communist Party in all spheres of society. Its removal would have meant depriving the party of its influence on the recruitment of new political cadres, specific mechanisms of instruction and control, and the parallel structure of party apparatus, state administration, bureaucracy, and state security.

The right of the party-state to subordinate all spheres of society to its direction and regulation prevented the pursuit of pragmatic and responsive policies and produced an artificial politicization of everyday life. The inherited centralism and authoritarianism, notwithstanding the signs of corruption and neo-feudal privileges, acted as a major impediment to the development of society and to the resolution of the economic, social, and cultural problems with which the GDR and the other socialist states had long been confronted. The key fact that society and political life were wholly subordinate to the party precluded any successful process of modernization or adaptation and resulted ultimately in the collapse of the old system.

Socialism of the Soviet type failed to display its superiority to capitalism. It proved unable to cast off the chains of Stalinism and to create a modern, working socialist society in its place. If anything, only a radical modernization of the system could have salvaged elements of the ideas which spawned the socialist movement. This historic opportunity has now been squandered, and not only in the GDR. This mechanism prevented real change and the adaptation of both the political and the social system to changing circumstances. As in other Soviet-type socialist countries, the GDR would have required a root-and-branch modernization and restructuring, which, in order to be successful, would have had to cast off the chains of the socio-economic, political, and cultural structures of society and the political system. This was the basic prerequisite for the successful modernization of the political, economic, and social system.

The developments in the GDR in 1989 were part of a more general historic development. The old regimes in Poland, Czechoslovakia, Hungary, Bulgaria, and Romania collapsed, while the Chinese leadership held on to power only by means of a massacre. The social and political crisis of the GDR was part of a general crisis of socialism in those countries upon which, after the war, the socio-economic and political system of the Soviet Union had been imposed. *Prima facie* it can be considered a crisis of a political and social order also beset by inefficient economic performance, even if economic decline did precipitate the political and social crisis. Seen in the wider context, however, it is the crisis of a premodern political and social system.

The ruling communist parties aimed at standardizing the societies they ruled and creating in their image a new socialist man. The reality both in the GDR and the other socialist countries was somewhat different: societies had successfully opposed the uniformity advocated by the leadership. In addition, the last twenty years have seen a process of cultural and social change not dissimilar to that of modern industrial societies: there was a differentiation in social structure and the old class conflict lost its importance; new 'cleavages' emerged; new values and modes of behavior came into view; the influences of international culture and civilization could no longer be held at bay, as had been possible in the early 1960s when the ruling SED attempted to prohibit Western television viewing. However, the Wall and closed borders prevented the population from participating actively in these developments. There was a growing sense of imprisonment, which fueled discontent. The SED response was either non-existent or insufficient.

On top of this, another factor – not without its dangers for orthodox circles – came into play after 1985: glasnost and perestroika in the Soviet Union. A process unique in world history took place and without recourse to war: the transformation from a dictatorship and its claims to hegemony to an enlightened authoritarianism with elements of democracy. The countries of the erstwhile socialist bloc could not remain unaffected. The year 1989 marked the collapse and overthrow of real socialism in Central and Eastern Europe.

–9–

The German Revolution of 1989 and German Unification

In the fall of 1989 hundreds of thousands of demonstrators took to the streets in East Germany and raised the cry, 'We are the people!' These mass demonstrations succeeded in overthrowing the country's communist regime. At the beginning of 1990 the new became, 'We are one people.' Within three months, the mood in East Germany had changed. After the Berlin Wall came down on November 9, those who had dared to oppose the dictatorship of the SED and who were longing for a democratic GDR became a minority. Now the people on the streets demanded the rapid unification of the two German states.

The 'people of the GDR' constituted itself for only a brief moment – when it swept away the old political order. Then this unified political entity broke up into its various component parts. The slogan 'We are the people!' as the maxim of a demo-cratic state and of its constitution was, in a way, a mirror image of the totalitarian state that had just been overthrown. It did not reflect the fact that modern societies are based on a differentiated set of interests, beliefs, values, and patterns of behavior that have to be represented in their plurality. Only a pluralistic political system based on common sense could provide the institutional framework needed for reconciling those societies that had undergone the experience of authoritarian communist rule.

In the short time between fall 1989 and the day of German Unity on October 3, 1990, political events in the GDR reflected three conflicting trends:

1. The process of political restructuring and differentiation led to the founding of a variety of parties, interest groups, clubs, etc. which sought an answer to the various problems faced by GDR citizens during this transitional period.
2. The process of transition was increasingly dominated by the wish to create as quickly as possible the prerequisites for the unification of the two German states. All political groups and the People's Chamber of the GDR, which had been freely elected on March 18,1990 attempted during these months to steer a course between the Scylla of a mere accession or takeover (in the GDR often in a historically problematic way, referring to the occupation of Austria by Nazi Germany in 1938, termed as *Anschluss* of the GDR to the Federal Republic) and the Charybdis of ensuring as firm a rooting as possible of the old structures.
3. Political forces in the GDR, both government and opposition, lost more and more of their freedom of movement. Their actions were determined by the circumstances

accompanying a permanent election campaign and by their superior partners in the West, and, last but not least. by a constant wave of migration from the East to the West.

If, in the weeks following the elections to the People's Chamber, the unification process visibly gathered speed, this was in all likelihood not only because of the worsening economic and social crisis in the GDR but also because a reassessment of the situation in world politics made as rapid an achievement of unity as possible appear desirable. The purpose was to use the window of opportunity which the revolutions in Central and Eastern Europe and the Soviet Union had opened.

The first freely elected parliament and the first democratically legitimized government of the GDR were confronted by the necessity of reaching, in the shortest possible time, three decisions of fundamental importance. Which path should the GDR follow in order to reach the goal of unity? What needed to be decided here was whether the unification of the two German states should be achieved via Article 146 of the Basic Law, which would have meant a longer process of state and constitution building, or by Article 23 of the Basic Law, which meant the accession of the GDR to the Federal Republic. Directly related to this was the question of whether the GDR should give itself a new constitution for this period of transition. Once a decision in favor of Article 23 had been reached, it was important to protect the interests of the citizens of the GDR during the process of unification. The debate about the form which unification should take – but above all about the dates of elections and about electoral procedures – led to endless controversies in both German states.

Were the Events of 1989 a Revolution?

If a revolution is seen in the tradition of the French and Russian revolutions, both dictated by violence, the answer to this question is no. With the exception of Romania, the revolutions of 1989 have broken this causal link. Given the collapse of the political system in the GDR, however, can the events of 1989/90 be seen as constituting a revolution? For the old elites who had always feared that their social experiment would end this way, the events were a counterrevolution, that is, the restoration of the old capitalist order.

If revolution is taken as the fundamental–not necessarily violent–overthrow of the political, economic, and social structures of a state, then surely the events of 1989 constituted a revolution. Socialist countries finally bade farewell to a secular utopia which had aimed to establish a just social order of equals but which ended the freedoms of civil society that had been painstakingly, albeit only partially, won since 1776 and 1789. The toppling of the SED leadership simultaneously marked the demise of a social experiment imposed by an external agency (the occupying forces). The Soviet model of power implemented in Central Europe after 1945 began to impede, not enhance, modernization in the developed countries, with the exception of the cultural sphere. The revolutions that took place in Central Europe and the GDR in 1989 were primarily of a compensatory nature, not a conservative one. They restored the conditions for a liberal democratic order and a market economy. In the GDR this became known as an 'abrogated revolution' in view of the specific national conditions which resulted in the dissolution of the GDR and its accession to the Federal Republic.

The death of the GDR was the logical result of the end of socialism. After November 9, 1989, when, in an unprecedented coup, the SED leadership opened the Berlin Wall, only a few groups were left to support the idea of an independent state named GDR. The slogans 'We are the people' and 'We are staying here' immediately changed to 'We are one people' and 'Germany united fatherland.' The pressure toward unification was rising from within. There was no broad support, however, for the idea of a new social and political experiment within the GDR. No coherent reform bloc was to be seen in GDR society, in contrast to Poland, Czechoslovakia, and Hungary. Has there ever been a social basis for reforming the socialist system? At the end of 1989 public opinion polls in the GDR showed a remarkable number of people who were of the opinion that some social advantages, such as housing and social policies, kindergartens, and social security, were worth defending. On the other hand, a growing number of people had no confidence in a future socialist experiment, the economic situation was considered disastrous, and expectations were running high that the Federal Republic would solve these problems one way or the other.

'We are the people' originally meant: we are against the old corrupt, authoritarian, centralist and inefficient regime, and we are united in the attempt to get rid of that regime. In early 1990 it became obvious that beyond that aim, which was achieved in an astonishingly short period of time, social and political interests were as different and divided as in all modern societies. The old antagonistic scheme (we the people versus a corrupt political leadership and an autocratic state, new social and political groups versus the SED, good versus evil) no longer applied.

Collapse and a New Beginning – the Citizens' Movements and Democratic Transition

Political groups appealed in the fall of 1989 for the establishment of a liberal and socially just society in the GDR and galvanized hundreds of thousands of people to take to the streets and call for a new beginning. However, it was only for a very brief period – if at all – that the aims of these groups coincided with popular opinion. This divergence only became apparent with hindsight because everyone was caught up in the cataclysmic events of the time. The general public was largely motivated by materialist concerns, while revolutionaries of citizens' movements were motivated by post-material values, and the reformist circles within the SED remained largely silent while they searched for an alternative stance. In the beginning, there was a grass-roots democratic movement united in its goal of achieving a free and open society.

However, once the authoritarian regime had been successfully and rapidly toppled, these movements were forced to confront serious issues that had previously been on the back burner. Were they to join in the struggle for power or agitate from the outside? The opposition faced a classic dilemma – it is far easier to criticize a state than run one. Unlike its Polish counterpart, the opposition in the GDR had never succeeded in forging an alliance between the opponents of the system, supported primarily by intellectuals, critical members of the party intelligentsia, and the workers. All past attempts at reform of party rule (in 1953, 1957, and the years after 1963) had failed for this reason.

Galvanized by the ballot-rigging scandal of the communal elections of May 1989, large numbers of grass-roots initiatives spread all over the country. The Protestant Church protected many of these groups and individuals against reprisals from the security services. Protestant ministers opened their churches for public discussions, organized by opposition groups. Because of the decisive influence church people played in the events, some analysts spoke of a protestant revolution.

The citizens' movements had emerged at a time when any political activity beyond the regulated forms of 'socialist democracy' was prohibited and subject to state repression. Evidence of this is provided in the (now public) reports of the Ministry for State Security, which warned the party leadership of the growing influence of these groups among the population. Their number was estimated at about 2,500. In mid-August 1989 the Church organization known as 'Rejection of the Principle and Practice of Demarcation' called for the formation of a broad movement to stand at the next elections as an 'identifiable alternative' to the SED and its Allied bloc parties.

It was no coincidence that in October/November 1989 New Forum became the symbol of change and rebellion. New Forum saw itself as a broad church on the left of the political spectrum and an umbrella organization for the opposition. It defined itself as a movement seeking to facilitate and stimulate a 'democratic dialogue' on questions affecting the whole of society. Their founding appeal stated that a democratic dialogue was inevitable on the role to be played by the rule of law, the economy, and culture. To this end, a political platform for the whole country had to be created, which would enable people irrespective of occupation, party or group affiliation to participate in the discussion and work out the vitally important social problems of the GDR.

On September 12, 1989 twelve people published an 'Appeal for Involvement in Personal Affairs.' Faced with the reluctance to reform state socialism and the ongoing crisis in the GDR, they appealed for the creation of an alliance of all reform-minded people: 'We invite all those who wish to join in a dialogue about the principles of a democratic restructuring of our country.' This appeal was the first public act of the 'Citizens' movement: Democracy Now.' It also contained 'ideas for a democratic restructuring of the GDR.' Democracy Now wanted to 'assist in the formation of a society based on solidarity and to democratize all spheres of life ... the continued development of a new socialism distinct from the one which became bogged down in the absolute dominance of the state.' Like other groups, Democracy Now aimed at a state founded on the basic consensus of society, a *res publica* of responsible citizenship, and the protection of the 'social achievements' of the GDR.

The citizens' movements which predated October 1989 – such as New Forum, Democracy Now and the Initiative for Peace and Human Rights – derived great moral authority from their willingness to speak openly and their long years of involvement in the opposition movement. The citizens' groups sought to bring about social dialogue on the various problems that had accumulated in the decades of bureaucratic socialist dictatorship. This dialogue would be the *sine qua non* for the creation of a civil society.

The dynamic of events was, however, overtaken by the need to set in place new, democratically legitimized institutions – first and foremost a parliament, a freely elected people's chamber (*Volkskammer*) – in order to prevent acollapse into anarchy and economic and social disintegration. This meant that the new movements were forced into making a decision before they were ready on whether to become a party or to remain a movement with corresponding forms of organization and decision-making. They opted to remain a movement, but one that would not ignore parliament.

This reluctance to reconstitute as parties naturally weakened the influence these groups wielded over political developments. During the revolutionary events of fall 1989 and the 'Round Table' discussions with the old regime, they exerted great influence on GDR political life at all levels. Not only were they central in the Round Table of the Hans Modrow government, but they also held sway in the mass media and within universities. This leadership, however, was obtained without ever having to secure the broader consent of the people. Initially, when attention was focused on the removal of the rubble of the old system, they could effectively articulate public interest. As the elections approached, it became clearer that, despite their moral integrity, these new groups could not in themselves gain a majority. They represented minority views, especially in their desire to follow an independent 'Third Way.'

The citizens' groups had been consciously founded as public forums. Their aim was to set in motion social dialogue, discourse, and deliberation about the many and varied problems that had accumulated during the decades of bureaucratic socialism. Given their origins, the various opposition groups were more interested in cultural questions and in grass-roots democracy than in achieving power. An attempt was made to combine the two aspects when the elections to the People's Chamber were brought forward, and efforts were undertaken in January 1990 to present a common front. But these quickly foundered. With the transformation of some groups into parties, the old consensus based on shared values fell away. Yet much that was held in common did survive the campaign and the elections. This derived from experiences gathered during the period prior to November 1989, when the immobility of the old SED leadership and its open support for the reactionary regimes in Romania and China increased the likelihood of growing repression in the GDR and the subjugation of any opposition by the use of force.

Dual Rule: the Old Regime and the New Political Forces

During the revolutionary changes in Eastern Europe, debate focused on two fundamental alternative courses: reform or rupture. The transition from authoritarianism to democracy tends, as was the case in the GDR, to be initiated by factions in the old regime which consider the possibility of reform leading to some form of political democracy. The opposition normally favors a fundamental break with the existing institutional order and political ideology. However, the strategy of a clean rupture is viable only in a revolutionary or potentially revolutionary situation. Paradoxically, transition is sometimes made possible by an 'elite settlement,' negotiated between the old elite and new political groups that advocate a clean break with the past.

The means used to achieve this form of agreement were 'Round Tables,' established in most of the communist countries in transition. Modeled on the Polish and Hungarian experience, the Round Table in the GDR was composed of representatives of opposition groups, the SED, and some old parties and organizations – all with equal rights. The opposition sought to use the Round Table as a means by which to veto and control government actions. As events unfolded, it turned into a form of parallel government which gave itself the right to advise the executive at any time. The Round Table was accorded certain *de facto* legislative and executive functions. In return, it also conferred a certain legitimacy on the government. This lasted until the elections of March 18, 1990. When the new political groups then called for a continuing role for the Round Table, they were reminded of the rules of the parliamentary system.

The institution of a Round Table intended to bring together all social and political groups for consultations was the most important demand of the opposition. By the time the Round Table had its first meeting on December 7, 1989, a dangerous power vacuum had come about. Various reactionary forces might seek to exploit this vacuum in order to restore the old order. While the demise of the SED threatened to deprive the government of its key support, the opposition did not have the vision, personnel or organization to assume power. The result was a 'dual rule' for the old institutions, the government and the rubber-stamp parliament, which gained a considerable independence over events, and the new opposition groups.

From early October a 'contact group' consisting of members of seven political groupings had been meeting clandestinely to debate possible forms of dialogue with the political authorities. The groupings included: the Initiative for Peace and Human Rights, New Forum, Democracy Now, Democratic Awakening, the Social Democratic Party, the Green Party, and the United Left. The invitation to the first sitting of the Round Table came from the Federation of Evangelical Churches, which played a decisive role as moderator. The pact between reform-minded sections of the old elites and the new elites was intended to fill the power vacuum and reduce the danger of violent internal unrest that had resulted from the insoluble contradiction between a political leadership prepared to negotiate and a floating mass unable to negotiate. Further Round Tables were set up at all levels of the state hierarchy and in many non-state institutions. Negotiations at the central Round Table in Berlin were conducted under the business – like auspices of church representatives, who did not eschew productive conflict. The early stages of negotiation revealed that the government, notwithstanding its many concessions, conceded little ground in a number of key areas, for example economic reform and structural reform of the state apparatus.

The initially obstructive stance adopted by government representatives at the Round Table (not only on the question of the state security service), and the government's reluctance to undertake fundamental political and economic emergency measures, underlined the impression that the government and the party supporting it were only prepared to offer concessions when compelled to do so. Further events undermined confidence in the government. A steady flow of revelations of corruption, abuse of office, and the general machinations of the state security service came to public attention. Economic crisis, mounting popular discontent, and clear moves by the erstwhile bloc parties (CDU, DBD, LDPD, NDPD) to jump the sinking ship of the SED fueled a further intensification of the crisis. The new prime minister, Hans Modrow (one of the very few reform-minded top politicians of the SED), tried to take control. He emphasized that, as head of government, he was responsible to the people, not a party. He announced a 'new chapter' in the process of 'revolutionary change.' He called on the Round Table to 'nominate persons who are willing to enter government as members of the government.' At the same time, he provided a government agenda for further legislation to be passed in the period leading up to the elections. This finally marked the transformation of the Round Table from a 'veto organ' to an organ of government.

In an attempt to avert the collapse of the political and economic order and the unforeseeable consequences it would have, on January 28 the government agreed – again *in camera* – with representatives of the Round Table to bring forward to March 18 the elections to parliament (*Volkskammer*) planned for May 6, 1990. The Communal elections in May 1989 – the rigging of which had greatly contributed to the popular protest later that year – were rescheduled for May 6, 1990. Both the Round Table and the *Volkskammer* consented to this proposal. On February 5, 1990, the new parties and movements entered the 'government of national responsibility' and delegated ministers, who brought the number of parties and political groups in government to thirteen. An assessment of this stage in the transition process is mixed. With the election of Modrow, the government was to safeguard changes introduced by the SED leadership under Egon Krenz and salvage what could still be saved. In this objective, the government failed.

The success of the role of parliament during this period of transition is also debatable. It provided a fractured reflection of change in GDR society. The *Volks-kammer* was never a driving force but represented the individual and collective contradictions of the personalities and institutions that in one way or another underpinned the old system. Given that, it is difficult to describe the *Volkskammer* as a parliamentary assembly. It never possessed the legitimacy of a parliament, nor did it deserve to do so. Despite these shortcomings, however, the *Volkskammer* did play an important role in the first critical phase of transition: it assisted greatly in creating a public realm and brought the rulers of the past to public account. The Round Table certainly played a constructive role in expediting change. It was not 'the' people but rather a transitory institution that made a major contribution to enabling the articulation of interests. The Round Table became a forum for the articulation of conflicts of interest between groups and helped pave the way for elections.

The campaigners, in particular the new political groups, had to learn the painful lesson that 'the people' soon went their own ways. In the initial phase dominated by the ultimate collapse of SED rule, particularly in its resolute stand against the retention of the state security service, the Round Table represented 'the people.' From the end of January, however, a paradoxical situation arose in which the Round Table and the government – for different reasons – acted as the representatives of an independent 'GDR identity,' while the majority of the people had long wanted the quickest possible end of that very identity.

The First Democratic Elections in East Germany

Prevented from participating in democratic elections for over forty years, the people of the GDR were called upon to do so on no fewer than four separate occasions in 1990: on March 18 for elections to the *Volkskammer*, on May 6 for the communal elections, on October 14 for elections to the regional parliaments in the newly reconstituted Länder, and on December 2 for the first all-German elections to the Bundestag.

The first free elections of the GDR took place on March 18, 1990 with parties and a new party system still in embryo. In total, twenty-four parties and groupings fielded candidates; there were also five joint lists.

The results illustrated that the voters were in favor of speedy unification of the two Germanys and that they displayed little willingness to break radically from established political forces. This was seen in the unexpected victory of the Alliance for Germany (a joint list by the Christian Democrats, the Christian Social Union and Democratic Awakening, a small citizens' group), the vote for the former bloc party CDU (40.9 percent), the poor showing of the SPD (21.9 percent), the relative success of the PDS (16.4 percent), and the modest showing for Alliance 90 (2.9 percent), without whom free elections would never have taken place. Most observers had assumed after the elections to the People's Chamber that voting behavior did not indicate firm party preferences. However, comparison of the election results reveals a remarkable stability in voting behavior. When the year 1990 ended, after four elections one could summarize by saying that no dramatic changes took place. Conservative-liberal majorities held stable. The party system in the eastern Länder had largely aligned itself to that in the old Federal Republic, with the sole exception of the PDS and Alliance 90, which succeeded in passing the 5 percent threshold at the federal elections. This secured representation of the citizens' movement and the Greens, who failed in the West because of their reluctance vis-à-vis unification.

One lasting effect could also be noticed at the federal elections: a decisive difference in party preferences in the West and in the East, and not only as to the PDS. Since the 1990 elections, federal elections were partly decided in the East. This was true for 1990 and again in 2002.

The Controversy about a New Constitution for the GDR

As in most other socialist countries which had shaken off their chains in 1989 and commenced on an uncertain journey toward a democratic order, the constitutional question also played an important role in the perishing GDR. The radical change in the GDR began as a mass citizen protest against the political and social circumstances and ended as a political revolution that swept away the old regime. As in most of the other countries, a transition phase existed in the GDR as well, in which the representatives of the old regime sat at one table with the new political powers in order to avoid a violent progression of events. The motives and goals of the participants were extremely different. The representatives of the SED and their Allies wanted to save as much of the old system as possible, while the new political groupings were divided. The opposition only had one goal in common: an aspiration for individual and civil rights to be based on a democratic order.

Throughout Central and Eastern Europe, citizens opted for a regime change that embraced free democratic order. However, the design of this new democracy differed from state to state. Similarly, decisions on new economic policies were widely varied. No new political group had a master plan for the future. Thus, the first and most pressing task was to agree upon the course for the political systems. Normally this happens within the framework of constitutional discussion. Appropriately, the regime changes in the socialist countries were called 'constitutional revolutions.' Change meant outlining the normative and institutional contours of the future economic and political order.

The central question in the first phase of the transition, quite rightly, was the shape of the future political order. First, the former political elite must be stripped of its power. Next, the political and legal conditions for a democratic progression had to be established. Democracy, civil rights, and political freedoms dominated the discussion. Questions about concrete politics were secondary concerns at this time. After many years of a non-existent social discourse on basic political questions, the constitutional discussion now played a critical, identity-forming role. For each post-communist country, the constitutional debate was a discussion about the self-image of the society and the construction of the new political order. It was also about the reconstruction of these Central and Eastern European nations' independence. The year 1989 marked the end of Soviet hegemony and the revival of independent nation states in Central and Eastern Europe.

In the first phase of the revolution, when the SED turned over some of its power to the citizens and gave up its *all-embracing grip on power* but still had control over important resources such as the army, secret service and public administration, it was necessary to strike out the leadership authority of the Communist Party from the constitution. The former socialist countries needed to pave a way for the constitutional developments required of a free democracy. Their path was blocked, however, by the former elites that still played a significant role in society, even after regime change. In addition, new democratic elites existed only in rudimentary form. The result was a set of constitutional documents riddled with contradictions and unable to withstand the test of time. A rift appeared between the emphasis on revolutionary reversal and the political reality of the post-revolutionary development period, which led to serious problems of legitimacy for the new democracy.

Constitutional politics played an important role in the post-communist states during three phases of development. In the first phase of radical change, the socialist constitutions were successively adjusted to fit the new circumstances, but remained in force. In the transition phase before the first free elections, provisional constitutions were written in some countries. Finally, after the first free elections, final versions of a democratic constitution were passed or provisional constitutions were rewritten. East Germany was spared this path of long and possibly crisis-filled political development to a democratic constitutional state, because only a quarter of a year after the revolutionary phase the signs of an accession to the Federal Republic, and with that the end of the GDR, were clearly seen.

Only during the period of transition was the GDR constitution of 1974 used as a basic framework. Cosmetic changes, eliminating phrases that gave supremacy to the SED for example, were immediately implemented. But as early as January 1990, the GDR parliament began to debate the constitutional framework of a revised or new GDR constitution. Concrete changes included the founding of joint-companies with Western businesses and of private businesses in the GDR. With these changes came a first step in the direction of a mixed economic order. The changes were tentative attempts to break with a Marxist-Leninist constitutional notion. A step-by-step repair process of the old socialist constitution was not, however, sufficient to shape the transition process. Therefore, the central Round Table created a commission to compose a new GDR constitution. In the spring of 1990 the commission presented a draft, which at first had great resonance. All parties that had participated in the Round Table supported this draft. The draft, which was considered a constitution for a democratic GDR, offered the prospect of an all-German constitution or an improved and modernized Basic Law. The Round Table draft emphasized the direct participation of all citizens in the business of government.

The freely elected People's Chamber faced the question of whether it should adopt this draft, in which the new political groups saw a commitment to the political aims of the fall of 1989. The People's Chamber rejected it. In a symbolic act, it deleted the preamble to the constitution in its first session. But then it could not agree on either the Round Table's draft constitution or a new draft. The coalition pact had left open the possibility of working out a new constitution for the GDR in which fundamental social rights, above all the right to work, to housing and to education, were to be anchored. If no new constitution could be devised, these aspects were to be incorporated in the Federal Republic's Basic Law. The coalition called for the unification process to be organized 'rapidly and in a responsible manner.' The rule of law would be a prerequisite and would be ensured by transitional arrangements that would take account of elements of both the old GDR constitution of 1949 and the Round Table's draft. But in fact this never happened.

At its fifteenth meeting on June 17, 1990, the People's Chamber approved new constitutional principles. These canceled all legal provisions in the GDR that placed the individual citizen or state institutions under an obligation to socialism, 'socialist law,' and 'democratic centralism.' In order to make possible monetary, economic and social union with the Federal Republic, they also determined that the GDR could transfer its sovereign rights to international institutions as well as institutions of the Federal Republic. The GDR was described as a 'free, democratic, federal, socially conscious and ecologically orientated state governed by the rule of law,' in which local self-government was guaranteed. The principles provided for free collective bargaining, economic freedom, private ownership, an independent judiciary, and the protection of the environment. They created the framework for the two most important documents which were to determine how the unification of the two German states was to be implemented: the 'State Treaty on Monetary, Economic and Social Union' of May 18, 1990 and the 'Unification Treaty' of August 31, 1990.

Although the letter document was attempting to seek a new constitution for the GDR before seeking unification, it is still of historic significance. This is not only because it was the final expression of a peaceful revolution, but also because many of the provisions of this text reflect both the positive tradition of the Federal Republic's Basic Law and a concept of modern constitutionalism which is more open vis-à-vis citizen's participation and positive basic rights than the Basic Law, written exactly forty years earlier.

Given the dictatorship of the past, it is understandable that certain provisions were included, such as freedom of movement, the ban on withdrawal of citizenship, or the protection of privacy. Provisions based on basic human decency were spelled out, such as to respect handicapped people or the elderly. Basic social rights such as tuition-free nursery schools and before- and after-school programs or the right to appropriate housing and subsidized housing were included as state goals. Other state goals included the equality of women, the right to a profession or job promotion/creation, and the protection of the environment.

In the light of the peaceful revolution in the GDR, the stress placed on the principle of representation and the plebiscite abstinence of the Basic Law of the Federal Republic seemed outdated. The draft of the Round Table underlined the importance of citizens' rights, such as freedom of association, and of direct participation of citizens in government affairs, and it recognized citizens' movements and their right to access state decision makers such as parliaments and the administration. The anchoring of these civil liberties in a bill of rights was a direct reaction to the experiences of autocracy in the GDR.

The draft constitution drew on the tradition of the Weimar constitution as well as the Basic Law. In an attempt to maintain what was understood as a GDR achievement, the constitution was oriented more toward the civil rights understanding of the Weimar constitution as opposed to the Basic Law. The latter remained the organizational godfather. Again, it is clear that the experience of SED authority also influenced the draft – it was designed to be more consequential than the Basic Law and not only as a constitution for the state, but also one for society. Characteristic of this was a small detail: the draft did not appeal to the 'people,' as had been common in German constitutional history, but referred in a republican tradition to the citizens of the GDR, who had declared themselves to be 'a constituency.' The constitution would be designed not as an authoritative settlement of sovereignty, but as a reciprocal promise designed by the citizens who through it constitute the civil society, and the constitution should be their way of life.

The Treaties of German Unification

Control of the budget is a prerequisite for autonomous action by a political community. In the early summer of 1990, the economic and social situation in the GDR had moved so threateningly close to the abyss that politicians saw no alternative to ending the sovereignty of the GDR except by handing over responsibility for fiscal policy to the Federal Republic. By approving the constitutional principles, the People's Chamber had created the necessary legal framework for concluding a 'State Treaty' between the Federal Republic and the GDR, which on July 1, 1990 brought into being a monetary, economic and social union. At the suggestion of the federal government, prior discussions had already taken place with the Modrow government from 20 February. At the time, talks were still being held about possible ways toward monetary union and a confederation of the two German states.

Later, however, tens of thousands were fleeing the GDR for the Federal Republic each month, attracted by better economic and social opportunities. The abolition of the GDR's currency and the introduction of the deutsche mark were intended to bring the flow of emigrants to a standstill and create the right conditions for the recovery of the GDR economy. But it was also a sign that the unification of Germany was to be completed quickly. *De facto* it meant the end of the GDR, and this is how it was seen by the majority of the population. It also meant the loss of a fundamental part of economic sovereignty and therefore also of political sovereignty. The introduction of the deutsche mark thus became the brand label of the unification process.

Many of the Federal Republic's laws immediately applied in the GDR. Old GDR laws were rescinded and the People's Chamber was obliged to pass new laws which ensured an orderly transition. Even before formal unification was completed, cooperation between authorities took place 'in accordance with international law,' the possibility of legal protection was created, and a mutual government commission was formed for the implementation of the State Treaty. The State Treaty was explicitly conceived as the first step on the path leading to the unification of the two German states. Its preamble declares that the parties to the treaty are determined 'to achieve immediately and in freedom the unification of Germany within a European peace order.'

The treaty ended all discussion about whether certain elements of the GDR's socio-economic system should be retained. It described the 'social market economy' as the economic system common to both states and even provided a definition: 'It is characterized in particular by private ownership, competition, the free setting of prices, and as a matter of principle the free movement of labor, capital, goods and services.' Only after the intervention of the GDR government was it also stipulated that this did not exclude the legal authorization of certain non-private forms of ownership, which would allow the participation of government or of other bodies in economic affairs as long as this did not discriminate against private bodies.

The GDR representatives also argued successfully for the inclusion in the treaty of the statement that 'social union forms an integrated whole with monetary and economic union.' The original formulation had specified that the 'social community' supplemented monetary and economic union. These statements were of concrete significance only to the extent that a series of measures was envisaged to soften the impact of a direct transition to a market economy. In particular, special provisions were made in the field of industrial law, and these remained in force in the eastern part of Germany even after reunification had formally taken place.

A controversial debate about the State Treaty was conducted in the People's Chamber. In particular, Alliance 90 and the PDS reproached the government for not having guaranteed the equal participation of GDR citizens and for simply taking over the political and social system of the Federal Republic. A representative of Alliance

90 stated in a session of the People's Chamber on the subject of the State Treaty that the GDR was being transferred to the Federal Republic 'under the domination of the social system which has developed there.' By contrast, the government coalition painted a positive picture of the opportunities that the treaty presented. Against the background of the catastrophic economic situation in the Länder of the former GDR, the expectations of the GDR government that the State Treaty would create the necessary framework for a rapid transition from a socialist command economy to a social market economy in all spheres of the economy, and that the restructuring of the economy and of agriculture would rapidly improve productivity at the workplace and in future create modern, secure jobs, were all but naïve.

At the signing of the treaty, the speech by the prime minister of the GDR included a statement that was later much quoted. It demonstrates the hope with which the introduction of the market economy was awaited: 'No one will be worse off than before. On the contrary!' And Federal Chancellor Helmut Kohl stressed that no one would be expected to suffer 'unreasonable hardships.' It was not just from the opposition side in the People's Chamber and in the Bundestag that this optimistic expectation was criticized. Important economic experts, for example from the German Federal Bank, had expressed reservations about whether the economy of the GDR could cope with the shock of the sudden impact of the laws of the market and believed that the consequences for the Federal Republic's economic competitiveness were unpredictable. That these reservations were justified became apparent shortly after economic and monetary union: the expected investment by Western firms did not take place; GDR firms which had previously been represented in Western markets because their prices were politically supported were no longer competitive; and COMECON, the Eastern common market, collapsed.

An objective discussion of these problems was rendered more difficult by the fact that the question of the social consequences of monetary union and the 'costs of unification' dominated the election campaign that then began. Not until the end of February 1991, when the GDR had been consigned to history and the gun-smoke of several election campaigns had dissipated, was it possible to comprehend fully the economic and social misery in what had once been the GDR. Only then did government and opposition begin seriously to consider what it would mean if the division of Germany into two states were replaced by a long-term economic and social division. In a statement to the Bundestag of his government's policy, Helmut Kohl demanded the achievement of equal living standards in the immediate years ahead, a demand which, a year previously, the SPD opposition had placed at the focus of its electoral campaign – and lost.

Germany's neighbors did not see the State Treaty as merely a document of economic and social provision. In it they quite rightly saw the first decisive step toward restoring Germany as one state. So it is not surprising that, even prior to unification, the question of Germany's border with Poland was brought up. The question of borders highlighted differences between the Federal Republic and the

GDR. While there was lively debate on the matter in the FRG and the federal government lost much credibility by long remaining silent on the matter, all political forces in the GDR were unanimous in the view that the western border of Poland was inviolable. The People's Chamber and the Bundestag approved, side by side with the State Treaty, a 'resolution on the German–Polish border' guaranteeing that the border will in future remain inviolable and that no territorial claims will be raised.

Although the State Treaty had *de facto* rescinded the sovereignty of the GDR, the latter continued to exist in international law. In a formal sense, the treaty was one between the Federal Republic and the GDR, but in real terms it was a constitutional treaty that nullified large parts of GDR law. If the planned accession of the GDR to the Federal Republic was not to be tantamount to a takeover, then the proper basis for an ordered accession would have to be created in a second state treaty. After long and agonizing public discussions about how and when accession should take place, the People's Chamber of the GDR announced on August 23 that formal accession of the GDR to the Federal Republic would indeed take place. This was on condition that the planned second treaty, the so-called 'Unification Treaty,' was ready, that the 'Two-Plus-Four Talks' between the two German states and the four powers responsible for finally ending World War II had reached the stage of finalizing the foreign policy and security policy preconditions for German unity, and that work on setting up Länder was sufficiently advanced to enable Land elections to take place on October 14. The Unification Treaty was signed on August 31. On September 23 both the Bundestag (440 votes in favor, 47 against, and 3 abstentions) and the People's Chamber (299 in favor, 80 against, and 1 abstention) approved it. The Bundesrat had given its unanimous approval on September 21.

While the first State Treaty was concerned above all with the reform of the economic system, the Unification Treaty embraced all other areas of the law – constitution, administrative law, criminal law, European Community law, international law, and so on. On approximately 900 typed pages almost everything was sorted out, from party law to dealing with *Stasi* files to the provisions of the law on the transport of seeds and other minor issues.

How to Unite Two Different Social and Political Systems?

The treaties of German unification were the product of industrious German officials and legislators. It transpired, however, that these regulations were not without considerable gaps. For instance, local authorities were scarcely considered in the Unification Treaty, and this subsequently led to serious problems. At the beginning of 1991 most local authorities in the new Länder were faced by bankruptcy. The Unification Treaty could also not ensure the rapid setting in place of an efficient administration. Not only were the necessary finances lacking. Of at least equal importance was the shortage of qualified personnel. To some extent, public administrations were having to work with the same people as before but now guided and controlled by western advisors.

The fundamental decisions within the treaty concerning public administration were as follows:

1. The establishment of five new states (Länder) by the GDR authorities in July 1990 was confirmed despite serious doubts about their size, economic performance, and potentialities and administrability – the five new Länder are the same size as North-Rhine Westphalia.
2. The new Länder gained responsibility for administrative bodies and other institutions and the administration of justice formerly conducted by central state institutions according to the federal principle.
3. Western Länder rendered administrative assistance.
4. Western Länder helped in establishing state authorities by sending experienced civil servants to the east.
5. The Federation made available the necessary budget resources for administrative assistance in the execution of technical responsibilities. The money came from the newly established German Unification Fund (*Fonds Deutsche Einheit*) and taxes.
6. For Berlin, which in fact became the sixth new Land, special provisions were put into place, especially a common responsibility for an all-Berlin government before the new Berlin constitution was passed in 1992.

These regulations and detailed specifications in the amendments of the treaty provided the legal framework and factual basis for the reconstruction of the public administration, the judiciary, and the educational system in East Germany. As can be seen in the new Länder, well-established and tested institutional structures were implemented.

Nonetheless, the adaptation of the West German constitutional and administrative system caused some serious problems as well. Initially, it was handled as if it were an exact blueprint for nearly every sector of society. Over time, however, it became apparent that West German legal norms, institutional structures, political procedures, and policies did not fit the specific needs of a post-communist system in transition. This could be seen in nearly every sector of society.

In order to finance the costs of unification, the federal government created the German Unification Fund on the capital market and secured special powers, valid until the end of 1994, to finance the states of the former GDR. This way, the new states were initially not included in the financial equalization scheme between the federal government and states, which was meant to avoid large disparities between poor and rich areas. The plan was drafted in order to save the citizens of the former GDR from the financial burden of unification, while bringing about quality of life improvements. Among other things, the Unification Treaty regulated that the new states would only receive 55 percent of the average sales tax per person compared with the full allotment received in the west. This was to be raised to 70 percent by 1994. At the end of February 1991 this provision and others in the Unification Treaty had to be revised to ensure no danger to the economic and social welfare future in the eastern states. By 2004 almost 1.3 Trillion deutsche marks were transferred (subtracting all paybacks) to the former GDR without a recognizable convincing structural concept.

While the material consequences of the Unification Treaty remained ambivalent, it created the conditions that saved East Germany from the many wrong turns and dead-ends that negatively influenced and stalled development in other post-communist neighboring countries. In particular, after initial adjustment problems, the legal and institutional transfer worked quite smoothly. The transfer of elites, for which the Unification Treaty also set the regulations, worked similarly. However, here the various mental barriers dependent on each individual special situation needed to be overcome. Underlying this, as soon became apparent, were unrealistic assumptions that the economy in the new Länder would very quickly experience a boom. In fact, the opposite was true. The transition from a centrally run economy to a market economy was proving so difficult, that at the beginning of 1991, the federal government had to radically rethink its policies. Major economic provisions of the Unification Treaty had proved to be illusory. The political success story which saw the realization of Germany's unity in one state had still to be followed by the economic and, above all, social unity guaranteed by the Basic Law.

The adaptation of the Western model produced new fissures in the former GDR within the party system, at the parliamentary level, and within interest groups. This led to the widespread sentiment, which still runs high in East Germany, that the former GDR was being marginalized – if not colonized – by the federal government. Even today nearly 60 percent of East Germans consider themselves second-class citizens.

The West German constitution and the Unification Treaty provided the institutional setting and legal procedures of government, political decision-making, and political participation. As with all regime changes, and in the early years of the Federal Republic as well, this does not automatically mean that a democratic system will succeed. Additional factors are of crucial importance. The consolidation of democracy is, to a great extent, due to favorable economic, social, and political circumstances. Compared to other former communist countries, the specific conditions under which East Germany conducted its transition to democracy were, despite all the shortcomings, extremely good. The accession of the GDR to the Federal Republic provided for a relatively smooth transition to democracy and a market economy. In most other post-communist countries this transition was accompanied by severe economic crisis, deprivation, and social conflicts.

–10–

Political Culture United?

When, at midnight on October 2, 1990, the national anthem rang out in front of the Reichstag in Berlin and the flag of the Federal Republic of Germany was raised, a long cherished dream became a reality – if one is to believe the official statements of politicians. A people divided for forty-five years by insurmountable borders was united again in one national state. The victorious powers of the Second World War had renounced their reserve powers regarding Germany as a whole and paved the way for unification.

As is often true with hindsight, it is easy to imbue the historical developments that led to unification with a certain logic and inevitability. But such an approach is mistaken. The simple truth is that, until the end of 1989, none of the participants, whether the Federal Republic of Germany or the Western powers or the Soviet Union, pursued an active policy aimed at unifying Germany, even though it was evident that a lasting peace in Europe was inconceivable without a solution to the 'German problem.' In spite of all efforts to achieve 'new thinking' in international relations, fear of the consequences of ending the post-war order established by force in central Europe was greater than the knowledge that this order was already rotten to the core. It required the spontaneous force of the masses in the countries of Central Europe and the German Democratic Republic to demonstrate this to their contemporaries.

Foreign observers saw more quickly and more clearly than the Germans themselves that the revolutionary changes in Central Europe and the upheavals in the GDR which resulted in German unification represented a problem for Germany's sense of its own identity. It took Germans a long time to recognize that the unification of the two German states had not solved this problem. After unity had been achieved, it could be seen that, in the euphoria that prevailed in 1990, it had been easy to underestimate the many difficulties that had to be overcome if the two German societies were to grow together. Politicians in the Federal Republic had acted without heeding to the skepticism expressed by many intellectuals regarding the problems to be expected in uniting two entirely different states *and* societies. Over more than forty years, the two Germanys had developed distinctly different political orders, economic and social systems, and political cultures.

Political Culture in West Germany

In 1949, when the two German states were born with very different ideas of socio-economic and political order, they were both faced with the task of creating a new political culture. Neither of them could simply adopt traditional patterns of politics, whether those of the Bismarckian and Wilhelmine German Reich or of the Weimar Republic.

When German democracy was founded after the war, the Western Allies and their German counterparts had a common goal: the establishment of a democratic order based on fundamental human rights as laid down in the UN Charter and the rule of law. As the political elites were discredited, only a few mostly elderly politicians from the Weimar Republic – many of them back from prisons, concentration camps or exile, others from what became known as 'internal exile' – could be trusted as partners in the building of a new democracy in Germany. In contrast to other sectors of society – such as the judicial system, education and the economy, where very little elite change took place – the political elites of post-war Germany were the only democrats the Allies could rely on and deal with. Building a democracy after a dictatorship is always difficult. But in the German case it was even more problematic since the majority of its citizens had supported the dictatorship and shunned democracy. Democracy as government of the people, by the people, and for the people, to use the Jeffersonian phrase, is simply not a realistic option under such circumstances. If one, nevertheless, believes in democracy and considers democracy as the only order to guarantee human rights and civil liberties, re-establishing a democratic system in Germany after the Nazi-dictatorship could only be an elite project – and that it was.

The fundamental decisions were taken by political elites, often appointed by the Allied government offices, sometimes elected, who, under instructions from the Allies, laid the ground for a representative political order and a 'social market economy.' The unconditional surrender of Nazi Germany and the obligation of the Western Allies to 'reeducate' the German people laid the very basis for a democratic Germany. The Federal Republic of Germany, founded as a democratic political system under the tutelage of the Western Allies, had to cope with antidemocratic and authoritarian traditions in German society and politics. The Germans complied with the new democratic system mainly because there was no alternative. They could not, as after the First World War, romanticize the old system, and the other alternative, communist rule as in East Germany, was by no means attractive – compliance was a rational choice. Democracy in West Germany got off to a good start under the democratically elected but nevertheless strong and paternalistic leadership of such charismatic political leaders as the conservative first chancellor, Konrad Adenauer, the liberal federal Ppesident, Theodor Heuß, and the leader of the Social-Democratic opposition, Kurt Schumacher.

Another crucial impetus after the war was the need for a quick economic recovery, one that could heal the wounds by rebuilding houses and cities and, above all, integrating more than 15 million refugees into the new society. Burden sharing (*Lastenausgleich*) was official government policy and became a fundamental feature of the new society. These factors led people to comply with the new order. Even if compliance had little, if anything, to do with firm convictions, it offered a starting point down the road to democracy. It took more than two decades before West German citizens became committed democrats rather than merely 'democratic opportunists,' a type that had dominated the 1950s.

A second critical element of the new political culture in the Federal Republic was anticommunism. With the onset of the Cold War, anticommunism and anti-totalitarianism became the binding force for the new democratic system. The new order was established as a 'militant democracy' not willing to give in to anti-democratic forces once again, as in 1933. As it were, the new enemy was the old one: communism. This made possible the integration of former combatants of the Nazi regime without causing doubts about the impact of this kind of reconciliation on the new democratic political order. Inclusion became the shibboleth of the time. However, the attempt to include former Nazis into economic, social, and cultural life had some side effects. Until the early 1960s the Federal Republic had no serious discussion of the Nazi past. West German political culture flourished and was at the same time permanently put in doubt by a collective amnesia.

The Cold War had other consequences. The confrontation with communism produced a political climate that was not favorable to an open and liberal society and what Ralf Dahrendorf has called the 'constitution of liberty.' Without a doubt, the Basic Law provided for freedom and liberty as no former German constitution had done, and the Federal Constitutional Court proved to be a stern defender of civil liberties (for example, in the famous Lüth verdict of 1958 on the centrality of free speech), but the political climate did not favor civic courage. Many a critic was suspected of being a 'fellow traveler' of communism and given the advice to leave West Germany for the East (*'geh doch rüber'*), if he or she did not agree with the commonly held beliefs or articulated a fundamental critique of the government.

When the American political scientists Gabriel A. Almond and Sydney Verba conducted a path-breaking comparative analysis of political culture in five countries (the United Kingdom, the United States, Italy, France, West Germany, and Mexico), they found a somewhat ambivalent situation in the new German democracy, mainly due to historical circumstances. In Germany a passive subject orientation persisted and had not yet been balanced by a participant orientation. Almond and Verba considered the Germans as a people more at ease in dealing with the output side of governmental activity, where government becomes administration rather than politics. Political life tended to be more formal than informal – exposure to mass media, voting, formal but inactive membership in voluntary associations.

When Almond and Verba repeated their study a decade later, they found remarkable differences: the beginnings of a civic culture. While democracy in the 1950s often meant no more than the formal procedures for electing political elites, decision-making and the division of powers, the 1960s brought a 'liberal revolution' in West German society. A new generation called for an expansion of citizens' rights, civil liberties and personal freedom, for political participation, and for more social chances for marginalized groups in society. The 1960s were marked by political scandals that suggested that authoritarian politics were again gaining ground. One of the most serious political crises of the Federal Republic was the so-called Spiegel crisis of 1962, which rocked the boat of the democratic system at the same time as the Cuba crisis pushed the world to the brink of nuclear war.

Der Spiegel magazine had reported on some inconsistencies in military planning, and the state authorities reacted by closing its offices and placing its editor and leading journalists under arrest. One of the authors of this article, Conrad Ahlers, was arrested in Spain, at that time a fascist country, due to the direct intervention of the minister of defense, the CSU politician Franz Joseph Strauß. After a public outcry the government nearly collapsed. Strauß had to leave office and a year later Adenauer resigned in the middle of a legislature. This marked the first time the German public had expressed its anger about an authoritarian style of leadership and a threat to independent journalism and freedom of expression. The Spiegel affair is widely seen as the watershed that divided the 'silent fifties' and the post-war Adenauer era with its authoritarian elements from a more liberal civil society. At the end of the 1960s a new generation rebelled against the status quo. The German youth and student movement was part of an international protest movement started in Berkeley, California, which spread throughout Europe. In May 1968 it nearly brought down the French Fifth Republic.

In Germany the protest movements had a specific edge to them because of its recent history. The generation of 1968 was the first to demand full knowledge of what had happened in Germany during the Nazi era and the Second World War. The 1968 uprising was a fundamental protest against authoritarian tendencies in Western democracies and against the American war in Vietnam. In West Germany, it was additionally a war of generations. This explains why these controversies were so bitter and relentless. It was about Nazi war crimes and the Shoah – not in a general way, but in a very personal way. 'What did you do?; why didn't you…?' It took years for the wounds to heal. Germany in the 1960s also witnessed the beginnings of a civil society, with new social, political, and cultural attitudes and lifestyles. These were the years of the cultural revolution.

A third basic principle underpinning the West German political system and political culture has been the quest for European unity. The very idea of a German nation state had been discredited by the Nazis. Germany was divided and nobody knew how long this division would last or whether there would ever be another opportunity for a united German polity. The vision of a federation of European states could substitute for the loss of national identity.

European integration was also meant as a decisive instrument for overcoming the fatal consequences of modern German history, the excesses of nationalism, and two world wars in the twentieth century. Again, it started as an elite project, initiated by politicians like Konrad Adenauer and Robert Schuman. But the project of a united Europe immediately captured the hearts and minds of a young generation that had witnessed war and hatred. They went to the borders and literally pushed aside barriers. This was the generation of people like Helmut Kohl, and it might explain the deep-rooted normative beliefs that European integration was the only way to avoid a return to the past with war and dictatorship.

For those who were politically socialized in the 1950s and early 1960s, a European federal state was a goal worth fighting for, even more so after 1961, when a German national state seemed impossible. The new *Ostpolitik* of the Brandt government (1969–74) provided an additional political vision that fascinated the German people. In former times, looking to the East in Germany meant alienation toward Western liberal and democratic ideas. *Ostpolitik*, in contrast, in no way jeopardized the integration of the Federal Republic into the West European community. It was meant and conducted as a policy to overcome the harshest consequences of German and European division. European enthusiasm in Germany also served as a sort of substitute for a lost national identity. In a world of nation states the Germans were confronted with their past and left with nothing positive to identify with. The idea of a united Europe, with Germany as an equal partner, offered a positive reference point for identification.

Looking back on nearly sixty years of Western-style democracy in West Germany, one has to come to the conclusion that, despite the heritage of German history, the Federal Republic has developed into a liberal, Europeanized and Westernized society with a stable democracy and a democratic political culture.

The Socialist Political Culture of the GDR

In contrast to West Germany, the German Democratic Republic (GDR) was an authoritarian, if not totalitarian, regime until its very end in 1989. Even after it formally gained sovereignty, it relied on the decisions of the Communist Party of the Soviet Union, and the SED's grip on power was secured by Soviet tanks. Its political culture has been a specific mix of authoritarian traditions of the German *Obrigkeitsstaat* and Soviet-style Marxism-Leninism, combined with elements of old working-class culture.

The GDR took the path of an 'antifascist democratic revolution' and thus brought about a radical break with the German political past. There were profound social and economic changes, such as land reform, the expropriation of large industries, and the transformation of education, to name only a few, and they created the preconditions for launching a new era of development toward a socialist society, one oriented toward the Soviet model. 'Learning from the Soviet Union,' the slogan went, 'means learning how to win.' The radical rupture with the past concealed the extent to which the 'revolution from above' failed to eliminate many a link to traditional German political culture.

Any attempt to analyze the traditions of the political culture in the GDR faces an obvious contradiction: an authoritarian political system invoked traditions in political culture which had been unable to put down roots at any time in German history before 1945. The political culture of the GDR rested essentially on four traditions. First, there was a distinct reform of the traditional authoritarian state. The *Obrigkeitsstaat* had been particularly prominent in Germany, a country without established democratic traditions. Second, the political system of the GDR had absorbed elements of the old workers' culture and incorporated them into the dominant political culture. Third, the SED assumed the right to exercise power as the representative of a movement committed to a political and cultural revolution. It also aimed at bringing about a communist society as the definitive answer to all problems people had suffered from since the early days of mankind. And finally, the political culture of the 'socialist' GDR differed greatly from that of other countries in the 'socialist camp' and was always influenced by national specifics, i.e. the division of the German people into two states and societies.

A further significant factor was at work: since the 1970s the GDR had been confronted with the cultural and political beliefs articulated by the 'new' social movements in the West. They derived from the fundamentally different tradition of historical protest movements, which the SED dismissed variously as antiprogressive, petit-bourgeois, romantic, or radical leftist. These influences played a key role in facilitating the emergence of a protest movement in the GDR. Authoritarianism had traditionally exerted a formative influence on German political culture. It established the principle of the division of state and society, the notion of the neutrality of the state conceived not as the result of a social contract but as the highest expression of authority and an independent institution endowed with superior and unlimited powers. The GDR had indisputably achieved a radical break with many of these beliefs. State and society were seen as a unit; society was organized by and through the state and its future was formed by central state planning. The state was not neutral but the instrument of the party. It was empowered by the historical mission of the Marxist-Leninist party to build socialism and communism.

The Soviet-style revolution from above, which took place in the GDR from 1948 on, left three central pillars of the authoritarian state intact, and put them in the service of the Marxist-Leninist party. The origins and justification of state authority were not based on the consent of the governed. State and society remained united, but the citizens had no voice in the determination of the goals of either one. This never diminished the role of the state as the highest authority vis-à-vis the citizenry, nor did the fact that it was an instrument of the party. Political absenteeism, however, was not seen as a virtue but as a violation of the moral code of a socialist society.

In its place, there arose the mobilization (not participation) of the masses for the goals of party and state, and criticism of the latter inevitably led to punishment. To a remarkable degree, Prussian authoritarianism and traditional modes of behavior rather than socialist ones patterned the political and social system.

The culture of the workers' movement, the second traditional element of GDR political culture, had its roots in preindustrial, peasant, handicraft, and urban-plebeian traditions. It was patterned on the manifold organizations of the workers' movement which included not only its political and social organization in parties and trade unions, but also its welter of leisure and sports organizations – singing clubs, nature societies, the different sports associations, cultural and educational undertakings – cooperatives, and mutual aid and self-help associations. The SED, however, took up only certain aspects of this line of tradition. While the Social Democratic branch of the workers' movement increasingly lost its sense of certainty in such a future after 1945, the Communists considered themselves the guarantors and executors of these 'historical laws of development.' They directed the working class, in whose name the SED thought it acted, to pursue the goals put forth by the party. The workers themselves had no role in their formulation. On the other hand, old forms of workers' solidarity survived in the GDR, such as had been developed during the long struggle for social and political rights, particularly in the world of factory work. Many of the rules of labor law, the stress on the workers' ethos, and the significance of traditions of work were carefully cultivated; later the regime attempted to develop them further and adapt them to the different social conditions. For instance, 'workers' honor' was a normative political concept in the 1940s and 1950s. Later it meant a new self-image of 'leading class' in a technical, scientifically informed socialist society.

The GDR saw itself as following squarely in the tracks of the communist world revolution, the traditions of the Leninist cultural revolution, which was not just a revolution of the socio-economic system but of the existing culture as well. To the extent that they had been realized at all, however, communist revolutions had been minority revolutions, brought about by a revolutionary elite whose ideas about the future were shared by the majority only in exceptional and passing moments. To put the revolutionary ideas into action, an educational dictatorship was required to overcome the traditional state of mind of the masses. Education, not experience, had to create the new socialist man (or woman). In the seventy years following the Russian October Revolution, and in the forty-odd years of the GDR (and Soviet occupation), the elite's time horizon had approached that of the citizenry. They still talked about achieving the communist society as a distant goal, but the day-to-day struggle was over mastering the many economic, social, and cultural problems – not to mention internal and external security threats from the forces of counterrevolution – for which the party could no longer offer ready solutions. The SED hid more and more behind the ritual incantations of the great goals and ideals of socialism without pointing a way out of the escalating economic, ecological, social, and cultural crisis.

Like the other socialist countries, the GDR was a teleological political culture which had lost its *telos* over the years. After years of dynamic social and political development, it had finally arrived at the problem of maintaining and securing its achievements. Everyday life was characterized by new political attitudes and modes of social behavior that were no longer patterned on utopian socialism and the goal of communism, but rather by 'real socialism.' Both the political leadership and the citizenry had settled down to living in the here and now.

This was unlikely to succeed in the long run, however, because the old institutional structures got in the way of the newly developing lifestyle. The socio-political structures for planning and directing the system (and the ideological legitimization of the movement) remained and continued to impose their goals authoritatively from above, with the help of the state and its forces. They had survived the death of the utopian faith. The SED never liked the idea of *citoyen* as part of the developed socialist system. Its hierarchical, authoritarian ideas of society placed narrow limits on the autonomy of individuals and social groups. It insisted that people understand their own life experience according to the official templates of interpretation. Citizens' everyday experiences, attitudes, feelings, and insights, however, were more and more in conflict with the official political culture and procedures of Marxism-Leninism. When the old faith died, the naked authoritarian power of the system became painfully visible to all, not just to its victims.

Unlike in other socialist countries, the political culture of the GDR was patterned by the special national situation of a Germany divided between East and West. Its very emphasis on being a different kind of Germany, separated by ideology and politics from the FRG – the presumed hotbed of fascism, capitalism, and Western NATO imperialism – tended to highlight the standards of comparison between the two. The everyday life and politics of the GDR's citizens were determined, even deformed, by the perpetual comparison with the FRG. The leadership never tired of stressing the social security in which GDR citizens could live, in contrast to the unemployment, material want, and other problems of capitalist society, such as crime and drugs. Many GDR citizens were forever comparing their situation with that of the FRG – especially after the opening of the borders to West German visitors in the early 1970s. Most GDR citizens never had the opportunity to see Western life for themselves until after the fall of the Wall. Until then, they relied on West German television, available in most parts of the GDR, and on the accounts of Western visitors to draw comparisons.

In the 'old days' many – if not in fact the majority of – East Germans had developed a somewhat unrealistic picture of 'the West.' They tended to compare their own situation with what they perceived to be the reality of the Federal Republic rather than with other, less well-off, market economies. This narrowed their perspective, and very few had the chance to make a true comparison due to travel restrictions. Only in the late 1980s were travel restrictions for the general public tangibly relaxed. About two million visitors per year could then gain their own impression of what life was like in the West. But for the vast majority of people in the East, their comparison was still based on their perception of Western society as conveyed by the Western mass media.

While the East Germans enjoyed the highest standard of living in COMECON, their unattainable political, economic, and cultural model was always the Federal Republic. Its image was ever present in television and yet out of reach. At the same time, their view was distorted by ideological slogans, the policy of disinformation, and the closed borders. Imagine the collective shock when, after November 9, 1989, they saw the 'promised land,' prosperous, clean, and orderly, and without political fear.

The Political Culture of Revolt

Observers of political and social developments in the GDR had long noticed the growing contradiction between the official political culture, with its tired rituals and slogans, and the everyday culture of the people. The first West German representative in the GDR, Günter Gaus, invented the phrase 'society of niches' (*Nischengesellschaft*) to describe how individuals had withdrawn from the impositions of the regime to the few private spaces they could create among friends, family, and non-political groups. From the beginning of the 1980s, more and more people sought the niche spaces of the churches and there became engaged in various new causes. It is important to be aware, however, of the marginal position of these groups in GDR society until the summer of 1980 and of their decline back into marginality within six months after the great explosion. For decades, the SED had worked at politicizing all of social life in the GDR in a never ending campaign of production and harvest battles and organized competitions. To believe the official propaganda, the policy of the party was a perpetual spur to daily positive action, as many examples could show.

Before 1989 there had been no organized opposition comparable to Charter 77 in Czechoslovakia or Solidarity in Poland. This distinguished the GDR from the other socialist countries. Charter 77 and Solidarity had roots in certain sectors of their respective countries. In the GDR most dissidents left the country and sometimes, as in the case of the prominent songwriter Wolf Biermann, the authorities even expelled opponents against their will.

To be sure, there had been various informal groups from the late 1970s working in the protected space of the churches, and these were not immune to penetration by the *Stasi* – as we have since learned. From about the mid-1980s there emerged a 'second public' represented by various forms of semi-legal and illegal publications. While – after the popular uprising of 1953 – the earlier opposition attempts had come from dissidents within the party, the new informal groups tended to be characterized by sub-cultural orientations and an avoidance of formal organization. They had no links to moderate groups of reformers within the SED. In addition, these groups had no binding ideology or political vision except that the prevailing political system and ideology were oppressive. What gave their political and cultural ideas such explosive power was their rejection of the party's monopoly on societal regulation, against which they claimed rights of privacy.

As had the earlier life reform movements and the Western new social movements, they postulated the autonomy of private circles of friends and living communities based on religious and secular beliefs, against the claims of the whole society. The power of human communities and their common sense and decency rather than opposing ideologies, such as previous dissidents had developed, overcame the party-centered political and social system. One could sharpen this thesis further by saying that the external events, the breakdown and transformation of Eastern socialist systems, forced individuals and groups to emerge from their respective niches and to organize themselves deliberately as a political opposition. They reached a breakthrough from a socially marginal position with the call to boycott the communal elections of spring 1989. The patent electoral fraud of the SED then sped up the erosion of loyalty. In this way, the groups contributed decisively to the revolutionary upheaval. Furthermore, the ecological, human rights, and peace groups, as well as the growing commitment of church representatives and groups, undermined the cultural hegemony of the party with the introduction of new and competing values and a reinterpretation of party dogma.

Another important difference from other socialist countries was that socialist ideas and concepts still played a decisive role in the democratic opposition of the GDR. There was a consensus far into the year 1989 that the roots of socialism in East Germany – its part in fighting fascism, its interest in peace, and especially the protection of egalitarian values – would remain after the overthrow of the communist regime. This accurately marks the point of departure of the groups that set out to make history in the summer of 1989: they wanted to transform the GDR into a real German Democratic Republic, a democracy under the rule of law, and they wanted to keep most of the 'social achievements' of the GDR, i.e. a social welfare state based on public ownership of the means of production and equal distribution of material goods and social chances for everyone.

Political Culture in United Germany

The events of 1989 and German unification in the following year formed a political and cultural constellation unprecedented in living memory: the incorporation of a socialist society into an established democratic system, which itself had been imposed by foreign occupiers on a people that had actively supported, or at least passively tolerated, the most criminal dictatorship in contemporary history. The political order of the Federal Republic originated from the experience of failure in the Weimar Republic and assimilated the lessons of the traumatic events of the Third

Reich. After 1989 the West German political system and culture had to digest the results and experiences of more than forty years of SED dictatorship, as well as the democratic revolution in the GDR. Fundamental differences between the Western and Eastern political cultures were, the main obstacle to uniting the two parts of Germany socially and culturally, and still are for the foreseeable future.

As significant as the economic differences were, the cultural divisions are more important than anything else because they are embedded more deeply in society, lasting for a generation or more. It is easy to see why political culture would be so different in both former states, given the antagonistic relationship they shared for so many years. When the GDR old regime collapsed in 1989, only octogenerians could have a living memory of democracy. East Germans had only a rudimentary knowledge and no practical experience of parliamentary democracy, democratic institutions, autonomous interest articulation, and civil society. In the revolutionary euphoria of fall 1989, many in East Germany believed that the seeds of a completely new political culture were beginning to bear fruit: the 'desire for justice, democracy, peace, and the protection and preservation of nature' was the driving force for the civil rights movement.

The end of the GDR brought in its wake the collapse of the institutional structure of official political culture. The people heaved a liberating sigh of relief and believed that they had rid themselves of all that had oppressed them for so long. They only gradually realized that they could not get rid of their past quickly, and that they had been more profoundly influenced by the old system than they had appreciated. Although the majority of East Germans wanted the end of the old system (as was evident in the free elections of March 1990), they now faced obvious difficulties in relinquishing it for good. This can scarcely be a cause for surprise, since the people in the old GDR were transposed unprepared into a new social reality which they knew only from hearsay but which had always been held up as an ideal.

Nonetheless, there were those who believed that the GDR offered the opportunity for creating a new, socialist society. Despite decades of disappointment, hope for an alternative to capitalism was stronger in the GDR than in any other socialist country. The collapse of communism again nurtured the hope that this goal could now at last be achieved. Both reform-minded SED members and members of the citizens' movements were left clutching at straws. Both groups sought to build a genuine socialism – a truly just society – from the rubble of socialism. But their view of the Federal Republic shared indisputable similarities with the view propagated by the Marxist-Leninists, whom they had never believed.

Other groups succumbed to the illusion that, by adopting the Western model of economic order, major problems would rapidly, if not immediately, be resolved. On March 18, 1990, the voters elected for rapid change – which meant more than simply getting their hands on the deutsche mark, as many Western observers remarked with a mixture of ignorance and arrogance frequently visible during the process of unification. Their decision represented the hope of expediting a radical break with the political, economic, social, and cultural past and living a life in political freedom and economic prosperity like the Germans in the West. It was only later that many people recognized the risks this would involve, for example to the obligation of the state to protect people from all the risks of life, as was taken for granted in the GDR.

Citizens of the former GDR only gradually became aware that they had pledged their lives to this radical transformation. Like many dictatorships before it, the authoritarian welfare state of Erich Honecker protected the population from the vicissitudes of world economic developments by means of demarcation (*Abgrenzung*) and the ruthless exploitation of natural and human resources. The price paid in terms of the near total demolition of the industrial infrastructure, the destruction of any industrial future for the country, and the exploitation of the natural world came to light only after the fall of the SED.

Even if no revolutionary change had taken place, the concealed economic and environmental crises would ultimately have come to light and precipitated a social crisis. As it happened, these crises were revealed simultaneously with the process of democratization after regime change and the integration of the GDR into the market economy. It is often too readily forgotten that the process of transition from authoritarianism to democracy is not the cause of the crisis. By the same token, the initially naïve trust in the power and will of politics could all too easily turn into disappointment, resignation, or apathy.

The hopes of spring 1990 were quickly dispelled and the great expectations disappointed. Optimism began to give way to resignation in the summer and early fall of 1990, as the economic situation again became grave and the currency union failed to produce the anticipated short-term improvements, resulting instead in an escalation of the fiscal crisis. Even today there is still a widespread resentment in East Germany that the dependency of the past has simply been replaced by another dependency. This is not unusual in the context of transitions from dictatorship to democracy.

The politically prudent if not (in view of the international political situation) imperative choice of accession of the GDR to the Federal Republic under Article 23 of the Basic Law had produced some serious side effects: it inevitably meant that familiar experience could not be preserved and that alien experience had to be adopted. The preservation of familiar experience did not mean salvaging the old political and economic structures. It meant instead that overnight entirely new norms, procedures and modes of behavior prevailed. This distinguished the process of transition in the GDR from that in Eastern Europe or from the replacement of a dictatorship which had not changed the capitalist order. As a result, life experience, behavior codes, social norms, and qualifications were invalidated *en masse* and replaced by new ones which could not be learned overnight in crash-course fashion. An entire society had to return to school, had to learn what its colleagues and teachers in the West had known for a long time.

A new social character was indeed required in the new German Länder, one that was fundamentally different from that of the old GDR. There, both party and state expected unwavering obedience in return for social security and modest prosperity.

In retrospect, the continuing exposure of the all-pervasive character of the instruments of repression, especially the former state security apparatus, the *Stasi*, appears to confirm the simple image that a ruling phalanx oppressed an entire society. It is not necessary to cite the numbers of the many people who played a role in such oppression in order to question this Manichean picture. The official ideology and the worldview propagated by the SED had a far deeper effect on the thoughts and actions of East Germans than many were prepared to admit after the system had broken down. With some resignation the writer Peter Schneider drew an historical parallel with this situation:

> Today we can see that hardly anyone in the GDR had his heart or at least his fist in communism. The whole GDR must have been a day clinic for ideologically abused adults. And we can now see that the SED and the other Bloc parties – just like the NSDAP in its time – were training grounds for clandestine resistance fighters who in fact worked with such secrecy that hardly anyone noticed anything until the end... The exercise I describe is by no means restricted to the GDR. It is passionately pursued on both sides of the border.

The collective suppression of the past could not succeed. It survived either in the form of newly found documents from the former SED or the *Stasi* which revealed the complicity of individuals or several politicians in the injustices of the past or, even more so, in the form of the inherited norms and behavior patterns of former citizens of the GDR, who, despite efforts to conform with the new situation, remained and sometimes still remain incompatible with their fellow citizens in the West. Peculiarities remain. Only the collapse of the communist system revealed that there was something approaching an independent social character in the GDR.

Compared to other former communist systems, East Germany was in a privileged position. The East Germans did not have to struggle over fundamental issues like the shape of the political, constitutional, and economic order. With its accession to the Federal Republic, East Germany automatically became a member of the European Union, and West Germans paid far more than 100 billion deutsche marks per year in support of the East German economy, infrastructure, and social welfare. However, all this could not bridge the mental gap between East and West. Both parts of Germany had, over the course of their partition, developed highly diverse and fundamentally different social characteristics that could not merge simply by amending laws and political structures. Indeed, differences still remain. East Germans grew up in a society characterized by a dichotomy between party-state and society, while West Germans were used to a liberal, pluralistic society and democratic political system. That is not to say that the vast majority of East Germans have not complied with democracy. But just as the example of West Germany after 1945 has demonstrated, the development of sustainable democratic norms, beliefs, and attitudes – all at the heart of civil society – is a generational task. When it comes to establishing democracy, time is a key factor.

The building of a civil society in most post-communist countries was hampered by a long lasting economic and social crisis. The same holds true in the case of East Germany. On the eve of the collapse of the communist system, the firm belief in a modern liberal society based on democratic ideals was generally accepted. But this did not always translate into active political participation. For many, democracy is still seen as a system of government, not as a system of self-government by the people.

Until the end of the 1960s, political scientists tended to regard democracy as a social mechanism that permits the largest possible part of the population to influence major decisions by choosing among contenders for political office. The line was drawn at the level which the 'normal' citizen was believed to be able and capable of reaching. The democratic citizen was to have his or her opportunity to participate. But there were limits to minimize the likelihood of unleashing the worst tendencies, as experienced in the Weimar Republic. This was the point of view held by the framers of the West German constitution, the *Grundgesetz*: they mistrusted what they called the 'unorganized will of the people.' The idea went that direct involvement of citizens in politics opens the space for irrationality and demagoguery. Therefore a strictly representative system was adopted in 1949.

It was the 'participatory revolution' of the late 1960s, and early 1970s which questioned the very basis of this assumption and asked for political participation and deliberation as the hallmarks of an open, pluralistic, and democratic society. Democratic institutions alone do not automatically lead to democratic participation. A number of factors must also be taken into account. The constitutional framework must provide an institutional setting within which social and political participation can effectively take place. The rules of the game must be clear. Participation must be seen as more than a formal procedure, as an integral part of the social and political process.

East Germany has become part of a political system and a political culture that has developed into an active democracy over the last thirty years or so, even though many of the dreams of a participatory democracy in the late 1960s did not come true. As the West German example has shown since World War II – and as again demonstrated in post-communist systems – democracies only provide the institutional setting and procedures for participation, no less and no more. There must be the persuasion within the *citizenry* that participation matters, in other words that formal procedures, i.e. the institutionalized citizens' rights to take part in politics, would alter the decision-making process and the political outcome.

The events of 1989 have brought Germany both state unity and social division. Until November 9, 1989, the majority of the German people were convinced that only politics and politicians were preventing them from living in a common polity. There was great reluctance to admit that more than forty years of division had produced a social and cultural separation. After 1990 it seemed as if the two German societies were drifting apart. This process has stopped, but there is still a cultural and mental divide between East and West. To overcome this divide will last a generation or even more. The 'German question' is not yet finally solved.

Appendix 1

Basic Law for the Federal Republic of Germany
May 23, 1949 (Federal Law Gazette, p. 1)
(BGBl III 100–1)
most recently amended by the amending law dated July 26, 2002 (BGBl I, p. 2863)

The Parliamentary Council, meeting in public session at Bonn am Rhein on May 23, 1949, confirmed that the Basic Law for the Federal Republic of Germany, which was adopted by the Parliamentary Council on May 8, 1949, was ratified in the week of May 16 to 22, 1949 by the parliaments of more than two thirds of the participating German Länder. By virtue of this fact the Parliamentary Council, represented by its Presidents, has signed and promulgated the Basic Law. The Basic Law is hereby published in the Federal Law Gazette pursuant to paragraph (3) of Article 145.

PREAMBLE

Conscious of their responsibility before God and man, Inspired by the determination to promote world peace as an equal partner in a united Europe, the German people, in the exercise of their constituent power, have adopted this Basic Law.
Germans in the Länder of Baden-Württemberg, Bavaria, Berlin, Brandenburg, Bremen, Hamburg, Hesse, Lower Saxony, Mecklenburg-Western Pomerania, North Rhine-Westphalia, Rhineland-Palatinate, Saarland, Saxony, Saxony-Anhalt, Schleswig-Holstein, and Thuringia have achieved the unity and freedom of Germany in free self-determination.
This Basic Law thus applies to the entire German people.

I. BASIC RIGHTS

Article 1 [Human dignity]
(1) Human dignity shall be inviolable. To respect and protect it shall be the duty of all state authority.
(2) The German people therefore acknowledge inviolable and inalienable human rights as the basis of every community, of peace and of justice in the world.
(3) The following basic rights shall bind the legislature, the executive, and the judiciary as directly applicable law.

Article 2 [Personal freedoms]

(1) Every person shall have the right to free development of his personality insofar as he does not violate the rights of others or offend against the constitutional order or the moral law.

(2) Every person shall have the right to life and physical integrity. Freedom of the person shall be inviolable. These rights may be interfered with only pursuant to a law.

Article 3 [Equality before the law]

(1) All persons shall be equal before the law.

(2) Men and women shall have equal rights. The state shall promote the actual implementation of equal rights for women and men and take steps to eliminate disadvantages that now exist.

(3) No person shall be favored or disfavored because of sex, parentage, race, language, homeland and origin, faith, or religious or political opinions. No person shall be disfavored because of disability.

Article 4 [Freedom of faith, conscience, and creed]

(1) Freedom of faith and of conscience, and freedom to profess a religious or philosophical creed, shall be inviolable.

(2) The undisturbed practice of religion shall be guaranteed.

(3) No person shall be compelled against his conscience to render military service involving the use of arms. Details shall be regulated by a federal law.

Article 5 [Freedom of expression]

(1) Every person shall have the right freely to express and disseminate his opinions in speech, writing, and pictures and to inform himself without hindrance from generally accessible sources. Freedom of the press and freedom of reporting by means of broadcasts and films shall be guaranteed. There shall be no censorship.

(2) These rights shall find their limits in the provisions of general laws, in provisions for the protection of young persons, and in the right to personal honor.

(3) Art and scholarship, research, and teaching shall be free. The freedom of teaching shall not release any person from allegiance to the constitution.

. . .

Article 8 [Freedom of assembly]

(1) All Germans shall have the right to assemble peacefully and unarmed without prior notification or permission.

(2) In the case of outdoor assemblies, this right may be restricted by or pursuant to a law.

Article 9 [Freedom of association]
(1) All Germans shall have the right to form corporations and other associations.
(2) Associations whose aims or activities contravene the criminal laws, or that are directed against the constitutional order or the concept of international understanding, shall be prohibited.
(3) The right to form associations to safeguard and improve working and economic conditions shall be guaranteed to every individual and to every occupation or profession. Agreements that restrict or seek to impair this right shall be null and void; measures directed to this end shall be unlawful. Measures taken pursuant to Article 12a, to paragraphs (2) and (3) of Article 35, to paragraph (4) of Article 87a, or to Article 91 may not be directed against industrial disputes engaged in by associations within the meaning of the first sentence of this paragraph in order to safeguard and improve working and economic conditions.

Article 10 [Privacy of correspondence, posts and telecommunications]
(1) The privacy of correspondence, posts and telecommunications shall be inviolable.
(2) Restrictions may be ordered only pursuant to a law. If the restriction serves to protect the free democratic basic order or the existence or security of the Federation or of a Land, the law may provide that the person affected shall not be informed of the restriction and that recourse to the courts shall be replaced by a review of the case by agencies and auxiliary agencies appointed by the legislature.

Article 11 [Freedom of movement]
(1) All Germans shall have the right to move freely throughout the federal territory.
(2) This right may be restricted only by or pursuant to a law, and only in cases in which the absence of adequate means of support would result in a particular burden for the community, or in which such restriction is necessary to avert an imminent danger to the existence or the free democratic basic order of the Federation or of a Land, to combat the danger of an epidemic, to respond to a grave accident or natural disaster, to protect young persons from serious neglect, or to prevent crime.

Article 12 [Occupational freedom; prohibition of forced labor]
(1) All Germans shall have the right freely to choose their occupation or profession, their place of work, and their place of training. The practice of an occupation or profession may be regulated by or pursuant to a law.
(2) No person may be required to perform work of a particular kind except within the framework of a traditional duty of community service that applies generally and equally to all.
(3) Forced labor may be imposed only on persons deprived of their liberty by the judgment of a court.

Article 12a [Compulsory military or alternative service]
(1) Men who have attained the age of eighteen may be required to serve in the Armed Forces, in the Federal Border Police, or in a civil defense organization.
(2) Any person who, on grounds of conscience, refuses to render military service involving the use of arms may be required to perform alternative service. The duration of alternative service shall not exceed that of military service. Details shall be regulated by a law, which shall not interfere with the freedom to make a decision in accordance with the dictates of conscience, and which shall also provide for the possibility of alternative service not connected with units of the Armed Forces or of the Federal Border Police.
(3) Persons liable to compulsory military service who are not called upon to render service pursuant to paragraph (1) or (2) of this Article may, when a state of defense is in effect, be assigned by or pursuant to a law to employment involving civilian services for defense purposes, including the protection of the civilian population; they may be assigned to public employment only for the purpose of discharging police functions or such other sovereign functions of public administration as can be discharged only by persons employed in the public service. The employment contemplated by the first sentence of this paragraph may include services within the Armed Forces, in the provision of military supplies, or with public administrative authorities; assignments to employment connected with supplying and servicing the civilian population shall be permissible only to meet their basic requirements or to guarantee their safety.
(4) If, during a state of defense, the need for civilian services in the civilian health system or in stationary military hospitals cannot be met on a voluntary basis, women between the ages of eighteen and fifty-five may be called upon to render such services by or pursuant to a law. They may under no circumstances be required to bear weapons.
(5) Prior to the existence of a state of defense, assignments under paragraph (3) of this Article may be made only if the requirements of paragraph (1) of Article 80a are met. In preparation for the provision of services under paragraph (3) of this Article that demand special knowledge or skills, participation in training courses may be required by or pursuant to a law. In this case the first sentence of this paragraph shall not apply.
(6) If, during a state of defense, the need for workers in the areas specified in the second sentence of paragraph (3) of this Article cannot be met on a voluntary basis, the right of German citizens to abandon their occupation or place of employment may be restricted by or pursuant to a law in order to meet this need. Prior to the existence of a state of defense, the first sentence of paragraph (5) of this Article shall apply mutatis mutandis.

Article 13 [Inviolability of the home]

(1) The home is inviolable.

(2) Searches may be authorized only by a judge or, when time is of the essence, by other authorities designated by the laws, and may be carried out only in the manner therein prescribed.

(3) If particular facts justify the suspicion that any person has committed an especially serious crime specifically defined by a law, technical means of acoustical surveillance of any home in which the suspect is supposedly staying may be employed pursuant to judicial order for the purpose of prosecuting the offense, provided that alternative methods of investigating the matter would be disproportionately difficult or unproductive. The authorization shall be for a limited time. The order shall be issued by a panel composed of three judges. When time is of the essence, it may also be issued by a single judge.

(4) To avert acute dangers to public safety, especially dangers to life or to the public, technical means of surveillance of the home may be employed only pursuant to judicial order. When time is of the essence, such measures may also be ordered by other authorities designated by a law; a judicial decision shall subsequently be obtained without delay.

(5) If technical means are contemplated solely for the protection of persons officially deployed in a home, the measure may be ordered by an authority designated by a law. The information thereby obtained may be otherwise used only for purposes of criminal prosecution or to avert danger and only if the legality of the measure has been previously determined by a judge; when time is of the essence, a judicial decision shall subsequently be obtained without delay.

(6) The Federal Government shall report to the Bundestag annually as to the employment of technical means pursuant to paragraph (3) and, within the jurisdiction of the Federation, pursuant to paragraph (4) and, insofar as judicial approval is required, pursuant to paragraph (5) of this Article. A panel elected by the Bundestag shall exercise parliamentary control on the basis of this report. A comparable parliamentary control shall be afforded by the Länder.

(7) Interferences and restrictions shall otherwise only be permissible to avert a danger to the public or to the life of an individual, or, pursuant to a law, to confront an acute danger to public safety and order, in particular to relieve a housing shortage, to combat the danger of an epidemic, or to protect young persons at risk.

...

Article 16 [Citizenship; extradition]

(1) No German may be deprived of his citizenship. Citizenship may be lost only pursuant to a law, and against the will of the person affected only if he does not become stateless as a result.

(2) No German may be extradited to a foreign country. A different regulation to cover extradition to a Member State of the European Union or to an international court of law may be laid down by law, provided that constitutional principles are observed.

Article 16a [Right of asylum]

(1) Persons persecuted on political grounds shall have the right of asylum.

(2) Paragraph (1) of this Article may not be invoked by a person who enters the federal territory from a member state of the European Communities or from another third state in which application of the Convention Relating to the Status of Refugees and of the Convention for the Protection of Human Rights and Fundamental Freedoms is assured. The states outside the European Communities to which the criteria of the first sentence of this paragraph apply shall be specified by a law requiring the consent of the Bundesrat. In the cases specified in the first sentence of this paragraph, measures to terminate an applicant's stay may be implemented without regard to any legal challenge that may have been instituted against them.

(3) By a law requiring the consent of the Bundesrat, states may be specified in which, on the basis of their laws, enforcement practices, and general political conditions, it can be safely concluded that neither political persecution nor inhuman or degrading punishment or treatment exists. It shall be presumed that a foreigner from such a state is not persecuted, unless he presents evidence justifying the conclusion that, contrary to this presumption, he is persecuted on political grounds.

(4) In the cases specified by paragraph (3) of this Article and in other cases that are plainly unfounded or considered to be plainly unfounded, the implementation of measures to terminate an applicant's stay may be suspended by a court only if serious doubts exist as to their legality; the scope of review may be limited, and tardy objections may be disregarded. Details shall be determined by a law.

(5) Paragraphs (1) through (4) of this Article shall not preclude the conclusion of international agreements of member states of the European Communities with each other or with those third states which, with due regard for the obligations arising from the Convention Relating to the Status of Refugees and the Convention for the Protection of Human Rights and Fundamental Freedoms, whose enforcement must be assured in the contracting states, adopt rules conferring jurisdiction to decide on applications for asylum, including the reciprocal recognition of asylum decisions.

Article 17 [Right of petition]

Every person shall have the right individually or jointly with others to address written requests or complaints to competent authorities and to the legislature.

Article 17a [Restriction of certain basic rights by laws respecting defense and alternative service]
(1) Laws respecting military and alternative service may provide that the basic right of members of the Armed Forces and of alternative service freely to express and disseminate their opinions in speech, writing, and pictures (first clause of paragraph (1) of Article 5), the basic right of assembly (Article 8), and the right of petition (Article 17) insofar as it permits the submission of requests or complaints jointly with others, be restricted during their period of military or alternative service.
(2) Laws respecting defense, including protection of the civilian population, may provide for restriction of the basic rights of freedom of movement (Article 11) and inviolability of the home (Article 13).

Article 18 [Forfeiture of basic rights]
Whoever abuses the freedom of expression, in particular the freedom of the press (paragraph (1) of Article 5), the freedom of teaching (paragraph (3) of Article 5), the freedom of assembly (Article 8), the freedom of association (Article 9), the privacy of correspondence, posts and telecommunications (Article 10), the rights of property (Article 14), or the right of asylum (Article 16a) in order to combat the free democratic basic order shall forfeit these basic rights. This forfeiture and its extent shall be declared by the Federal Constitutional Court.

Article 19 [Restriction of basic rights]
(1) Insofar as, under this Basic Law, a basic right may be restricted by or pursuant to a law, such law must apply generally and not merely to a single case. In addition, the law must specify the basic right affected and the Article in which it appears.
(2) In no case may the essence of a basic right be affected.
(3) The basic rights shall also apply to domestic artificial persons to the extent that the nature of such rights permits.
(4) Should any person's rights be violated by public authority, he may have recourse to the courts. If no other jurisdiction has been established, recourse shall be to the ordinary courts. The second sentence of paragraph (2) of Article 10 shall not be affected by this paragraph.

II. THE FEDERATION AND THE LÄNDER

Article 20 [Basic institutional principles; defense of the constitutional order]
(1) The Federal Republic of Germany is a democratic and social federal state.
(2) All state authority is derived from the people. It shall be exercised by the people through elections and other votes and through specific legislative, executive, and judicial bodies.

(3) The legislature shall be bound by the constitutional order, the executive and the judiciary by law and justice.

(4) All Germans shall have the right to resist any person seeking to abolish this constitutional order, if no other remedy is available.

Article 20a [Protection of natural living conditions and animals]
The State, in a spirit of responsibility for future generations, also protects the natural living conditions and the animals within the framework of the constitutional rules through the legislation and as provided by the laws through the executive power and the administration of justice.

Article 21 [Political parties]
(1) Political parties shall participate in the formation of the political will of the people. They may be freely established. Their internal organization must conform to democratic principles. They must publicly account for their assets and for the sources and use of their funds.

(2) Parties that, by reason of their aims or the behavior of their adherents, seek to undermine or abolish the free democratic basic order or to endanger the existence of the Federal Republic of Germany shall be unconstitutional. The Federal Constitutional Court shall rule on the question of unconstitutionality.

(3) Details shall be regulated by federal laws.

Article 22 [The flag]
The federal flag shall be black, red, and gold.

Article 23 [The European Union]
(1) With a view to establishing a united Europe, the Federal Republic of Germany shall participate in the development of the European Union that is committed to democratic, social, and federal principles, to the rule of law, and to the principle of subsidiarity, and that guarantees a level of protection of basic rights essentially comparable to that afforded by this Basic Law. To this end the Federation may transfer sovereign powers by a law with the consent of the Bundesrat. The establishment of the European Union, as well as changes in its treaty foundations and comparable regulations that amend or supplement this Basic Law, or make such amendments or supplements possible, shall be subject to paragraphs (2) and (3) of Article 79.

(2) The Bundestag and, through the Bundesrat, the Länder shall participate in matters concerning the European Union. The Federal Government shall keep the Bundestag and the Bundesrat informed, comprehensively and at the earliest possible time.

(3) Before participating in legislative acts of the European Union, the Federal Government shall provide the Bundestag with an opportunity to state its position. The Federal Government shall take the position of the Bundestag into account during the negotiations. Details shall be regulated by a law.

(4) The Bundesrat shall participate in the decision-making process of the Federation insofar as it would have been competent to do so in a comparable domestic matter, or insofar as the subject falls within the domestic competence of the Länder.

(5) Insofar as, in an area within the exclusive competence of the Federation, interests of the Länder are affected, and in other matters, insofar as the Federation has legislative power, the Federal Government shall take the position of the Bundesrat into account. To the extent that the legislative powers of the Länder, the structure of Land authorities, or Land administrative procedures are primarily affected, the position of the Bundesrat shall be given the greatest possible respect in determining the Federation's position consistent with the responsibility of the Federation for the nation as a whole. In matters that may result in increased expenditures or reduced revenues for the Federation, the consent of the Federal Government shall be required.

(6) When legislative powers exclusive to the Länder are primarily affected, the exercise of the rights belonging to the Federal Republic of Germany as a member state of the European Union shall be delegated to a representative of the Länder designated by the Bundesrat. These rights shall be exercised with the participation and concurrence of the Federal Government; their exercise shall be consistent with the responsibility of the Federation for the nation as a whole.

(7) Details respecting paragraphs (4) through (6) of this Article shall be regulated by a law requiring the consent of the Bundesrat.

Article 24 [International organizations]
(1) The Federation may by a law transfer sovereign powers to international organizations.

(1a) Insofar as the Länder are competent to exercise state powers and to perform state functions, they may, with the consent of the Federal Government, transfer sovereign powers to trans-frontier institutions in neighboring regions.

(2) With a view to maintaining peace, the Federation may enter into a system of mutual collective security; in doing so it shall consent to such limitations upon its sovereign powers as will bring about and secure a lasting peace in Europe and among the nations of the world.

(3) For the settlement of disputes between states, the Federation shall accede to agreements providing for general, comprehensive, and compulsory international arbitration.

Article 25 [International law and federal law]
The general rules of international law shall be an integral part of federal law. They shall take precedence over the laws and directly create rights and duties for the inhabitants of the federal territory.

Article 26 [Ban on preparations for war of aggression]

(1) Acts tending to and undertaken with intent to disturb the peaceful relations between nations, especially to prepare for a war of aggression, shall be unconstitutional. They shall be made a criminal offence.

(2) Weapons designed for warfare may be manufactured, transported, or marketed only with the permission of the Federal Government. Details shall be regulated by a federal law.

. . .

Article 28 [Federal guarantee of Land constitutions and of local self-government]

(1) The constitutional order in the Länder must conform to the principles of a republican, democratic, and social state governed by the rule of law, within the meaning of this Basic Law. In each Land, county, and municipality the people shall be represented by a body chosen in general, direct, free, equal, and secret elections. In county and municipal elections, persons who possess citizenship in any member state of the European Community are also eligible to vote and to be elected in accord with European Community law. In municipalities a local assembly may take the place of an elected body.

(2) Municipalities must be guaranteed the right to regulate all local affairs on their own responsibility, within the limits prescribed by the laws. Within the limits of their functions designated by a law, associations of municipalities shall also have the right of self-government according to the laws. The guarantee of self-government shall extend to the bases of financial autonomy; these bases shall include the right of municipalities to a source of tax revenues based upon economic ability and the right to establish the rates at which these sources shall be taxed.

(3) The Federation shall guarantee that the constitutional order of the Länder conforms to the basic rights and to the provisions of paragraphs (1) and (2) of this Article.

. . .

Article 30 [Division of authority between the Federation and the Länder]

Except as otherwise provided or permitted by this Basic Law, the exercise of state powers and the discharge of state functions is a matter for the Länder.

Article 31 [Supremacy of federal law]

Federal law shall take precedence over Land law.

Article 32 [Foreign relations]

(1) Relations with foreign states shall be conducted by the Federation.

(2) Before the conclusion of a treaty affecting the special circumstances of a Land, that Land shall be consulted in timely fashion.

(3) Insofar as the Länder have power to legislate, they may conclude treaties with foreign states with the consent of the Federal Government.

...

III. THE BUNDESTAG
Article 38 [Elections]
(1) Members of the German Bundestag shall be elected in general, direct, free, equal, and secret elections. They shall be representatives of the whole people, not bound by orders or instructions, and responsible only to their conscience.
(2) Any person who has attained the age of eighteen shall be entitled to vote; any person who has attained the age of majority may be elected.
(3) Details shall be regulated by a federal law.

Article 39 [Convening and legislative term]
(1) Save the following provisions, the Bundestag shall be elected for four years. Its term shall end when a new Bundestag convenes. New elections shall be held no sooner than forty-six months and no later than forty-eight months after the legislative term begins. If the Bundestag is dissolved, new elections shall be held within sixty days...

Article 42 [Proceedings; voting]
(1) Sessions of the Bundestag shall be public. On the motion of one tenth of its Members, or on the motion of the Federal Government, the public may be excluded by a two-thirds majority. The motion shall be voted upon at a session not open to the public.
(2) Decisions of the Bundestag shall require a majority of the votes cast unless this Basic Law otherwise provides.
The rules of procedure may permit exceptions with respect to elections to be conducted by the Bundestag.
(3) Truthful reports of public sessions of the Bundestag and of its committees shall not give rise to any liability.

Article 43 [Attendance of members of the Federal Government and of the Bundesrat]
(1) The Bundestag and its committees may require the appearance of any member of the Federal Government.
(2) The members of the Bundesrat and of the Federal Government as well as their representatives may attend all sessions of the Bundestag and of its committees. They shall have the right to be heard at any time.

Article 44 [Investigative committees]

(1) The Bundestag shall have the right, and on the motion of one quarter of its Members the duty, to establish an investigative committee, which shall take the requisite evidence at public hearings. The public may be excluded.

(2) The rules of criminal procedure shall apply mutatis mutandis to the taking of evidence. The privacy of correspondence, posts and telecommunications shall not be affected.

(3) Courts and administrative authorities shall be required to provide legal and administrative assistance.

(4) The decisions of investigative committees shall not be subject to judicial review. The courts shall be free to evaluate and rule upon the facts that were the subject of the investigation.

Article 45 [Committee on the European Union]

The Bundestag shall appoint a Committee on European Union Affairs. It may authorize the committee to exercise the rights of the Bundestag under Article 23 vis-à-vis the Federal Government.

Article 45a [Committees on Foreign Affairs and Defense]

(1) The Bundestag shall appoint a Committee on Foreign Affairs and a Committee on Defense.

(2) The Committee on Defense shall also have the powers of an investigative committee. On the motion of one quarter of its members it shall have the duty to make a specific matter the subject of investigation.

(3) Paragraph (1) of Article 44 shall not apply to defense matters.

Article 45b [Parliamentary Commissioner for the Armed Forces]

A Parliamentary Commissioner for the Armed Forces shall be appointed to safeguard basic rights and to assist the Bundestag in exercising parliamentary control over the Armed Forces. Details shall be regulated by a federal law.

Article 45c [Petitions Committee]

(1) The Bundestag shall appoint a Petitions Committee to deal with requests and complaints addressed to the Bundestag pursuant to Article 17.

(2) The powers of the Committee to consider complaints shall be regulated by a federal law.

...

IV. THE BUNDESRAT

Article 50 [Functions]

The Länder shall participate through the Bundesrat in the legislation and administration of the Federation and in matters concerning the European Union.

Article 51 [Composition]

(1) The Bundesrat shall consist of members of the Land governments, which appoint and recall them. Other members of those governments may serve as alternates.

(2) Each Land shall have at least three votes; Länder with more than two million inhabitants shall have four, Länder with more than six million inhabitants five, and Länder with more than seven million inhabitants six votes.

(3) Each Land may appoint as many members as it has votes. The votes of each Land may be cast only as a unit and only by Members present or their alternates.

...

Article 53 [Attendance of members of the Federal Government]

The members of the Federal Government shall have the right, and on demand the duty, to participate in sessions of the Bundesrat and of its committees. They shall have the right to be heard at any time. The Bundesrat shall be kept informed by the Federal Government with regard to the conduct of its affairs.

IVa. THE JOINT COMMITTEE

Article 53a [Composition; rules of procedure; right to information]

(1) The Joint Committee shall consist of Members of the Bundestag and Members of the Bundesrat; the Bundestag shall provide two thirds and the Bundesrat one third of the committee members. The Bundestag shall designate Members in proportion to the relative strength of the various parliamentary groups; they may not be members of the Federal Government. Each Land shall be represented by a Bundesrat Member of its choice; these Members shall not be bound by instructions. The establishment of the Joint Committee and its proceedings shall be regulated by rules of procedure to be adopted by the Bundestag and requiring the consent of the Bundesrat.

(2) The Federal Government shall inform the Joint Committee about its plans for a state of defense. The rights of the Bundestag and its committees under paragraph (1) of Article 43 shall not be affected by the provisions of this paragraph.

V. THE FEDERAL PRESIDENT

Article 54 [Election]

(1) The Federal President shall be elected by the Federal Convention without debate. Any German who is entitled to vote in Bundestag elections and has attained the age of forty may be elected.

(2) The term of office of the Federal President shall be five years. Reelection for a consecutive term shall be permitted only once.

(3) The Federal Convention shall consist of the Members of the Bundestag and an equal number of members elected by the parliaments of the Länder on the basis of proportional representation.

(4) The Federal Convention shall meet not later than thirty days before the term of office of the Federal President expires or, in the case of premature termination, not later than thirty days after that date. It shall be convened by the President of the Bundestag.

(5) After the expiration of a legislative term, the period specified in the first sentence of paragraph (4) of this Article shall begin when the Bundestag first convenes.

(6) The person receiving the votes of a majority of the members of the Federal Convention shall be elected. If after two ballots no candidate has obtained such a majority, the person who receives the largest number of votes on the next ballot shall be elected.

(7) Details shall be regulated by a federal law.

Article 55 [Incompatibility]

(1) The Federal President may not be a member of the government or of a legislative body of the Federation or of a Land.

(2) The Federal President may not hold any other salaried office, or engage in any trade or profession, or belong to the management or supervisory board of any enterprise conducted for profit.

...

Article 58 [Countersignature]

Orders and directions of the Federal President shall require for their validity the countersignature of the Federal Chancellor or of the competent Federal Minister. This provision shall not apply to the appointment or dismissal of the Federal Chancellor, the dissolution of the Bundestag under Article 63, or a request made under paragraph (3) of Article 69.

Article 59 [Representation of the Federation]

(1) The Federal President shall represent the Federation in terms of international law. He shall conclude treaties with foreign states on behalf of the Federation. He shall accredit and receive envoys.

(2) Treaties that regulate the political relations of the Federation or relate to subjects of federal legislation shall require the consent or participation, in the form of a federal law, of the bodies responsible in such a case for the enactment of federal law. In the case of executive agreements the provisions concerning the federal administration shall apply mutatis mutandis.

Article 60 [Appointment and dismissal of federal judges, federal civil servants, and military officers; pardon]

(1) The Federal President shall appoint and dismiss federal judges, federal civil servants, and commissioned and non-commissioned officers of the Armed Forces, except as may otherwise be provided by a law.

(2) He shall exercise the power to pardon individual offenders on behalf of the Federation.

(3) He may delegate these powers to other authorities.

(4) Paragraphs (2) to (4) of Article 46 shall apply to the Federal President mutatis mutandis.

Article 61 [Impeachment before the Federal Constitutional Court]

(1) The Bundestag or the Bundesrat may impeach the Federal President before the Federal Constitutional Court for willful violation of this Basic Law or of any other federal law. The motion of impeachment must be supported by at least one quarter of the Members of the Bundestag or one quarter of the votes of the Bundesrat. The decision to impeach shall require a majority of two thirds of the Members of the Bundestag or of two thirds of the votes of the Bundesrat. The case for impeachment shall be presented before the Federal Constitutional Court by a person commissioned by the impeaching body.

(2) If the Federal Constitutional Court finds the Federal President guilty of a willful violation of this Basic Law or of any other federal law, it may declare that he has forfeited his office. After the Federal President has been impeached, the Court may issue an interim order preventing him from exercising his functions.

VI. THE FEDERAL GOVERNMENT

Article 62 [Composition]

The Federal Government shall consist of the Federal Chancellor and the Federal Ministers.

Article 63 [Election and appointment of the Federal Chancellor]

(1) The Federal Chancellor shall be elected by the Bundestag without debate on the proposal of the Federal President.

(2) The person who receives the votes of a majority of the Members of the Bundestag shall be elected. The person elected shall be appointed by the Federal President.

(3) If the person proposed by the Federal President is not elected, the Bundestag may elect a Federal Chancellor within fourteen days after the ballot by the votes of more than one half of its Members.

(4) If no Federal Chancellor is elected within this period, a new election shall take place without delay, in which the person who receives the largest number of votes shall be elected. If the person elected receives the votes of a majority of the Members of the Bundestag, the Federal President must appoint him within seven days after the election. If the person elected does not receive such a majority, then within seven days the Federal President shall either appoint him or dissolve the Bundestag.

Article 64 [Appointment and dismissal of Federal Ministers]

(1) Federal Ministers shall be appointed and dismissed by the Federal President upon the proposal of the Federal Chancellor.

(2) On taking office the Federal Chancellor and the Federal Ministers shall take the oath provided for in Article 56 before the Bundestag.

Article 65 [Authority within the Federal Government]

The Federal Chancellor shall determine and be responsible for the general guidelines of policy. Within these limits each Federal Minister shall conduct the affairs of his department independently and on his own responsibility. The Federal Government shall resolve differences of opinion between Federal Ministers. The Federal Chancellor shall conduct the proceedings of the Federal Government in accordance with rules of procedure adopted by the Government and approved by the Federal President.

Article 65a [Command of the Armed Forces]

Command of the Armed Forces shall be vested in the Federal Minister of Defense.

Article 66 [Incompatibility]

Neither the Federal Chancellor nor a Federal Minister may hold any other salaried office, or engage in any trade or profession, or belong to the management or, without the consent of the Bundestag, to the supervisory board of an enterprise conducted for profit.

Article 67 [Constructive vote of no confidence]

(1) The Bundestag may express its lack of confidence in the Federal Chancellor only by electing a successor by the vote of a majority of its Members and requesting the Federal President to dismiss the Federal Chancellor. The Federal President must comply with the request and appoint the person elected.

(2) Forty-eight hours shall elapse between the motion and the election.

Article 68 [Vote of confidence; dissolution of the Bundestag]

(1) If a motion of the Federal Chancellor for a vote of confidence is not supported by the majority of the Members of the Bundestag, the Federal President, upon the proposal of the Federal Chancellor, may dissolve the Bundestag within twenty-one days. The right of dissolution shall lapse as soon as the Bundestag elects another Federal Chancellor by the vote of a majority of its Members.

(2) Forty-eight hours shall elapse between the motion and the vote.

Article 69 [Deputy Federal Chancellor; tenure of members of the Federal Government]
(1) The Federal Chancellor shall appoint a Federal Minister as his deputy.
(2) The tenure of office of the Federal Chancellor or of a Federal Minister shall end in any event when a new Bundestag convenes; the tenure of office of a Federal Minister shall also end on any other occasion on which the Federal Chancellor ceases to hold office.
(3) At the request of the Federal President the Federal Chancellor, or at the request of the Federal Chancellor or of the Federal President a Federal Minister, shall be obliged to continue to manage the affairs of his office until a successor is appointed.

VII. LEGISLATIVE POWERS OF THE FEDERATION

Article 70 [Division of legislative powers between the Federation and the Länder]
(1) The Länder shall have the right to legislate insofar as this Basic Law does not confer legislative power on the Federation.
(2) The division of authority between the Federation and the Länder shall be governed by the provisions of this Basic Law respecting exclusive and concurrent legislative powers.

Article 71 [Exclusive legislative power of the Federation: definition]
On matters within the exclusive legislative power of the Federation, the Länder shall have power to legislate only when and to the extent that they are expressly authorized to do so by a federal law.

Article 72 [Concurrent legislative power of the Federation: definition]
(1) On matters within the concurrent legislative power, the Länder shall have power to legislate so long as and to the extent that the Federation has not exercised its legislative power by enacting a law.
(2) The Federation shall have the right to legislate on these matters if and to the extent that the establishment of equal living conditions throughout the federal territory or the maintenance of legal or economic unity renders federal regulation necessary in the national interest.
(3) A federal law may provide that federal legislation that is no longer necessary within the meaning of paragraph (2) of this Article may be superseded by Land law.

Article 73 [Subjects of exclusive legislative power]
The Federation shall have exclusive power to legislate with respect to:
1. foreign affairs and defense, including protection of the civilian population;
2. citizenship in the Federation;
3. freedom of movement, passports, immigration, emigration, and extradition;

4. currency, money, and coinage, weights and measures, and the determination of standards of time;

5. the unity of the customs and trading area, treaties respecting commerce and navigation, the free movement of goods, and the exchange of goods and payments with foreign countries, including customs and border protection;

6. air transport;

6a. the operation of railways wholly or predominantly owned by the Federation (federal railways), the construction, maintenance, and operation of tracks belonging to federal railways as well as the imposition of charges for the use of such tracks;

7. postal and telecommunication services;

8. the legal relations of persons employed by the Federation and by federal corporations under public law;

9. industrial property rights, copyrights, and publishing;

10. cooperation between the Federation and the Länder concerning (a) criminal police work, (b) protection of the free democratic basic order, existence, and security of the Federation or of a Land (protection of the constitution), and (c) protection against activities within the federal territory which, by the use of force or preparations for the use of force, endanger the external interests of the Federal Republic of Germany, as well as the establishment of a Federal Criminal Police Office and international action to combat crime;

11. statistics for federal purposes.

Article 74 [Subjects of concurrent legislation]
(1) Concurrent legislative powers shall extend to the following subjects:

1. civil law, criminal law, and corrections, court organization and procedure, the legal profession, notaries, and the provision of legal advice;

2. registration of births, deaths, and marriages;

3. the law of association and assembly;

4. the law relating to residence and establishment of aliens;

4a. the law relating to weapons and explosives;

5. [repealed]

6. matters concerning refugees and expellees;

7. public welfare;

8. [repealed]

9. war damage and reparations;

10. benefits for persons disabled by war and for dependents of deceased war victims as well as assistance to former prisoners of war;

10a. war graves and graves of other victims of war or despotism;

11. the law relating to economic affairs (mining, industry, energy, crafts, trades, commerce, banking, stock exchanges, and private insurance);

11a. the production and utilization of nuclear energy for peaceful purposes, the construction and operation of facilities serving such purposes, protection against hazards arising from the release of nuclear energy or from ionizing radiation, and the disposal of radioactive substances;

12. labor law, including the organization of enterprises, occupational safety and health, and employment agencies, as well as social security, including unemployment insurance;

13. the regulation of educational and training grants and the promotion of research;

14. the law regarding expropriation, to the extent relevant to matters enumerated in Articles 73 and 74;

15. the transfer of land, natural resources, and means of production to public ownership or other forms of public enterprise;

16. prevention of the abuse of economic power;

17. the promotion of agricultural production and forestry, ensuring the adequacy of the food supply, the importation and exportation of agricultural and forestry products, deep-sea and coastal fishing, and preservation of the coasts;

18. real estate transactions, land law (except for laws respecting development fees), and matters concerning agricultural leases, as well as housing, settlement, and homestead matters;

19. measures to combat dangerous and communicable human and animal diseases, admission to the medical profession and to ancillary professions or occupations, as well as trade in medicines, drugs, narcotics, and poisons;

19a. the economic viability of hospitals and the regulation of hospital charges;

20. protective measures in connection with the marketing of food, drink, and tobacco, essential commodities, feedstuffs, agricultural and forest seeds and seedlings, and protection of plants against diseases and pests, as well as the protection of animals;

21. maritime and coastal shipping, as well as navigational aids, inland navigation, meteorological services, sea routes, and inland waterways used for general traffic;

22. road traffic, motor transport, construction and maintenance of long-distance highways, as well as the collection of tolls for the use of public highways by vehicles and the allocation of the revenue;

23. non-federal railways, except mountain railways;

24. waste disposal, air pollution control, and noise abatement;

25. state liability;

26. human artificial insemination, analysis and modification of genetic information, as well as the regulation of organ and tissue transplantation.

(2) Laws adopted pursuant to clause 25 of paragraph (1) of this Article shall require the consent of the Bundesrat.

Article 74a [Concurrent legislative power of the Federation: remuneration, pensions, and related benefits of members of the public service]

(1) Concurrent legislative power shall also extend to the remuneration, pensions, and related benefits of members of the public service who stand in a relationship of

service and loyalty defined by public law, insofar as the Federation does not have exclusive legislative power pursuant to clause 8 of Article 73.

(2) Federal laws enacted pursuant to paragraph (1) of this Article shall require the consent of the Bundesrat.

(3) Federal laws enacted pursuant to clause 8 of Article 73 shall likewise require the consent of the Bundesrat, insofar as they contemplate standards for the structure or computation of remuneration, pensions, and related benefits including the classification of positions, or minimum or maximum rates, that differ from those provided for in federal laws enacted pursuant to paragraph (1) of this Article.

(4) Paragraphs (1) and (2) of this Article shall apply mutatis mutandis to the remuneration, pensions, and related benefits of judges of the Länder. Paragraph (3) of this Article shall apply mutatis mutandis to laws enacted pursuant to paragraph (1) of Article 98.

Article 75 [Areas of federal framework legislation]

(1) Subject to the conditions laid down in Article 72, the Federation shall have power to enact provisions on the following subjects as a framework for Land legislation:

1. the legal relations of persons in the public service of the Länder, municipalities, or other corporate bodies under public law, insofar as Article 74a does not otherwise provide;

1a. general principles respecting higher education;

2. the general legal relations of the press;

3. hunting, nature conservation, and landscape management;

4. land distribution, regional planning, and the management of water resources;

5. matters relating to the registration of residence or domicile and to identity cards;

6. measures to prevent expatriation of German cultural assets.

Paragraph (3) of Article 72 shall apply mutatis mutandis.

(2) Only in exceptional circumstances may framework legislation contain detailed or directly applicable provisions.

(3) When the Federation enacts framework legislation, the Länder shall be obliged to adopt the necessary Land laws within a reasonable period prescribed by the law.

...

Article 77 [The legislative process]

(1) Federal laws shall be adopted by the Bundestag. After their adoption the President of the Bundestag shall submit them to the Bundesrat without delay.

(2) Within three weeks after receiving an adopted bill, the Bundesrat may demand that a committee for joint consideration of bills, composed of Members of the Bundestag and of the Bundesrat, be convened. The composition and proceedings of this committee shall be regulated by rules of procedure adopted by the Bundestag and requiring the consent of the Bundesrat. The Members of the Bundesrat on this

committee shall not be bound by instructions. When the consent of the Bundesrat is required for a bill to become law, the Bundestag and the Federal Government may likewise demand that such a committee be convened. Should the committee propose any amendment to the adopted bill, the Bundestag shall vote on it a second time.

(2a) Insofar as its consent is required for a bill to become law, the Bundesrat, if no request has been made pursuant to the first sentence of paragraph (2) of this Article or if the mediation proceeding has been completed without a proposal to amend the bill, shall vote on the bill within a reasonable time.

(3) Insofar as its consent is not required for a bill to become law, the Bundesrat, once proceedings under paragraph (2) of this Article are completed, may within two weeks object to a bill adopted by the Bundestag. The time for objection shall begin, in the case described in the last sentence of paragraph (2) of this Article, upon receipt of the bill as readopted by the Bundestag, and in all other cases upon receipt of a communication from the chairman of the committee provided for in paragraph (2) of this Article to the effect that the committee's proceedings have been concluded.

(4) If the objection is adopted by the majority of the votes of the Bundesrat, it may be rejected by a decision of the majority of the Members of the Bundestag. If the Bundesrat adopted the objection by a majority of at least two thirds of its votes, its rejection by the Bundestag shall require a two-thirds majority, including at least a majority of the Members of the Bundestag.

Article 78 [Passage of federal laws]

A bill adopted by the Bundestag shall become law if the Bundesrat consents to it, or fails to make a demand pursuant to paragraph (2) of Article 77, or fails to enter an objection within the period stipulated in paragraph (3) of Article 77, or withdraws such an objection, or if the objection is overridden by the Bundestag.

Article 79 [Amendment of the Basic Law]

(1) This Basic Law may be amended only by a law expressly amending or supplementing its text. In the case of an international treaty respecting a peace settlement, the preparation of a peace settlement, or the phasing out of an occupation regime, or designed to promote the defense of the Federal Republic, it shall be sufficient, for the purpose of making clear that the provisions of this Basic Law do not preclude the conclusion and entry into force of the treaty, to add language to the Basic Law that merely makes this clarification.

(2) Any such law shall be carried by two thirds of the Members of the Bundestag and two thirds of the votes of the Bundesrat.

(3) Amendments to this Basic Law affecting the division of the Federation into Länder, their participation on principle in the legislative process, or the principles laid down in Articles 1 and 20 shall be inadmissible.

...

Article 80a [Application of legal provisions in a state of tension]

(1) If this Basic Law or a federal law respecting defense, including protection of the civilian population, provides that legal provisions may be applied only in accordance with this Article, their application, except when a state of defense has been declared, shall be permissible only after the Bundestag has determined that a state of tension exists or has specifically approved such application. The determination of a state of tension and specific approval in the cases mentioned in the first sentence of paragraph (5) and the second sentence of paragraph (6) of Article 12a shall require a two-thirds majority of the votes cast.

(2) Any measures taken pursuant to legal provisions by virtue of paragraph (1) of this Article shall be rescinded whenever the Bundestag so demands.

(3) Notwithstanding paragraph (1) of this Article, the application of such legal provisions shall also be permissible on the basis of and in accordance with a decision made by an international body within the framework of a treaty of alliance with the approval of the Federal Government. Any measures taken pursuant to this paragraph shall be rescinded whenever the Bundestag, by the vote of a majority of its Members, so demands.

Article 81 [Legislative emergency]

(1) If, in the circumstances described in Article 68, the Bundestag is not dissolved, the Federal President, at the request of the Federal Government and with the consent of the Bundesrat, may declare a state of legislative emergency with respect to a bill, if the Bundestag rejects the bill although the Federal Government has declared it to be urgent. The same shall apply if a bill has been rejected although the Federal Chancellor had combined it with a motion under Article 68.

(2) If, after a state of legislative emergency has been declared, the Bundestag again rejects the bill or adopts it in a version the Federal Government declares unacceptable, the bill shall be deemed to have become law to the extent that it receives the consent of the Bundesrat. The same shall apply if the Bundestag does not pass the bill within four weeks after it is reintroduced.

(3) During the term of office of a Federal Chancellor, any other bill rejected by the Bundestag may become law in accordance with paragraphs (1) and (2) of this Article within a period of six months after the first declaration of a state of legislative emergency. After the expiration of this period, no further declaration of a state of legislative emergency may be made during the term of office of the same Federal Chancellor.

(4) This Basic Law may neither be amended nor abrogated nor suspended in whole or in part by a law enacted pursuant to paragraph (2) of this Article.

Article 82 [Promulgation, publication, and entry into force]

(1) Laws enacted in accordance with the provisions of this Basic Law shall, after countersignature, be certified by the Federal President and promulgated in the Federal

Law Gazette. Statutory instruments shall be certified by the agency that issues them and, unless a law otherwise provides, shall be promulgated in the Federal Law Gazette.

(2) Every law or statutory instrument shall specify the date on which it shall take effect. In the absence of such a provision, it shall take effect on the fourteenth day after the day on which the Federal Law Gazette containing it was published.

VIII. THE EXECUTION OF FEDERAL LAWS AND THE FEDERAL ADMINISTRATION

Article 83 [Distribution of authority between the Federation and the Länder]
The Länder shall execute federal laws in their own right insofar as this Basic Law does not otherwise provide or permit.

Article 84 [Execution by the Länder in their own right and federal oversight]
(1) Where the Länder execute federal laws in their own right, they shall regulate the establishment of the authorities and their administrative procedure insofar as federal laws enacted with the consent of the Bundesrat do not otherwise provide.

(2) The Federal Government, with the consent of the Bundesrat, may issue general administrative rules.

(3) The Federal Government shall exercise oversight to ensure that the Länder execute federal laws in accordance with the law. For this purpose the Federal Government may send commissioners to the highest Land authorities and, with their consent or, where such consent is refused, with the consent of the Bundesrat, also to subordinate authorities.

(4) Should any deficiencies that the Federal Government has identified in the execution of federal laws in the Länder not be corrected, the Bundesrat, on application of the Federal Government or of the Land concerned, shall decide whether that Land has violated the law. The decision of the Bundesrat may be challenged in the Federal Constitutional Court.

(5) With a view to the execution of federal laws, the Federal Government may be authorized by a federal law requiring the consent of the Bundesrat to issue instructions in particular cases. They shall be addressed to the highest Land authorities unless the Federal Government considers the matter urgent.

Article 85 [Execution by the Länder on federal commission]
(1) Where the Länder execute federal laws on federal commission, establishment of the authorities shall remain the concern of the Länder, except insofar as federal laws enacted with the consent of the Bundesrat otherwise provide.

(2) The Federal Government, with the consent of the Bundesrat, may issue general administrative rules. It may provide for the uniform training of civil servants and other salaried public employees. The heads of intermediate authorities shall be appointed with its approval.

(3) The Land authorities shall be subject to instructions from the competent highest federal authorities. Such instructions shall be addressed to the highest Land authorities unless the Federal Government considers the matter urgent. Implementation of the instructions shall be ensured by the highest Land authorities.

(4) Federal oversight shall extend to the legality and appropriateness of execution. For this purpose the Federal Government may require the submission of reports and documents and send commissioners to all authorities.

Article 86 [Federal administration]
Where the Federation executes laws through its own administrative authorities or through federal corporations or institutions established under public law, the Federal Government shall, insofar as the law in question contains no special provision, issue general administrative rules. The Federal Government shall provide for the establishment of the authorities insofar as the law in question does not otherwise provide.

Article 87 [Subjects of direct federal administration]
(1) The foreign service, the federal financial administration, and, in accordance with the provisions of Article 89, the administration of federal waterways and shipping shall be conducted by federal administrative authorities with their own administrative substructures. A federal law may establish Federal Border Police authorities and central offices for police information and communications, for the criminal police, and for the compilation of data for purposes of protection of the constitution and of protection against activities within the federal territory which, through the use of force or acts preparatory to the use of force, endanger the external interests of the Federal Republic of Germany.

(2) Social insurance institutions whose jurisdiction extends beyond the territory of a single Land shall be administered as federal corporations under public law. Social insurance institutions whose jurisdiction extends beyond the territory of a single Land but not beyond that of three Länder shall, notwithstanding the first sentence of this paragraph, be administered as Land corporations under public law, if the Länder concerned have specified which Land shall exercise supervisory authority.

(3) In addition, autonomous federal higher authorities as well as new federal corporations and institutions under public law may be established by a federal law for matters on which the Federation has legislative power. When the Federation is confronted with new responsibilities with respect to matters on which it has legislative power, federal authorities at intermediate and lower levels may be established, with the consent of the Bundesrat and of a majority of the Members of the Bundestag, in cases of urgent need.

...

Article 88 [The Federal Bank]

The Federation shall establish a note-issuing and currency bank as the Federal Bank. Within the framework of the European Union, its responsibilities and powers may be transferred to the European Central Bank that is independent and committed to the overriding goal of assuring price stability.

...

Article 91 [Internal emergency]

(1) In order to avert an imminent danger to the existence or free democratic basic order of the Federation or of a Land, a Land may call upon police forces of other Länder, or upon personnel and facilities of other administrative authorities and of the Federal Border Police.

(2) If the Land where such danger is imminent is not itself willing or able to combat the danger, the Federal Government may place the police in that Land and the police forces of other Länder under its own orders and deploy units of the Federal Border Police. Any such order shall be rescinded once the danger is removed, or at any time on the demand of the Bundesrat. If the danger extends beyond the territory of a single Land, the Federal Government, insofar as is necessary to combat such danger, may issue instructions to the Land governments; the first and second sentences of this paragraph shall not be affected by this provision.

VIIIa. JOINT TASKS

Article 91a [Participation of the Federation pursuant to federal legislation]

(1) In the following areas the Federation shall participate in the discharge of responsibilities of the Länder, provided that such responsibilities are important to society as a whole and that federal participation is necessary for the improvement of living conditions (joint tasks):

1. extension and construction of institutions of higher learning, including university clinics;

2. improvement of regional economic structures;

3. improvement of the agrarian structure and of coastal preservation.

(2) Joint tasks shall be defined in detail by a federal law requiring the consent of the Bundesrat. This law shall include general principles governing the performance of such tasks.

(3) The law referred to in paragraph (2) of this Article shall provide for the procedure and institutions required for joint overall planning. The inclusion of a project in the overall plan shall require the consent of the Land in whose territory it is to be carried out.

(4) In cases to which subparagraphs 1 and 2 of paragraph (1) of this Article apply, the Federation shall finance one half of the expenditure in each Land. In cases to

which subparagraph 3 of paragraph (1) of this Article applies, the Federation shall finance at least one half of the expenditure, and the proportion shall be the same for all Länder. Details shall be regulated by the law. The provision of funds shall be subject to appropriation in the budgets of the Federation and the Länder.

(5) Upon request the Federal Government and the Bundesrat shall be informed about the execution of joint tasks.

Article 91b [Cooperation between the Federation and the Länder pursuant to agreements] Pursuant to agreements, the Federation and the Länder may cooperate in educational planning and in the promotion of research institutions and research projects of supraregional importance. The apportionment of costs shall be regulated by the relevant agreement.

IX. THE JUDICIARY

Article 92 [The courts]

The judicial power shall be vested in the judges; it shall be exercised by the Federal Constitutional Court, by the federal courts provided for in this Basic Law, and by the courts of the Länder.

Article 93 [Federal Constitutional Court: jurisdiction]

(1) The Federal Constitutional Court shall rule:

1. on the interpretation of this Basic Law in the event of disputes concerning the extent of the rights and duties of a supreme federal body or of other parties vested with rights of their own by this Basic Law or by the rules of procedure of a supreme federal body;

2. in the event of disagreements or doubts respecting the formal or substantive compatibility of federal law or Land law with this Basic Law, or the compatibility of Land law with other federal law, on application of the Federal Government, of a Land government, or of one third of the Members of the Bundestag;

2a. in the event of disagreements whether a law meets the requirements of paragraph (2) of Article 72, on application of the Bundesrat or of the government or legislature of a Land;

3. in the event of disagreements respecting the rights and duties of the Federation and the Länder, especially in the execution of federal law by the Länder and in the exercise of federal oversight;

4. on other disputes involving public law between the Federation and the Länder, between different Länder, or within a Land, unless there is recourse to another court;

4a. on constitutional complaints, which may be filed by any person alleging that one of his basic rights or one of his rights under paragraph (4) of Article 20 or under Article 33, 38, 101, 103, or 104 has been infringed by public authority;

4b. on constitutional complaints filed by municipalities or associations of municipalities on the ground that their right to self-government under Article 28 has been infringed by a law; in the case of infringement by a Land law, however, only if the law cannot be challenged in the constitutional court of the Land;
5. in the other instances provided for in this Basic Law.
(2) The Federal Constitutional Court shall also rule on such other matters as may be assigned to it by a federal law.

...

XI. TRANSITIONAL AND CONCLUDING PROVISIONS

Article 116 [Definition of "German"; restoration of citizenship]
(1) Unless otherwise provided by a law, a German within the meaning of this Basic Law is a person who possesses German citizenship or who has been admitted to the territory of the German Reich within the boundaries of December 31, 1937 as a refugee or expellee of German ethnic origin or as the spouse or descendant of such person.
(2) Former German citizens who between January 30, 1933 and May 8, 1945 were deprived of their citizenship on political, racial, or religious grounds, and their descendants, shall on application have their citizenship restored. They shall be deemed never to have been deprived of their citizenship if they have established their domicile in Germany after May 8, 1945 and have not expressed a contrary intention.

...

Article 144 [Ratification of the Basic Law]
(1) This Basic Law shall require ratification by the parliaments of two thirds of the German Länder in which it is initially to apply.
(2) Insofar as the application of this Basic Law is subject to restrictions in any Land listed in Article 23 [since repealed] or in any part thereof, such Land or part thereof shall have the right to send representatives to the Bundestag in accordance with Article 38 and to the Bundesrat in accordance with Article 50.

Article 145 [Promulgation of the Basic Law]
(1) The Parliamentary Council, with the participation of the members for Greater Berlin, shall confirm the ratification of this Basic Law in public session and shall certify and promulgate it.
(2) This Basic Law shall take effect at the end of the day on which it is promulgated.
(3) It shall be published in the Federal Law Gazette.

Article 146 [Duration of validity of the Basic Law]

This Basic Law, which since the achievement of the unity and freedom of Germany applies to the entire German people, shall cease to apply on the day on which a constitution freely adopted by the German people takes effect.

(Source: *http://www.bundesregierung.de/static/pdf/GG_engl_Stand_26_07_02.pdf*)

Appendix 2

Treaty of August 31, 1990 between the Federal Republic of Germany and the German Democratic Republic on the Establishment of German Unity (Unification Treaty)

On August 31, 1990 Wolfgang Schäuble, Federal Minister of the Interior, and GDR State Secretary Günther Krause signed the Unification Treaty in East Berlin. The Treaty entered into force upon the GDR's accession to the Federal Republic on October 3, 1990. This date was chosen by the GDR Volkskammer on August 23, 1990.

The Federal Republic of Germany and the German Democratic Republic,

Resolved to achieve in free self-determination the unity of Germany in peace and freedom as an equal partner in the community of nations,

Mindful of the desire of the people in both parts of Germany to live together in peace and freedom in a democratic and social federal state governed by the rule of law,

In grateful respect to those who peacefully helped freedom prevail and who have unswervingly adhered to the task of establishing German unity and are achieving it,

Aware of the continuity of German history and bearing in mind the special responsibility arising from our past for a democratic development in Germany committed to respect for human rights and to peace,

Seeking through German unity to contribute to the unification of Europe and to the building of a peaceful European order in which borders no longer divide and which ensures that all European nations can live together in a spirit of mutual trust,

Aware that the inviolability of frontiers and of the territorial integrity and sovereignty of all states in Europe within their frontiers constitutes a fundamental condition for peace,

Have agreed to conclude a Treaty on the Establishment of German Unity, containing the following provisions:

CHAPTER I

EFFECT OF ACCESSION

ARTICLE 1

LÄNDER

(1) Upon the accession of the German Democratic Republic to the Federal Republic of Germany in accordance with Article 23 of the Basic Law taking effect on 3 October 1990 the Länder of Brandenburg, Mecklenburg-Western Pomerania, Saxony, Saxony-Anhalt and Thuringia shall become Länder of the Federal Republic of Germany.[1] The establishment of these Länder and their boundaries shall be governed by the provisions of the Constitutional Act of 22 July 1990 on the Establishment of Länder in the German Democratic Republic (Länder Establishment Act) (Law Gazette I, No. 51, p. 955) in accordance with Annex II.

(2) The 23 boroughs of Berlin shall form Land Berlin.

ARTICLE 2

CAPITAL CITY, DAY OF GERMAN UNITY

(1) The capital of Germany shall be Berlin. The seat of the parliament and government shall be decided after the establishment of German unity.

(2) October 3 shall be a public holiday known as the Day of German Unity.

CHAPTER II

BASIC LAW

ARTICLE 3

ENTRY INTO FORCE OF THE BASIC LAW

Upon the accession taking effect, the Basic Law of the – Federal Republic of Germany, as published in the Federal Law Gazette Part III No. 100–1, and last amended by the Act of 21 December 1983 (Federal Law Gazette I, p. 1481), shall enter into force in the Länder of Brandenburg, Mecklenburg-Western Pomerania, Saxony, Saxony-Anhalt and Thuringia and in the part of Land Berlin where it has not been valid to date,[2] subject to the amendments arising from Article 4, unless otherwise provided in the Treaty.

ARTICLE 4

AMENDMENTS TO THE BASIC LAW RESULTING FROM ACCESSION

The Basic Law of the Federal Republic of Germany shall be amended as follows:

1. The Preamble shall read as follows:

'Conscious of their responsibility before God and men,

Animated by the resolve to serve world peace as an equal partner in a united Europe, the German people have adopted, by virtue of their constituent power, this Basic Law.

The Germans in the Länder of Baden-Württemberg, Bavaria, Berlin, Brandenburg, Bremen, Hamburg, Hesse, Lower Saxony, Mecklenburg-Western Pomerania, North-Rhine/Westphalia, Rhineland-Palatinate, Saarland, Saxony, Saxony-Anhalt, Schleswig-Holstein and Thuringia have achieved the unity and freedom of Germany in free self-determination. This Basic Law is thus valid for the entire German People.'

2. Article 23 shall be repealed.

3. Article 51 (2) shall read as follows:

'(2) Each Land shall have at least three votes; Länder with more than two million inhabitants shall have four, Länder with more than six million inhabitants five, and Länder with more than seven million inhabitants six votes.'[3]

4. The existing text of Article 135a[4] shall become paragraph 1. The following paragraph shall be inserted after paragraph 1:

'(2) Paragraph 1 above shall be applied mutatis mutandis to liabilities of the German Democratic Republic or its legal entities as well as to liabilities of the Federation or other corporate bodies and institutions under public law which are connected with the transfer of properties of the German Democratic Republic to the Federation, Länder and communes (Gemeinden), and to liabilities arising from measures taken by the German Democratic Republic or its legal entities.'

5. The following new Article 143 shall be inserted in the Basic Law:

'Article 143

(1) Law in the territory specified in Article 3 of the Unification Treaty may deviate from provisions of this Basic Law for a period not extending beyond 31 December 1992 in so far as and as long as no complete adjustment to the order of the Basic Law can be achieved as a consequence of the different conditions. Deviations must not violate Article 19 (2)[5] and must be compatible with the principles set out in Article 79 (3).[6]

(2) Deviations from sections II, VIII, VIIIa, IX, X and XI are permissible for a period not extending beyond December 31, 1995.

(3) Notwithstanding paragraphs 1 and 2 above, Article 41 of the Unification Treaty and the rules for its implementation shall remain valid in so far as they provide for the irreversibility of interferences with property in the territory specified in Article 3 of the said Treaty.'

6. Article 146 shall read as follows:

'Article 146

This Basic Law, which is valid for the entire German people following the achievement of the unity and freedom of Germany, shall cease to be in force on the day on which a constitution adopted by a free decision of the German people comes into force.'

ARTICLE 5

FUTURE AMENDMENTS TO THE CONSTITUTION

The Governments of the two Contracting Parties recommend to the legislative bodies of the united Germany[7] that within two years they should deal with the questions regarding amendments or additions to the Basic Law as raised in connection with German unification, in particular

– with regard to the relationship between the Federation and the Länder in accordance with the Joint Resolution of the Minister Presidents of July 5, 1990,[8]

– with regard to the possibility of restructuring the Berlin/Brandenburg area in derogation of the provisions of Article 29 of the Basic Law[9] by way of an agreement between the Länder concerned,

– with considerations on introducing state objectives into the Basic Law, and

– with the question of applying Article 146 of the Basic Law and of holding a referendum in this context.

…

CHAPTER III

HARMONIZATION OF LAW

ARTICLE 8

EXTENSION OF FEDERAL LAW

Upon the accession taking effect, federal law shall enter into force in the territory specified in Article 3 of this Treaty unless its area of application is restricted to certain Länder or parts of Länder of the Federal Republic of Germany and unless otherwise provided in this Treaty, notably Annex I.

ARTICLE 9

CONTINUED VALIDITY OF LAW OF THE GERMAN DEMOCRATIC REPUBLIC

(1) Law of the German Democratic Republic valid at the time of the signing of this Treaty which is Land Law according to the distribution of competence under the

Basic Law shall remain in force in so far as it is compatible with the Basic Law, notwithstanding Article 143, with the federal law put into force in the territory specified in Article 3 of this Treaty and with the directly applicable law of the European Communities, and unless otherwise provided in this Treaty. Law of the German Democratic Republic which is federal law according to the distribution of competence under the Basic Law and which refers to matters not regulated uniformly at the federal level shall continue to be valid as Land Law under the conditions set out in the first sentence pending a settlement by the federal legislator ...

ARTICLE 10

LAW OF THE EUROPEAN COMMUNITIES

(1) Upon the accession taking effect, the Treaties on the European Communities together with their amendments and supplements as well as the international agreements, treaties and resolutions which have come into force in connection with those Treaties shall apply in the territory specified in Article 3 of this Treaty.

(2) Upon the accession taking effect, the legislative acts enacted on the basis of the Treaties on the European Communities shall apply in the territory specified in Article 3 of this Treaty unless the competent institutions of the European Communities enact exemptions. These exemptions are intended to take account of administrative requirements and help avoid economic difficulties.

(3) Legislative acts of the European Communities whose implementation or execution comes under the responsibility of the Länder shall be implemented or executed by the latter through provisions under Land Law.

CHAPTER IV

INTERNATIONAL TREATIES AND AGREEMENTS

ARTICLE 11

TREATIES OF THE FEDERAL REPUBLIC OF GERMANY

The Contracting Parties proceed on the understanding that international treaties and agreements to which the Federal Republic of Germany is a contracting party, including treaties establishing membership of international organizations or institutions, shall retain their validity and that the rights and obligations arising therefrom, with the exception of the treaties named in Annex I, shall also relate to the territory specified in Article 3 of this Treaty. Where adjustments become necessary in individual cases, the all-German government shall consult with the respective contracting parties.

ARTICLE 12

TREATIES OF THE GERMAN DEMOCRATIC REPUBLIC

(1) The Contracting Parties are agreed that, in connection with the establishment of German unity, international treaties of the German Democratic Republic shall

be discussed with the contracting parties concerned with a view to regulating or confirming their continued application, adjustment or expiry, taking into account protection of confidence, the interests of the states concerned, the treaty obligations of the Federal Republic of Germany as well as the principles of a free, democratic basic order governed by the rule of law, and respecting the competence of the European Communities.

(2) The united Germany shall determine its position with regard to the adoption of international treaties of the German Democratic Republic following consultations with the respective contracting parties and with the European Communities where the latter's competence is affected.

(3) Should the united Germany intend to accede to international organizations or other multilateral treaties of which the German Democratic Republic but not the Federal Republic of Germany is a member, agreement shall be reached with the respective contracting parties and with the European Communities where the latter's competence is affected.

CHAPTER V

PUBLIC ADMINISTRATION AND THE ADMINISTRATION OF JUSTICE

ARTICLE 13

FUTURE STATUS OF INSTITUTIONS

(1) Administrative bodies and other institutions serving the purposes of public administration or the administration of justice in the territory specified in Article 3 of this Treaty shall pass under the authority of the government of the Land in which they are located. Institutions whose sphere of activities transcends the boundaries of a Land shall come under the joint responsibility of the Länder concerned. Where institutions consist of several branches each of which is in a position to carry out its activities independently, the branches shall come under the responsibility of the government of the respective Land in which they are located. The Land government shall be responsible for the transfer of winding-up. Section 22 of the Länder Establishment Act of July 22, 1990 shall remain unaffected.

(2) To the extent that before the accession took effect the institutions or branches mentioned in paragraph 1, first sentence, performed tasks that are incumbent upon the Federation according to the distribution of competence under the Basic Law they shall be subject to the competent supreme federal authorities. The latter shall be responsible for the transfer of winding-up.

(3) Institutions under paragraph 1 and 2 above shall also include such

1. cultural, educational, scientific and sports institutions,

2. radio and television establishments as come under the responsibility of public administrative bodies.

...

Notes

1. On August 23, 1990 the East German Volkskammer voted in favor of the accession of the German Democratic Republic to the Federal Republic of Germany with effect from October 3, 1990. 363 of the 400 members were present, 294 voted for, 62 against, and there were 7 abstentions.

2. I.e. East Berlin.

3. Old version: ,Each Land shall have at least three votes; Länder with more than 2 million inhabitants shall have four, Länder with more than 6 million inhabitants five votes.'

4. Article 135a of the Basic Law concerns the procedure for settling the liabilities of the German Reich and the former Land of Prussia as well as a number of cases of the immediate post-war era.

5. Article 19 (2) of the Basic Law: 'In no case may the essential content of a basic right be encroached upon.'

6. Article 79 (3) of the Basic Law: 'Amendments of the Basic Law affecting the division of the Federation into Länder, the participation of the Länder in legislation, or the basic principles laid down in articles 1 and 20, shall be inadmissible.' Article 1 concerns human dignity and the state's duty to protect it. Article 20 relates to the fundamental structure of the state and the right to resist anyone seeking to abolish the constitutional order.

7. The legislative bodies of the Federal Republic of Germany are the German Bundestag as the directly elected parliament and the Bundesrat (Federal Council) representing the Länder (federal states).

8. Decision of the Minister Presidents of the Länder amending the number of votes of each Land in the Bundesrat.

9. Article 29 of the Basic Law concerns the reorganization of the federal territory through the formation of new Länder.

(Source: *The Unification of Germany in 1990. A Documentation*. Bonn: Press and Information Office of the Federal Government, 1991)

Appendix 3

Treaty of September 12, 1990 on the Final Settlement with Respect to Germany

The Federal Republic of Germany, the German Democratic Republic, the French Republic, the Union of Soviet Socialist Republics, the United Kingdom of Great Britain and Northern Ireland and the United States of America,

Conscious of the fact that their peoples have been living together in peace since 1945;

Mindful of the recent historic changes in Europe which make it possible to overcome the division of the continent;

Having regard to the rights and responsibilities of the Four Powers relating to Berlin and to Germany as a whole, and the corresponding wartime and post-war agreements and decisions of the Four Powers;

Resolved in accordance with their obligations under the Charter of the United Nations to develop friendly relations among nations based on respect for the principle of equal rights and self-determination of peoples, and to take other appropriate measures to strengthen universal peace;

Recalling the principles of the Final Act of the Conference on Security and Cooperation in Europe, signed in Helsinki;

Recognizing that those principles have laid firm foundations for the establishment of a just and lasting peaceful order in Europe;

Determined to take account of everyone's security interests;

Convinced of the need finally to overcome antagonism and to develop cooperation in Europe;

Confirming their readiness to reinforce security, in particular by adopting effective arms control, disarmament and confidence-building measures; their willingness not to regard each other as adversaries but to work for a relationship of trust and co-operation and accordingly their readiness to consider positively setting up appropriate institutional arrangements within the framework of the Conference on Security and Cooperation in Europe;

Welcoming the fact that the German people, freely exercising their right of self-determination, have expressed their will to bring about the unity of Germany as a state so that they will be able to serve the peace of the world as an equal and sovereign partner in a united Europe;

Convinced that the unification of Germany as a state with definitive borders is a significant contribution to peace and stability in Europe;

Intending to conclude the final settlement with respect to Germany;

Recognizing that thereby, and with the unification of Germany as a democratic and peaceful state, the rights and responsibilities of the Four Powers relating to Berlin and to Germany as a whole lose their function;

Represented by their Ministers for Foreign Affairs who, in accordance with the Ottawa Declaration of February 13, 1990, met in Bonn on May 5, 1990, in Berlin on June 22, 1990, in Paris on July 17, 1990 with the participation of the Minister for Foreign Affairs of the Republic of Poland, and in Moscow on September 12, 1990;

Have agreed as follows;

ARTICLE 1

(1) The united Germany shall comprise the territory of the Federal Republic of Germany, the German Democratic Republic and the whole of Berlin. Its external borders shall be the borders of the Federal Republic of Germany and the German Democratic Republic and shall be definitive from the date on which the present Treaty comes into force. The confirmation of the definitive nature of the borders of the united Germany is an essential element of the peaceful order in Europe.

(2) The united Germany and the Republic of Poland shall confirm the existing border between them in a treaty that is binding under international law.

(3) The united Germany has no territorial claims whatsoever against other states and shall not assert any in the future.

(4) The Governments of the Federal Republic of Germany and the German Democratic Republic shall ensure that the constitution of the united Germany does not contain any provision incompatible with these principles. This applies accordingly to the provisions laid down in the preamble, the second sentence of Article 23, and Article 146 of the Basic Law for the Federal Republic of Germany.[1]

(5) The Governments of the French Republic, the Union of Soviet Socialist Republics, the United Kingdom of Great Britain and Northern Ireland and the United States of America take formal note of the corresponding commitments and declarations by the Governments of the Federal Republic of Germany and the German Democratic Republic and declare that their implementation will confirm the definitive nature of the united Germany's borders.

ARTICLE 2

The Governments of the Federal Republic of Germany and the German Democratic Republic reaffirm their declarations that only peace will emanate from German soil. According to the constitution of the united Germany, acts tending to and undertaken with the intent to disturb the peaceful relations between nations, especially to prepare for aggressive war, are unconstitutional and a punishable offence.[2] The Governments of the Federal Republic of Germany and the German Democratic Republic declare that the united Germany will never employ any of its weapons except in accordance with its constitution and the Charter of the United Nations.

ARTICLE 3

(1) The Governments of the Federal Republic of Germany and the German Democratic Republic reaffirm their renunciation of the manufacture and possession of and control over nuclear, biological and chemical weapons. They declare that the united Germany, too, will abide by these commitments. In particular, rights and obligations arising from the Treaty on the Non-Proliferation of Nuclear Weapons of 1 July 1968 will continue to apply to the united Germany.

(2) ...

(3) ...

ARTICLE 4

(1) The Governments of the Federal Republic of Germany, the German Democratic Republic and the Union of Soviet Socialist Republics state that the united Germany and the Union of Soviet Socialist Republics will settle by treaty the conditions for and the duration of the presence of Soviet armed forces on the territory of the present German Democratic Republic and of Berlin as well as the conduct of the withdrawal of these armed forces which will be completed by the end of 1994, in connection with the implementation of the undertaking of the Federal Republic of Germany and the German Democratic Republic referred to in paragraph 2 of Article 3 of the present Treaty.

(2) The Governments of the French Republic, the United Kingdom of Great Britain and Northern Ireland and the United States of America take note of this statement.

ARTICLE 5

(1) Until the completion of the withdrawal of the Soviet armed forces from the territory of the present German Democratic Republic and of Berlin in accordance with Article 4 of the present Treaty, only German territorial defense units which are not integrated into the alliance structures to which German armed forces in the rest of German territory are assigned will be stationed in that territory as armed forces of the united Germany. During that period and subject to the provisions of paragraph 2

of this Article, armed forces of other states will not be stationed in that territory or carry out any other military activity there.

(2) For the duration of the presence of Soviet armed forces in the territory of the present German Democratic Republic and of Berlin, armed forces of the French Republic, the United Kingdom of Great Britain and Northern Ireland and the United States of America will, upon German request, remain stationed in Berlin by agreement to this effect between the Government of the united Germany and the Governments of the states concerned...

(3) ...

ARTICLE 6

The right of the united Germany to belong to alliances, with all the rights and responsibilities arising therefrom, shall not be affected by the present Treaty.

ARTICLE 7

(1) The French Republic, the Union of Soviet Socialist Republics, the United Kingdom of Great Britain and Northern Ireland and the United States of America hereby terminate their rights and responsibilities relating to Berlin and to Germany as a whole. As a result, the corresponding, related quadripartite agreements, decisions and practices are terminated and all related Four Power institutions are dissolved.

(2) The united Germany shall have accordingly full sovereignty over its internal and external affairs.

...

AGREED MINUTE

to the Treaty on the Final Settlement with respect to Germany of September 12, 1990.

Any questions with respect to the application of the word 'deployed' as used in the last sentence of paragraph 3 of Article 5 will be decided by the government of the united Germany in a reasonable and responsible way taking into account the security interests of each Contracting Party as set forth in the preamble.

Notes

1   This requirement was fulfilled by the provisions of Article 4 amending the Basic Law.

2   Article 26 of the Basic Law reads: 'Acts tending to and undertaken with the intent to disturb the peaceful relations between nations, especially to prepare for aggressive war, shall be unconstitutional. They shall be made a punishable offence.'

(Source: *The Unification of Germany in 1990. A Documentation.* Bonn: Press and Information Office of the Federal Government, 1991)

Suggestions for Further Reading

Textbooks

Beyme, Klaus von (2004): *Das politische System der Bundesrepublik Deutschland. Eine Einführung*. Wiesbaden: Verlag Sozialwissenschaften.

Dalton, Russel J. (1993): *Politics in Germany*. New York: HarperCollins College Publishers.

Facts about Germany. Published by the Press and Information Office of the Federal Government. https://www.tatsachen-neber-deutschland.de/389.0.html

Glaeßner, Gert-Joachim (1999): *Demokratie und Politik in Deutschland*. Opladen: Leske+Budrich.

Hancock, M. Donald (1989): *West Germany. The Politics of Democratic Corporatism*. Chatham NJ: Chatham House Publishers.

Padgett, Stephen/William E. Paterson/Gordon Smith, eds. (2003): *Developments in German Politics 3*. Basingstoke: Palgrave Macmillan.

Sontheimer, Kurt/Wilhelm Bleek (2002): *Grundzüge des politischen Systems Deutschlands*. Munich: Piper Verlag.

Chapter 1

Glees, Anthony (1996): *Reinventing Germany. German Political Development since 1945*. Oxford: Berg.

Görtemaker, Manfred (1999): *Geschichte der Bundesrepublik Deutschland. Von der Gründung bis zur Gegenwart*. München: C.H. Beck.

Krisch, Henry (1974): *German Politics under Soviet Occupation*. New York: Columbia University Press.

Politics and Government in Germany 1944–1994. Basic Documents. Providence/Oxford: Berghan Books.

Pultzer, Peter (1995): *German Politics 1945–1995*. Oxford: Oxford University Press.

Turner, Henry (1987): *The Two Germanys since 1945*. New Haven/London: Yale University Press.

Chapter 2

Basic Law for the Federal Republic of Germany, May 23, 1949 (*Federal Law Gazette* BGBl III 100–1; http://www.bundesregierung.de/static/pdf/GG_engl_ Stand_26_07_02.pdf)

Degenhart, Christoph (1998): *Staatsrecht I: Staatszielbestimmungen, Staatsorgane, Staatsfunktionen.* Heidelberg: C. F. Müller Verlag.

Glaeßner, Gert-Joachim/Werner Reutter/Charlie Jefferey, eds. (2001): *Verfassungspolitik und Verfassungswandel. Deutschland und Großbritannien im Vergleich.* Opladen: Westdeutscher Verlag.

Pieroth, Bodo/Bernhard Schlink (1998): *Staatsrecht II: Grundrechte.* Heidelberg: C. F. Müller Verlag.

Starck, Christian, ed. (1983): *Main Principles of the German Basic Law. 1st World Congress on the Modern Constitution. Selected Papers.* Baden-Baden: Nomos.

Chapter 3

Guggenberger, Bernd/Tine Stein, eds. (1991): *Die Verfassungsdiskussion im Jahr der deutschen Einheit.* Munich: Carl Hanser.

Quint, Peter E. (1997): *The Imperfect Union. Constitutional Structures of German Unification.* Princeton NJ: Princeton University Press.

Chapter 4

Bender, Peter (1986): *Neue Ostpolitik. Vom Mauerbau bis zum Moskauer Vertrag.* Munich: Deutscher Taschenbuch Verlag.

Hacke, Christian (1993): *Die Außenpolitik der Bundesrepublik Deutschland. Weltmacht wider Willen?* Frankfurt a.M./Berlin: Ullstein Verlag.

Herbst, Ludolf (1996): Option für den Westen. Vom Marshallplan bis zum deutschfranzösischen Vertrag. Munich: Deutscher Taschenbuch Verlag.

Kirchner, Emil J./James Sperling, eds. (1992): The Federal Republic of Germany and NATO: 40 Years After: New York: St. Martin's Press.

McAdams, A. James (1985): East Germany and Détente: Building Authority after the Wall. Cambridge: Cambridge University Press.

Szabo, Stephen F. (1992): *The Diplomacy of German Unification.* New York: St. Martin's Press.

Zelikow, Philip/Condoleezza Rice (1997): *Germany Unified and Europe Transformed. A Study in Statecraft.* Cambridge MA: London Harvard University Press.

Chapter 5

Beyme, Klaus von (1998): *The Legislator. German Parliament as a Center of Political Decision Making.* Aldershot: Ashgate.

Conradt, David P. (2001): *The German Polity.* New York/London: Longman.

Helms, Ludger, ed. (2000): *Institutions and Institutional Change in the Federal Republic of Germany.* Houndmills, Basingstoke: Macmillan.

Hesse, Jens Joachim/Thomas Ellwein (1997): *Das Regierungssystem der Bundesrepublik Deutschland.* Opladen: Westdeutscher Verlag.

Katzenstein, Peter (1987): *Policy and Politics in West Germany. The Growth of a Semisovereign State.* Philadelphia: Temple University Press.

Schindler, Peter (1999): *Datenhandbuch zu Geschichte des Deutschen Bundestages 1949 bis 1999.* 3 Vols. Baden-Baden: Nomos.

Sturm, Roland/Heinrich Pehle (2001): *Das neue deutsche Regierungssystem. Die Europäisierung von Institutionen, Entscheidungsprozessen und Politikfeldern.* Oplanden: Leske+Budrich.

Chapter 6

Clemens, Clay/William E. Paterson, eds. (1998): *The Kohl Chancellorship. German Politics Special Issue.* London: Frank Cass.

Dalton, Russel J., ed. (1993): *The New Germany Votes: Unification and the Creation of a New German Party System.* Providence RI/Oxford: Berg.

Egle, Christoph/Tobias Ostheim/Reimut Zohlnhöfer, eds. (2003): *Das Rot-Grüne Projekt. Eine Bilanz der Regierung Schröder 1998–2002.* Wiesbaden: Westdeutscher Verlag.

Niclauß, Karlheinz (2004): *Kanzlerdemokratie. Regierungsführung von Konrad Adenauer bis Gerhard Schröder.* Paderborn: Ferdinand Schöningh.

Padgett, Stephen, ed. (1994): *Adenauer to Kohl. The Development of the German Chancellorship.* London: Hurst & Company.

Padgett, Stephen/Thomas Saalfeld, eds. (1999): *Bundestagswahl '98. End of an Era? German Politics Special Issue*. London: Frank Cass.

Reutter, Werner, ed. (2003): *Germany on the Road to 'Normalcy': Policies and Politics of the Red-Green Federal Government (1998–2002)*. New York etc.: Palgrave Macmillan.

Roberts, Geoffrey K., ed. (1996): *Superwahljahr: The German Elections in 1994*. London: Frank Cass.

Chapter 7

Allen, Christopher S., ed. (1999): *Transformation of the German Political Party System. Institutional Crisis or Democratic Renewal?* New York/Oxford: Berghan.

Beyme, Klaus von (2000): *Parteien im Wandel. Von den Volksparteien zu den professionalisierten Wählerparteien*. Wiesbaden: Verlag für Sozialwissenschaften.

Lösche, Peter (1993): *Kleine Geschichte der deutschen Parteien*. Stuttgart: Kohlhammer.

Mintzel, Alf/Heinrich Oberreuter, eds. (1992): *Parteien in der Bundesrepublik Deutschland*. Opladen: Leske+Budrich.

Niclauß, Karlheinz (2002): *Das Parteiensystem der Bundesrepublik Deutschland*. Paderborn: Schöningh.

Padgett, Stephen, ed. (1993): *Parties and Party Systems in the New Germany*. Aldershot: Dartmouth.

Roberts, Geoffrey K. (1997): *Party Politics in the New Germany*. London/Washington: Pinter.

Chapter 8

Beyme, Klaus von/Hartmut Zimmermann, eds. (1984): *Policymaking in the German Democratic Republic*. Aldershot: Gower.

Childs, David/Thomas A. Baylis/Marilyn Rueschemeyer, eds. (1989): *East Germany in Comparative Perspective. Conference on the GDR in the Socialist World*. London: Routledge.

Glaeßner, Gert-Joachim (1989): *Die andere deutsche Republik. Gesellschaft und Politik in der DDR*. Opladen: Westdeutscher Verlag.
Krisch, Henry (1985): *The German Democratic Republic. The Search for Identity*. Boulder CO/London: Westview Press.

Chapter 9

Deutsche Einheit. Sonderedition aus den Akten des Bundeskanzleramtes 1989/90. Dokumente zur Deutschlandpolitik. Munich: Oldenbourg.
Glaessner, Gert-Joachim (1992): *The Unification Process in Germany. From Dictatorship to Democracy*. London: Pinter.
Grix, Jonathan (2000): *The Role of the Masses in the Collapse of the GDR*. Houndmills, Basingstoke: Macmillan.
Jarausch, Konrad H. (1994): *The Rush to German Unity*. New York: Oxford University Press.
Merkl, Peter H. (with a contribution by Gert-Joachim Glaessner) (1993): *German Unification in the European Context*. University Park: The Pennsylvania State University Press.
The Unification of Germany in 1990. A Documentation (1991). Bonn: Press and Information Office of the Federal Government.

Chapter 10

Baker, Kendall L./Russell J. Dalton/Kai Hildebrandt (1981): *Germany Transformed. Political Culture and the New Politics*. Cambridge, MA London: Harvard University Press.
Childs, David (2001): *The Fall of the GDR. Germany's Road to Unity*. Harlow: Longman.
Flockton, Chris/Eva Kolinsky, eds. (1999): *Recasting East Germany. Social Transformation after the GDR*. London: Frank Cass.
Glaeßner, Gert-Joachim, ed. (1996): *Germany after Unification. Coming to Terms with the Recent Past*. Amsterdam/Atlanta GA: Rodopi.
Jarausch, Konrad H., ed. (1997): *After Unity. Reconfiguring German Identities*. Providence/Oxford: Berghan.

Niedermayer, Oskar/Klaus von Beyme, eds. (1996) *Politische Kultur in Ost- und Westdeutschland*. Wiesbaden: Westdeutscher Verlag.

Schoenbaum, David/Elizabeth Pond (1996): *The German Question and Other German Questions*. Basingstoke/New York: Macmillan.

Weidenfeld, Werner/Karl Rudolf Korte, eds. (1999): *Handbuch zur deutschen Einheit*. Frankfurt a.M./New York: Campus Verlag.

Zimmer, Matthias, ed. (1997): *Germany Phoenix in Trouble?* Edmonton: University of Alberta Press.

URLs

Government

http://www.bundesregierung.de/

Federal President

http://www.bundespraesident.de/

Chancellor's Office

http://www.bundeskanzler.de/

Foreign Ministry

http://www.auswaertiges-amt.de/www/de/index_html

Federal Parliament

http://www.bundestag.de/
http://www.bundesrat.de/

Federal Constitutional Court

http://www.bundesverfassungsgericht.de/

Political parties

http://www.cdu.de/
http://www.csu.de/
http://www.fdp.de/
http://www.gruene.de/
http://www.spd.de/
http://sozialisten.de/

Index